Insurgent Testimonies

Insurgent Testimonies

Witnessing Colonial Trauma in Modern and Anglophone Literature

Nicole M. Rizzuto

FORDHAM UNIVERSITY PRESS
NEW YORK 2015

Visit us online at www.fordhampress.com.

Library of Congress Cataloging-in-Publication Data

Rizzuto, Nicole M.
Insurgent testimonies : witnessing colonial trauma in modern and Anglophone literature / Nicole M. Rizzuto. — First edition.
pages cm
Includes bibliographical references and index.
ISBN 978-0-8232-6781-1 (cloth : alk. paper) —
ISBN 978-0-8232-6782-8 (pbk. : alk. paper)
1. English literature—20th century—History and criticism.
2. Commonwealth literature (English)—History and criticism.
3. Imperialism in literature. 4. War in literature. 5. Psychic trauma in literature. 6. Justice, Administration of, in literature.
7. Nationalism and literature—English-speaking countries.
8. Literature and society—English-speaking countries.
I. Title.
PR478.153R59 2016
820.9'0091—dc23

2015006026

Printed in the United States of America
17 16 15 5 4 3 2 1
First edition

for Helen Morrissey Rizzuto and Thomas Rizzuto

CONTENTS

ACKNOWLEDGMENTS

Many people have helped bring this book into existence. I am grateful to Gayatri Chakravorty Spivak for her great generosity and for mentoring me over the years, and I thank Bruce Robbins and Carol Jacobs as well for their continued support of my work. Conversations with Benjamin Conisbee Baer, Nicholas Boggs, Rosalind Galt, Jeff Gatrall, Jeannie Im, Heather Lukes, Mina Rajagopolan, Lily Saint, and Penny Vlagopoulos enabled me to reframe earlier ideas and move forward in new directions. These true and lasting friends have also offered invaluable comments on argument, structure, and style throughout the research and writing processes.

Colleagues and students at the various institutions at which I have taught while developing the book have been a source of intellectual inspiration and growth. The students in the graduate seminars I led at New York University's John W. Draper Master's Program in the Humanities and Social Thought and at Oklahoma State University helped me reformulate my uses of the concepts of testimony and trauma so as to engage more effectively the ethics and politics of the literatures I examine. In the English department at OSU, Linda Austen and Martin Wallen read early drafts and offered not only incisive comments but much encouragement along the way. They, Brian Price, and Meghan Sutherland provided an intellectual and social haven for testing out my ideas and challenging them. Colleagues in the English Department at Georgetown have offered advice at other stages in the book's development. The members of our junior faculty writing group helped me hone my articulations of interventions I hope to make. Lori Merish and Ricardo Ortiz guided me through institutional thickets while reading drafts. My Georgetown colleagues Nathan Hensley, Caetlin Benson-Allot, and

Samantha Pinto, as well as colleagues working outside of Georgetown, Sangeeta Ray, Peter Kalliney, and Seth Perlow, were kind and careful readers of different chapters. Their comments helped me improve each one of these.

I am grateful to the editors and editorial staff at Fordham University Press for their help in transforming the manuscript into a book. I thank Helen Tartar for supporting the project. Helen died a week after she had finalized the approval that put the book under contract; her untimely death was a blow to her family and friends, of course, but also to the many authors who have worked with her over the years and to the readers who have learned so much from that work. I thank Tom Lay and Richard Morrison for taking on the project at different points to guide it toward publication. I am indebted to the anonymous readers for their comments and suggestions. I am grateful to Fordham's managing editor, Eric Newman, and I also thank my student Samantha Reid for her care with the source-checking process. All errors that remain are of course my own.

Earlier versions of pieces of two chapters appeared in journals. I thank *Twentieth-Century Literature* and *College Literature* for permissions to reprint these. I also thank Georgetown University for awarding me a grant-in-aid to help fund the publication of the book.

My family has been an enduring source of support and joy even (or especially) when the writing process has been its most challenging. Mark, Dee Dee, and Declan enrich my life by helping me see the world differently and do so often in hilarious ways. Topher Lundell has been a singular companion whose patience, wit, and humor are unparalleled. I am grateful that he has always been game when the possibility of pursuing my career involved moving across many states during a relatively short span of time. Finally, I dedicate this book to my parents, Helen Morrissey Rizzuto and Thomas Rizzuto, whose creativity and curiosity continually inspire me and whose love, support, and friendship made it possible.

Insurgent Testimonies

INTRODUCTION

Challenging Ruptures

Testimonial Insurgencies, Spectral Witnesses

> To articulate the past historically does not mean to recognize it "the way it really was." . . . It means to seize hold of a memory as it flashes up at a moment of danger.
>
> —WALTER BENJAMIN, "Theses on the Philosophy of History"

In this book, I examine how British, Caribbean, and African Anglophone writing elaborates an ethics and politics of witnessing events in imperial modernity that generated crises in historical memory.[1] During the second half of the nineteenth century and the first half of the twentieth, insurgencies erupted in imperial states and colonies around the world, including Britain's. At the time of such conflicts, England was confronting social and political unrest within its borders, undergoing cultural and economic shifts accompanying the growth and decline of empire, participating in geopolitical realignments of Europe and the global "East" and "West," and fighting in world wars. Britain relied on legislation, trials, changes in policing, and extraordinary techniques such as indefinite detention and torture to restore or maintain order while also attempting to protect cherished narratives of national cohesion and imperial benevolence that would secure it from charges of totalitarianism and barbarism leveled at other imperial powers. The writings collected here depict these historical events and their aftereffects as traumas that compromise such narratives. Such events are traumatic not only because they caused great pain, both physical and psychological, to individuals but because they brought to crisis representations of collective pasts, called into question the conceptual and affective underpinnings of nations, and challenged the legitimacy of empires.

The fiction and nonfiction I consider orchestrate testimonies to insurgencies, wars, and varied forms of social and political agitation while engaging cultural, state, legal, and literary discourses that sought to control them. But these works also orchestrate testimony *as* insurgent, in the narrow and general senses of the word. As such, testimony disrupts established orders, is not institutionally recognized, rises up and overflows borders, and is difficult to contain. *Insurgent Testimonies* draws into constellation works from different nations and literary-historical periods to analyze how testimony crosses and displaces boundaries between literary, legal, documentary, and autobiographical domains and thereby interrupts the dominant representations of colonial history these works also often ratify, indeed reinforce.

My aim is not to offer a comprehensive survey of testimony to trauma in twentieth-century Anglophone literature but to construct a particular genealogy of witnessing as it intersects with moments in which the stability of nations and empires as economic, cultural, and social formations were perceived to be under heightened threat. The cause of the threat is different in each of the works I consider, but in every case it is fundamentally connected to anticolonial struggle. These diverse struggles were both "successful" and "unsuccessful," some organized and sustained under the mantle of national liberation, others sporadic and unlinked to claims for national sovereignty. Each struggle was also coterminous with other intranational and international conflicts whose structural relationship to them, these texts indicate, was often obscured. Viewed together, the writing of the Ukrainian-born Joseph Conrad, the Anglo-Irish Rebecca West, the Jamaicans H. G. de Lisser and V. S. Reid, and the Kenyan Ngũgi wa Thiong'o testify to contested events in colonial modernity in ways that question premises underlying approaches to trauma in modernist studies and trauma and memory studies. Their modes of witnessing also invite us to reassess divisions and classifications in literary studies that generate such categories as modernist, colonial, postcolonial, national, and world literatures.

Critics working on trauma in modernist studies and those working in trauma and memory studies have tended to focus on the effects of what are often considered the greatest ruptures of the twentieth century, the two world wars. I depart from tenets of modernist studies, which centralizes the impact of World War I on the formation of English modernism, and from methods in the field of trauma and memory studies, which long traced the impact of World War II and the Shoah on continental European literary forms. I contend that acute as well as chronic disruptions to imperial and national power and the legal and extralegal responses they inspired shape the formal practices of literatures from the modernist, colonial, and postcolonial periods. To do so, I analyze a particular body of work that has generally fallen beyond the purview of explorations of trauma, testimony, and law: novels, novellas, autobiographical and critical writings, and trial reports published in the first seventy years of the twentieth century.[2] This writing appears between the great nineteenth-century novels of the legal profession—Walter Scott's *Heart of Midlothian*, Charles Dickens's *Bleak House*, Anthony Trollope's *Orley Farm*—and the vast body of contemporary literature that addresses suspensions of rights under neocolonialism, apartheid, and post-9/11 U.S. imperialism. Composed outside of continental Europe, this work also mostly predates the wealth of post-Holocaust poetry and prose that has attracted critical analyses since the 1990s.[3] The overlooked itineraries of testimony in literatures of this time and from these places challenge the dominant definition of trauma as rupture. The deployment of this definition has diverted attention from modernism's imbrication in colonial histories. It has also strengthened periodizing models that separate modernist from postcolonial literatures.

The narrative strategies that alternately enact and suppress insurgent testimony in the works of the modernist period analyzed here demonstrate that the structural violence of imperialism inhabiting everyday life in both colonies and metropoles is often forgotten in the midst of the spectacular violence of world war. Criticism's articulation of the First World War as the exemplary rupture of modernity perpetuates this amnesia. Concentration on the Great War's role in defining modernist and countermodernist articulations of memory, consciousness, and culture began with Paul Fussell's landmark study *The Great War and Modern Memory* and was followed by the important scholarship of Modris Ecksteins, Samuel Hynes, Vincent Sherry, and feminist revisions of the period by Sandra Gilbert and Susan Gubar, Bonnie Kime Scott, Trudi Tate, Margaret Higonnet, and others.[4] Arguing that the war was the rupture that made modernism possible, Fussell writes, "The Great War was perhaps the last to be conceived as taking place within a seamless, purposeful 'history' involving a coherent stream of time running from past through present to future," maintaining that it "took place in what was, compared with ours, a static world, where the values appeared stable and where the meanings of abstractions seemed permanent and reliable." Before the war "there was no *Waste Land* . . . no *Ulysses*, no Mauberly, no *Cantos*, no Kafka, no Proust, no Waugh, no Auden, no Huxley, no Cummings, no *Women in Love* or *Lady Chatterly's Lover*."[5] This line of argument is reconfigured in the decades succeeding the publication of Fussell's study. Most recently, the textual effects of the experience of the battlefield have been paralleled to those of the experience of the European metropolis, the Georgian strategies of the war poets connected to the strategies of modernist civilian writers such as D. H. Lawrence.[6] Whether used to distinguish modernism from realist war testimonials or to read modernist fragmentation as reflective of the real, the foregrounding of war eclipses the effects of colonial life and history on modernist form.[7] Depicting the war as rupture explicitly or implicitly characterizes the prewar past, the time of colonial conquest, consolidation, and resistances to these, as "static" rather than dynamic or violent.

Such arguments express a temporal imaginary that takes modernism at its word when it claims to "make it new" and a spatial imaginary that posits a gap between metropole and colonies. Others, however, have dispelled these mythic visions. Jay Winter argues that "the view that there was a 'modernist' moment in literary history, beginning in the 1860s, maturing before 1914, but coming of age after the Great War" is a dream of order; "to array the past in such a way is to invite distortion by losing a sense of its messiness, its non-linearity, its vigorous and stubbornly visible incompatibilities."[8] Modernist and Great War culture and literature did not exclusively perform a radical break with the past or abide by Ezra Pound's commandment to make it new. In mourning and rememoration, writers often availed themselves of earlier aesthetic techniques and practices, Winter asserts. The performance of testimony in Conrad's and West's works composed during the war illustrate that both authors do so. This performance also questions the ideology that situates modernism, and modernity, as rupture, an ideology that Fredric Jameson critiques and attributes to modernism's commentators and periodizers. Jameson contends that a dialectic of rupture and periodization recurs throughout modernity and comes to define it: "the foregrounding of continuities, the insistent and unwavering focus on the seamless passage from past to present, slowly turns into a consciousness of a radical break, while at the same time the enforced attention to a break gradually turns the latter into a period in its own right."[9] Jameson was also one of the first critics to expose how a perceived rupture between the spaces of the metropole and colonies organizes modernist literature, demonstrating that British modernism reveals its reliance upon colonialism and its inability to raise this reliance to the level of textual consciousness.[10] The last decades have seen an increasing number of studies explore how British modernism alternately registers and obscures the imperial formations that enable it.[11] None, however, has focused on how testimony labors to raise histories of colonial trauma, violence, and law to the level of textual consciousness. Attending to this labor clarifies the Eurocentric perspective underwriting the theory of modernism, and modernity, as rupture.

That the conceptualization of trauma as rupture is thoroughly entrenched, and that modernity is often conflated with trauma, is suggested by the fact that even the critic of the ideology of modernity-as-rupture promulgates it while using the language of trauma. On the one hand, Jameson proposes that "modernity" is a trope of rewriting, a "rhetorical effect" that returns throughout history.[12] On the other hand, he insists that this trope possesses a singular referent. Instead of World War I, this referent is what he describes as the traumatic break that initiates the capitalist world system, which subsumes all differences under the standardization of a universal market order.[13] In a passage whose significance he minimizes by calling it a "parenthesis" and whose language of trace, ghostliness, and abstraction appears to convey modernity as irreducibly tropological, Jameson negates this argument. He claims that we can

> restore the social and historical meaning of the rewriting operation by positioning it as a trace and an abstraction from a real historical event and trauma, one which can be said to amount to a rewriting and a surcharging of the social itself in its most concrete form. This is the moment of the overcoming of feudalism by capitalism, and of the aristocratic social order of castes and blood by the new bourgeois order which at least promised social and juridical equality and political democracy. This is to locate the referent of "modernity" in a new way, via the ancient ghostly forms of experience itself rather than in some one-to-one

> correspondence between the alleged concept and its equally alleged object. . . . In any case—and this is the deeper justification for tracing the formal operations of the trope of modernity back to its traumatic historical emergence—our situation at the beginning of the twenty-first century has nothing to do with this any longer.[14]

Abiding by his own premise that "we cannot not periodize,"[15] Jameson adduces modernity as the consequence of a "real" new beginning, "experience itself." His term for the rupture in history, the moment of the overcoming of feudalism by capitalism, is trauma.

Analyzing the speech act of testimony makes clear the problems with conceptualizing trauma in terms of rupture. As psychoanalysis tells us, testimony does not re-present events as "real, historical traumas"; rather, it figures traumas as sites of struggle over representation and over what constitutes reality and history. Freud never wrote a single or unified theory of trauma, but he elaborated the concept through discussions of different topics: dreams, accident neuroses, castration anxiety, and exile under fascism and religious persecution.[16] His discussion of *Nachträglichkeit*, translated as "aftereffect," theorizes that trauma is relayed through (re)telling and, therefore, is always spread across multiple times. In the process of secondary revision, trauma is figured through contingencies of enunciation and subject to the pressures that initiate that enunciation. Trauma is the effect of testimony, of which it is also a cause. Every trauma is internally split, haunted by another time, that of a potential testimony to it in the messianic formulations of the future anterior in which trauma "will have been," will have happened. Every testimony is haunted by the time of the historically specific event outside the present of its enunciation, which it figures. The psychoanalytic theorization of trauma thus elucidates the problem with viewing a past as either entirely continuous *or* discontinuous with a present that activates testimony. This theorization can function as a reminder for the work of literary criticism that periods are not self-enclosed. Testimony in the writings I examine discloses how ruptures claimed to constitute periods dissimulate relations between pasts and presents.

Employing as one critical apparatus the morphology of testimony psychoanalysis elaborates helps restore the importance of imperial trauma to the formal procedures of modernist and Anglophone literatures. It is worth pointing out, however, that the institution of psychoanalysis also consolidated patriarchal, colonialist, and heteronormative narratives of subjectivity and historical development. As feminist, postcolonial, and queer theorists have taught us, using psychoanalytic models to counter such narratives also means setting psychoanalysis against itself in key ways. In recent years, others have questioned the value of trauma theory for reading postcolonial and contemporary literature and culture.[17] I maintain that the psychoanalytic theory of trauma provides a critique of temporality useful for broadly describing the structure of historicity formally articulated in the writings I examine. My specific readings of texts, however, while informed by trauma theory's critiques of temporality and experience, are not solely framed by them. To address the singular enactments of testimony in the works I consider, it is necessary to turn to other critical methodologies. For example, in an idiom distinct from the psychoanalytic, Walter Benjamin, too, questions modes of temporalizing that render a past either entirely continuous or discontinuous with a present. This questioning is undertaken not with the clinical goals of healing or working through trauma but rather to articulate a critical method aimed at fomenting social and political justice.

Instead of as breaks, totalities, or periods, testimony in fiction and nonfiction written during particular moments of imperial decline codes earlier scenes of colonial conflict as something like what Benjamin calls dialectical images, that is, pasts of oppression that issue forth in a "moment of danger." These literary works do not "recover" such pasts. Staged through testimony, these pasts resist the apprehension of homogenous time that guides historicist projects of recovery. Benjamin directs his philosophical critiques of positivism and historicism toward political ends: the resistance to fascism and the control of "ruling classes." While his famous call to blast open the continuum of history prescribes the critical method through a language of violent disruption, what is blasted out of this continuum is not a totality or bounded period but, rather, a monad in which "is crystallized all the tensions of past, present, future together, at a standstill [*Stillstellung*]"[18] and that therefore offers "a revolutionary chance in the fight for the oppressed past." Giving a chance to a past described not, in Freudian terms, as "repressed" but "oppressed" (*unterdruckt*—the word Benjamin uses to depict, in Marxist terms, classes in struggle) requires that one encounter the monad as dialectical image. He defines the pedagogical aim of the *Arcades Project*, therefore, as training the "image-making medium within us."[19] The potential critical force of every image is that it is suffused by the now-time, *Jetzeit*, which is not the present but rather undoes phenomenologies of presence: "What distinguishes images from the 'essences' of phenomenology is their historical index. . . . Image is dialectics at a standstill." The dialectical image is activated in a contingent moment that forms a constellation with this what-has-been; thus, "to articulate the past historically does not mean to recognize it 'the way it really was' (Ranke). It means to seize hold of a memory as it flashes up at a moment of danger. Historical materialism wishes to retain that image of the past which unexpectedly appears to man singled out by history at a moment of danger. The danger affects both the content of the tradition and its receivers."[20] Benjamin announces the critical gesture of wresting the memory from "the conformism of tradition" in terms of class struggle, but de Lisser, Conrad, West, Reid, and Ngũgi demonstrate how class struggle is necessarily crosshatched by gender, sexual, race, and ethnic struggles as well. Each work's compositional context—the Russian Revolution of 1905 and coincident anticolonial revolt in Russian peripheries, including Poland; World Wars I and II; uprisings against Crown colony rule in Jamaica; and the emerging neocolonial state in Kenya—is a moment of danger that spurs other, earlier moments to flash up or surge forth as dialectical images.

Because the form of testimony and the events it figures are incompatible with the logic of rupture used to characterize the aesthetic practices of modernism and the historical situations said to condition them—a logic that has been used in both similar and different ways to characterize Holocaust writings and the Shoah[21]—examining texts that stage traumatic testimony encourages, if not demands, a transnational approach with a dilated temporal perspective. Conrad, West, de Lisser, Reid, and Ngũgi reimagine revolutions, insurgencies, counterinsurgencies, treason, and war as tears in the fabric of the nation and empire, but the formal practices that constitute testimony relate that each of these events is enmeshed within historical processes that predate them and is the product of contemporaneous forces that extend beyond the particular region, nation, or continent in which they are shown to occur. Drawing together Conrad's autobiographical and political "Polish" writings and novel of the Russian revolution of 1905, *Under Western Eyes*; West's World War I novel, *The Return of the Soldier*, and post–World War II trial reports collected in *The Meaning of Treason*; de Lisser's historical romance *Revenge: A Tale of Old Jamaica* and Reid's epic novel *New Day* and young-adult novel *Sixty-Five*, all of which recount the Morant Bay rebellion of 1865 in Jamaica; and Ngũgi's novel about the Kenya Emergency, *A Grain of Wheat*, which I situate in the context of his critical writings on African literature and his prison writing, *Detained*, allows us to put into practice what Michael Rothberg calls "multidirectional memory." As Rothberg persuasively argues, the study of trauma is enriched by an approach that seeks out connections across time and space while preserving differences. This critical practice "posits collective memory as partially disengaged from exclusive versions of cultural identity and acknowledges how remembrance both cuts across and binds together diverse spatial, temporal, and cultural sites."[22]

The works I analyze use a variety of textual strategies to bear witness to these crises in memory, including those typically identified as modernist, though only two authors would traditionally be classified as modernists and even they are not the most canonical examples of this type. Participating in ongoing critical endeavors to rethink what the term "modernism" means in the era of the new modernist studies, I turn to West and Conrad because their writings complicate received ideas about what modernism is or does. Among these is that modernism is skeptical of Enlightenment narratives that uphold nationalism as a spiritual ideal, and that it reflects a secular alienated and atomistic subjectivity produced by capitalist modernity. Each author's interest in testimony as both literary and legal acts is coupled with ambivalent attitudes toward nationalism as a basis for community. This ambivalence betrays contradictory responses to imperialism and demonstrates how a boundary between secular and religious discourse is rendered precarious by testimony.

West's works are written across high and late modernist, as well as postmodernist periods, but do not fit neatly into any of these periodizing categories. As Bernard Schweizer asserts, "West's modernist work places less emphasis on the concept of artistic crisis than it does on notions of political, cultural, and spiritual crisis," and he proposes that this "makes her work less susceptible to traditional readings of modernism as a movement driven by aesthetic and formal imperatives."[23] West's vocations as journalist and travel writer, who documented journeys through 1930s Yugoslavia and 1960s Mexico, and as a reporter of many important trials in the United States, Britain, and postwar Germany, influenced her approach to literary form and shaped her views on nationalism, imperialism, and anti-imperialism. West's political views shifted across her career. Although she was never a member of the Bloomsbury group, her earlier writing shares some of the perspectives of its figures. *The Return of the Soldier* criticizes nationalist discourses for ratifying uneven social and class structures within England and ties these structures to imperial interests and the suppression of labor movements abroad. Over the next two decades, West's perspectives moved away from those of modernist vanguards. She became critical of communism and other forms of leftist internationalism including the cosmopolitanist ethos of Bloomsbury. She interpreted this ethos as antinationalist and the result of unexamined privilege. Witnessing the repression and destruction of nationalities in the Balkans made her sympathetic to nationalism as an affective mode and led her to see it as a form of resistance to imperial domination.[24] But her acculturation as an Anglo-Irish subject, combined with anxieties about the consequences of accelerating imperial contraction in the postwar period, seems to have made her less than sympathetic to other nationalisms—those targeting British rather than Eastern European powers. In her reports on the treason trials in England, West derides the anticolonial nationalism of the Irish, whom she treats as subhuman and therefore lacking the right to national independence.

Conrad's experiences traveling throughout the colonial world and his status as a colonial subject helped mold his writing, too, which, like West's, departs in certain ways from modernist practices and politics. Conrad was the son of a leading Polish revolutionary of the most radical faction of anticolonialists, which notably did not articulate their program in ethnonationalist terms. Apollo Korzienowski was exiled by the Russian state and died while Conrad was very young, and, consequently, Conrad was raised by a maternal uncle who was highly critical of his father's revolutionary agenda. Conrad left Poland and became a citizen and supporter of the British empire and a critic of incipient globalization and emerging cosmopolitical alliances. Divided attitudes toward imperial nationalism drive his fictional and autobiographical responses to revolution in Russia and anticolonial revolt in Poland. These attitudes are crystallized in the enactment of confession in *Under Western Eyes* and the 1915 essay "Poland Revisited." Those works' employment of literary impressionism and other techniques read as modernist, but their use of confession positions them within a tradition of secular and religious expression that precedes the modernist period, is largely absent from modernist practice, and then returns in the postwar West in a multitude of discursive forms.

West's and Conrad's writings' concerns with law, testimony, and justice during struggles against imperial power connects them to the works of de Lisser, Reid, and Ngũgi. These are more forgotten than canonical texts of colonial and postcolonial literature. This fact might be attributed to their subjects and their treatments of them. These novels lack the plots and thematics often found in highly anthologized and popular Anglophone fiction: narratives of migration and diaspora detailing the difficulties of negotiating identity and existence among foreign communities, for example, or representations of encounters between global and minority cultures in a "modernity at large." By contrast, *Revenge*, *New Day*, *Sixty-Five*, and *A Grain of Wheat* center on insurgencies and counterinsurgencies that take place within the space of a colony and that were rooted in economic factors as much as, if not more so than, contestations over culture. Moreover, their range of responses to these events defies what we have come to expect from postcolonial literature.

Revenge (1919) and *New Day* (1949) were published decades prior to independence in Jamaica, and *Sixty-Five* (1960) two years before it. It is not only that they make insurgency their topic but also how they address it that distinguishes these texts from canonical postcolonial fiction, understood as literature written after as well as during the colonial era that takes a critical stance toward colonialism. Reid's works are highly ambivalent toward the ends of empire, and de Lisser's is opposed to Jamaican independence. These attitudes are conveyed through narrative strategies that attempt to vindicate English law. According to the Jamaica Royal Commission and the Victorian writers and jurists whose arguments, I contend, *Revenge*, *New Day*, and *Sixty-Five* engage, English law has been tarnished by the excessively brutal and lengthy suppression of the Morant Bay rebellion under Governor Edward Eyre's command. The formal protocols of witnessing in de Lisser's and Reid's novels dissect the legal concept of necessity that was at the foundation of British emergency law and at the heart of the debates about whether the counterinsurgency was justifiable. These debates occurred during what became known as the Governor Eyre controversy in England. This slippery legal concept has reemerged as the site of controversy again in the twenty-first century, having become the focus of criticisms of the practices of policing and detention in the ongoing U.S. war on terror. The question the Morant Bay rebellion raised, which has been raised again, is whether the concept of necessity should be based on imminent threat or on deterrence.[25] That all three novels have fallen out of print and have garnered little to no critical attention in decades evinces they are incompatible with the Anglophone/World Literature market today and illegible within the discipline of postcolonial literary studies. But this fiction should be revisited, I maintain, because it ruminates on how justifications for legal violence intersect with uneven class and race formations. It permits us to see, then, that contemporary questions about the use of legitimate versus illegitimate force possess a history and a buried literary history.

Unlike de Lisser and Reid, Ngũgi is a world-renowned author today; nevertheless, his novel *A Grain of Wheat* had only recently come back into print in the beginning of the twenty-first century. This reprinting of a work about the years of the Emergency, during which the screening and detention in concentration camps and villages of tens of thousands of Kikuyu occurred, is timely. Details of the brutality and scope of the counterinsurgency were buried in British archives for decades and first unearthed in the early 2000s by historians whose studies have since punctured the British "counterinsurgency myth": that the empire was engaged in a campaign to win hearts and minds with the goal of rehabilitating insurgents. Not until 2011, under pressure from the Kenyan government, had England begun to address in legal form its crimes under the Emergency. Ngũgi's novel has returned to print in its revised version, which was first published in 1986. The original work, which appeared in 1967, has not. That text, which I examine here, portrays the violence of the counterinsurgency as well as that of the Kenya Land and Freedom fighters in graphic terms. The rhetoric through which violence is justified creates discomfiting overlaps and complicities among colonial, neocolonial, and even anticolonial formations. Ngũgi exposes the violence of British law in its enactment of a state of exception. This enactment normalizes indefinite detention and compelled confession, techniques of governance the Kenyan leaders will use after independence. The novel's strategic management of silence and speech critiques these techniques and signals Ngũgi's attempts to end a cycle of traumatic repetitions of betrayal that plague Kenyan colonial and postcolonial history. At times, however, the text delivers its critique of violence and betrayal by justifying national independence in a language of natural rights, rights based on biological or bare life. Use of this language risks perpetuating the legacy of colonial thought the work sets out to destroy.

The connections that emerge among these modernist, colonial, and postcolonial writings are not produced by the plotting of transcultural encounters in colonial spaces or "contact zones," therefore. Rather, these connections are produced by formal enactments of testimony to "missed encounters," or traumas, in colonial history.[26] These enactments refute claims by scholars that a particular style proffers a more ethical response to trauma than another, for instance, modernist or postmodernist experimentation or, conversely, documentary and "conventional" narrative forms associated with traditions such as realism and naturalism.[27] Moreover, these authors' deployments of diverse styles and various discourses challenge monolithic notions of an engaged literature of the postcolonial period that would contrast with a metropolitan modernism thought to be defined by difficulty, self-reflection, and experimentalism. West and Conrad eschew markers of innovation such as stream of consciousness and fragmented narratives and use techniques found in literary, journalistic, and popular genres whose grammars stress continuity more than discontinuity and convey a sense of coherence rather than disorientation. Instead of aspiring toward aesthetic autonomy and self-reflection, these works are directed outward: through testimony, they broach actual historical events. Ngũgĩ's and Reid's novels appear during eras in which fiction often portrayed the material conditions of everyday life through vernacular modes in the hopes of galvanizing a people toward independence and nation building. But *New Day* and *A Grain of Wheat* also employ tactics identified with cosmopolitan high modernism: nonlinear narratives, shifts in perspective, and epic forms. Raymond Williams argued that such features express modernism's "metropolitan perception" and were a consequence of upheavals in traditional social structures accompanying deracination and migration to the European metropolis in the beginning of the twentieth century.[28] The settings of Reid's and Ngũgĩ's texts are not the European or even the colonial metropolis, however, but the rural estates, towns, and detention villages of the colony. What impels their formal tactics is not migration and deracination but upheavals *within* the colony or nation that are the effects of transnational, cultural, and legal forces on it.

Although Ngũgi and Reid use what could be described as modernist tactics, their works also require that we define the term "modernism" differently from the ways critical models have defined it in the past: as a recognizable category of texts associated with a specific set of aesthetic practices thought to originate in Europe and diffuse outward to colonies and former colonies, where they are copied or recycled.[29] Jessica Berman offers an alternative to this reading of modernism in her study of ethics, politics, and transnational modernism. She argues that "modernism . . . stands for a dynamic set of relationships, practices, problematics, and cultural engagements with modernity rather than a static canon of works, a given set of formal devices, or a specific range of beliefs," and she proposes that "modernist narrative might best be seen as a constellation of rhetorical actions, attitudes, or aesthetic occasions, motivated by the particular and varied situations of economic, social, and cultural modernity worldwide, and shaped by the ethical and political demands of those situations."[30] This understanding of modernist narrative is capacious enough to describe the strategies of works that stand outside traditionally defined high modernist and late modernist periods as well as canons. It has the added value of disputing entrenched ideas about modernism understood as works that feature a particular set of formal devices—namely that modernism is inherently colonialist or Eurocentric or, contrarily, that it inherently challenges colonial ideologies and Eurocentricisms.[31] Envisioning modernist narrative forms as flexible, plural, and emerging in response to national and transnational forces that both foreclose and aim toward justice enables us to draw connections between literatures of different periods. These connections emerge otherwise than on the basis of empirically verifiable information, for instance, that Ngũgi wa Thiong'o read and revised Conrad's works throughout his fiction and, specifically, rewrote *Under Western Eyes* as *A Grain of Wheat*. As Nicholas Brown reminds us in his study of modernism and African literature, a framework that seeks to analyze relationships among modernist and postcolonial literatures cannot be based on "influence."[32] This category has functioned to position colonial and postcolonial writing as secondary and belated responses to European literature. I would add, moreover, that it assumes we know what modernism and postcolonial literature are—an assumption my analyses of these colonial and postcolonial novels also questions by treating them not as copies but as works whose own historical pressures induce their formal portrayals of these events.

It is not my aim to relabel and reperiodize these novels of coloniality and postcoloniality *as* modernism, however, that is, to subject them to classificatory schemas of new modernist studies. It is true that compelling arguments have been made for a "weak theory" of modernism that would enable a broadening of critical approaches and promote attention to literary and cultural works that are not typically included in this category.[33] But I decline to reclassify the Jamaican and Kenyan texts I consider as modernism because today the term modernism does not register the oppositional stance that the terms colonial and postcolonial literature still do. Retaining these terms, which evoke histories of marginalization and assimilation, encourages us to question why certain texts resist or fall outside institutionally and culturally dominant circuits of criticism and publication. Retaining these terms also encourages us to notice when the influence model returns to literary studies in other guises. Reid's, de Lisser's, and Ngũgi's works cannot easily enter these circuits because they express the force of the nation and nationalism linguistically, rhetorically, and ideologically and because their orchestrations of globality are not articulated in the culturalist terms of an expansive worldliness but rather in economic terms of constrictive depredation. "Modernism" in its most recent manifestations—appended to the word "global" and also occupying a central position in studies of world literature—has enabled the model of influence to regain ground while also establishing divisions and hierarchies between world literature and national literature and between cosmopolitanism and nationalism. According to Pascale Casanova's influential theory of world literature, Anglo-European modernism serves as the example that writers from the colonies attempt to reproduce when they seek to break out of local, national, or regional constraints and enter the "world republic of letters."[34] This argument reduces colonial and postcolonial literature to instances of mimicry of metropolitan modernism and reduces world literature to literature that dominates the global market and has somehow divested itself of the specificities of the "local" through which it has been constituted and also resists. While studies of global modernism do not necessarily frame their inquiries in terms of a work's position in the world republic of letters, attention is increasingly paid to texts that are thought to enact a global perspective, to articulate modes of identification and belonging and an ethics and politics that reach beyond the nation.[35]

A transnational approach to literatures of imperial modernity enables us to see how testimony troubles the privileging of the global over the national and illuminates how a world increasingly structured by transnational and cosmopolitical forces also provokes the emergence of nationalisms in different forms.[36] This approach allows us to examine how, for Ngũgi and Reid, the nation-state is an aspirational form and nationalism an affective mode with which to challenge the legitimacy of the colonial and neocolonial state and expose the violence inhabiting dispensations of sovereign power. It also permits us to explore how for de Lisser, Conrad, and West an era marked by world wars, shifting geopolitical alliances, declining nation-states, imperial retrenchment, and incipient globalization can awaken or reawaken imperial nationalisms and ethnonationalism as reaction-formations. In their writings, such reaction-formations disavow the violence of imperial law as it struggles to legitimate its power while delegitimating the claims of those who challenge it.

Examining works written from the metropole as well as the colony and postcolony at moments in which a nation's borders are particularly porous, or are not yet formed, or are under assault allows for both a broader and a more nuanced view of the processes through which literature responds to trauma. The effort to transnationalize trauma studies and facilitate critical encounters between trauma theory and postcolonial histories and literatures has gained momentum in recent years through the scholarship of Victoria Burrows, Sam Durrant, Anne Whitehead, Stef Craps, and Michael Rothberg.[37] Gabriele Schwab both adds to and modifies Rothberg's transnational theory and practice of multidirectional memory, which posits memory as generous rather than competitive and as generative of connections among rather than conflicts between traumatic histories. Schwab analyzes "haunting legacies," conflicting representations of collective memory that come into view by comparing victims' and perpetrators' responses to historical trauma.[38] As they testify to the nation as an ongoing project under constant revision as it hyphenates with the state and is reshaped through various economic and cultural modes of transnationalism, these writings both enact instances of multidirectional memory and also illustrate how haunting legacies engender clashes between antagonistic and uneven forces—dominant and subaltern, perpetrator and victim. Neither the modernist nor the colonial and postcolonial texts neatly align with, or stage, categories of dominant and subaltern or perpetrator and victim, however. Insurgent testimony conjures specters that displace these categories as it elaborates and negotiates impasses between ethics and politics.

In his second sustained response to Levinasian ethics,[39] Jacques Derrida writes of the aporetic and dissymmetrical relation without relation between ethics and politics and justice and law as a mode of spectral witnessing. Emmanuel Levinas asserts that ethics, as "first philosophy," precedes ontology. In glossing Levinas's theory of ethics as an underived responsibility to others that both comes before and also exceeds the prescriptions of the socius, law, or the state and that Levinas articulates as the unique encounter with the unique in the face to face, Derrida figures this encounter as testimony.

> If the face to face with the unique engages the infinite ethics of my responsibility for the other in a sort of *oath before the letter*, an unconditional respect or fidelity, then the ineluctable emergence of the third, and with it, of justice, would signal an initial perjury. . . . such perjury is not accidental and secondary, but is as originary as the experience of the face. Justice would begin with this perjury. (Or at least, justice as law; even if justice remains transcendent or heterogeneous to law, these two concepts must not be dissociated: justice demands law, and law does not wait).[40]

Levinas maintains that the ethical is the singular and incalculable responsibility to another, which cannot be mediated by law or the state. Derrida agrees with Levinas that there can be no dialectical synthesis of or mediation between the infinite and incalculable responsibility to others and the calculus of the state, between the ethical and political, or between justice and law. The first term of each of these couples exceeds the economy of mediation and synthesis. No political or legal action can be verified as just or ethical; the effects of actions cannot be entirely controlled or calculated. Yet, Derrida insists, every ethical encounter is haunted by the demands of the calculus from the very beginning. If the ethical is an oath, a promise that binds one to and makes one responsible to and for others, a promise that precedes consciousness or choice, the political is the perjury that necessarily haunts this originary scene as specter and interrupts, simultaneously, this supposedly "prior" ethical relation that nonetheless remains discontinuous with the political. Derrida also challenges Levinas's privileging of the ethical over the political by arguing that without law and the calculus, without perjury, there is no possibility of anything like justice or ethics taking place, even though these institutions also enable the spectral "pervertibility" of ethics and justice: hence the aporetic relation between ethics and politics, justice and law. "This spectral 'possibility' is the impossibility of controlling, deciding, or determining a limit, the impossibility of situating, by means of criteria, norms or rules, a tenable threshold separating pervertibility from perversion," Derrida asserts. He relates that "this possible hospitality to the worst" that testimony as perjury enables "is necessary so that good hospitality can have a chance, the chance of letting the other come." In betraying, by responding to, an other, testimony conjures specters that occasion other responses and responsibilities.

In each of the writings I examine, the insurgent staging of testimony conjures spectral witnesses, events and subjects that are focal points of negotiations between ethics and politics. And at times, it is the very institutions that seek to contain testimony, as well as insurgency, that enable or facilitate these conjurations: the courtroom, the confessional, the police ministry, the detention center. These works relate, also, that "just as the law is not simply a reactive institution that codifies existing social relations," as Joseph Slaughter reminds us, "literature is not simply a medium for re-presenting those formations."[41] Literature and testimony are both irreducible to institutions that organize and deploy them, and they can break the frames that appear to contain them. Shoshana Felman's insight in her and Dori Laub's classic study of testimony is borne out in different ways in Conrad's, West's, de Lisser's, Reid's, and Ngũgi's writings: "As a performative speech act, testimony in effect addresses what in history is *action* that exceeds any substantialized significance, and . . . dynamically explodes any conceptual reifications and any constative delimitations."[42] Though enlisted in the service of providing evidence, testimony cannot be reduced to evidentiary report and exceeds such "constative de-limitations."

When I say that testimony in these works conjures specters, I do so with the various meanings of "conjure" in mind. These meanings signal that testimony convokes communities whose members are not "naturally" affiliated, as communities of race, blood, or nation are often imputed to be, nor are they gathered together by rational choice or consensus. These communities emerge as an effect of speech acts of law and the state as well as an effect of acts not decreed, indeed even forbidden, by law and state. The *OED* relates that conjure is derived from the

> Middle English, < Old French *conjurer* (*conjurer*) = Provençal *conjurar*, Spanish *conjurar*, Italian *congiurare* < Latin *conjūrāre* to swear together, to band, combine, or make a compact by oath, to conspire, etc., < *con-* tog ether + *iūrāre* to

> swear, make oath. The stress-mutation in Old French *conju'rer, con'jure*, gave two corresponding forms *'conjure, con'jure* in Middle English, of which the former was by far the more usual, and has come down in senses.

The definitions are broken into three main categories: "I. To swear together; to conspire. II. To constrain by oath, to charge or appeal to solemnly. III. To invoke by supernatural power, to effect by magic or jugglery." These definitions summarize the ways testimony convokes communities throughout the texts I address. The first definition relates that conjuring endeavors to interrupt administrative, state, or legal domains; the second situates conjuring within such domains; and the third denotes that conjuring breaks with codes of reason, operates outside the limits of the rational and secular, when it summons community. The communities that testimony convokes are those of the nation, empire, and people as "imagined" and "imaginary" social formations (although no less material in their effects) as well as the subaltern-on-the-way to the people that have been thrown into crisis by colonial and neocolonial trauma and war, insurgency and counterinsurgency.[43] It is to these amorphous and shifting communities that testimony, as acts launched within the forums of law and the state, as well as those that break out of those forums, also responds.

Having sketched in some detail the outline of the book, I end this introductory chapter by turning to a work whose staging of testimony exemplifies that in the works that follow: E. M. Forster's 1924 novel, *A Passage to India*. This text serves as an example because it is both similar to and different from those I address in the next four chapters. It is similar because although it is composed only a few years after World War I, the trauma to which it attests is not the effects of that war alone but also those of an imperial rule whose claims to legitimacy have become increasingly vulnerable as the consequence of state violence and a strengthening anticolonial movement. It is different because unlike the fiction and nonfiction I discuss in the next chapters, its examination of how colonial law attempts to manage an occluded event has received a fair amount of critical attention.[44]

The novel depicts a struggle between colonial law and insurgent testimony that dramatizes the irreducibility of ethics to politics yet confuses clear limits between them. *A Passage to India* convokes spectral witnesses in the midst of growing unrest in colonial India. An imputed but occluded act of violence generates a trial that sets the struggle in motion: an Indian man is accused of raping an English woman in the Marabar Caves. In the novel, the caves metonymize India. The formal articulation of the alleged rape and its adjudication in the court indicate British anxieties about colonial masculinities in the midst of ever more vocal anticolonial resistance. This articulation and adjudication also point to an increased anxiety about Britain's (self-)image as a benevolent empire. This image has become threatened by Britain's recent efforts to implement a state of exception in the colony.

The transformation of the state of exception from a phenomenon of wartime to a condition of peacetime constitutes a historical shift in modernity, and it is one backdrop against which *A Passage to India* is composed. Giorgio Agamben describes this shift in which the state of exception becomes a "technique of government rather than an exceptional measure,"[45] transforming liberal democracies and exposing their tendencies toward the "'liquidation of democracy.'"[46] Agamben asserts that during World War I and the years immediately after it, "one of the essential characteristics of the state of exception—the provisional abolition of the distinction among legislative, executive, and judicial powers—here shows its tendency to become a lasting practice of government."[47] The philosopher discusses England in this context but does not consider how Britain's deployments of states of exception in its colonies in response to anticolonial resistance play a role in this transformation of modern biopower and sovereignty.[48]

Forster writes the novel in the immediate aftermath of a brutal show of force in the colony, the Amritsar Massacre of 1919. British soldiers fired into a crowd of ten thousand unarmed demonstrators, killing 379 people and wounding over one thousand others. This violence, though excessive, was not exceptional in the juridical sense of the term. That is, it was not, *but could have been*, authorized by the very legislation of a state of exception against which the protestors were demonstrating: the Rowlatt Acts. These acts extended World War I emergency powers into the colonies during peacetime to combat "subversive activities," allowing trials without juries and detention without trial in certain political cases. The acts were never implemented. Martial law was declared following the massacre, and other acts of state violence including beatings and floggings followed, but the massacre also gave rise to Gandhi's movement of noncooperation, which successfully thwarted the implementation of the acts.

A Passage to India makes no mention of the Rowlatt Acts, the mass demonstration, or the massacre, but its handling of colonial law and portrayal of an India that baffles that law's attempts to get hold of it can be read as a meditation on Britain's waning power and changing reputation from benevolent to malevolent imperial power. Forster's elaboration of testimony as a mode contained within institutions such as the trial, and also uncontainable by them, tells a story about how literature responds to historical trauma that will recur in singular ways throughout this book.

Through its treatment of the Marabar Caves, the novel relates English characters' desires to comprehend and get hold of India, a place that seems destined always to elude their grasp. Eventually the caves become a site of failed comprehension that compels the intervention of colonial law. The English woman Adela Quested, who is in India visiting her fiancé with her future mother-in-law, Mrs. Moore, accuses the Indian Aziz of raping her when they travel together to the caves. Before they visit them, Adela eagerly demands information about the caves from Aziz and others. Her demand sets off a vertiginous process that ends in failure. The stakes of comprehending the caves are great, for by accessing them, according to Adela, she will finally discover the "*real* India."[49] She implores the Hindu Professor Godbole and Muslim Aziz to describe these Jain caves: "Tell me everything you will, or I shall never understand India" (79). Aziz, failing to present them, encourages Godbole, "do describe them" (79). Godbole more than acquiesces to filling the role of native informant, it seems, insisting, "it will be a great honor" (79). But Adela's desire to "understand India" is left unsatisfied.

> "There is an entrance in the rock in which you enter, and through the entrance is the cave."
>
> "Something like the caves at Elephanta?"
>
> "Oh no, not at all; at Elephanta there are sculptures of Siva and Parvati. There are no sculptures at Marabar."
>
> "They are immensely holy, no doubt," said Aziz, to help on the narrative.
>
> "Oh no, oh no."
>
> "Still, they are ornamented in some way."
>
> "Oh no."
>
> "Well, why are they so famous? We all talk of the famous Marabar Caves. Perhaps that is our empty brag."
>
> "No, I should not quite say that."

"Describe them to this lady, then."

"It will be a great pleasure." He forewent the pleasure, and Aziz realized he was keeping back something about the caves.

(80)

It is unclear whether the novel's dramatization of Adela's desire and Godbole's refusal to satisfy it criticizes or consolidates colonialist vision. Although Aziz labors to "help on the narrative," Godbole, who masquerades as an informant, stymies it at every point. The power of silence and withholding is harnessed by the Hindu colonial subject against both Adela and the Muslim character, whom the novel presents throughout as more proximate to the English. Significantly, the passage does not relate that Godbole *cannot* represent the caves but that he *chooses* not to, perhaps even at his own expense; he "forewent the pleasure." One might of course read that claim as ironic, but one might just as well read it as the desire to interrupt desire. That the novel declines to represent the caves not only through Godbole's perspective but also the narrator's suggests that one point of this exchange might be to make readers aware that their own desires can coincide with colonial desires to objectify, to freeze a complex place into an image and insert it into a body of knowledge in order to master it. But this scene might, on the contrary, support scholars' contentions, most notably Edward Said's and Sara Suleri's, that Forster's depiction of India as exorbitant to representation codes this place as irrational, a "muddle," as the narrative frequently derides.[50]

As muddle, I would argue, India also appears exorbitant to modernity and justice, a place that requires colonial knowledge and legal systems to provide both. The performative contradiction the scene cited above rehearses by declaring the caves immediately representable while refusing to represent them is repeated in reverse later in the novel. Here, the narrator's ethnographic voice and focalization render the caves overdetermined:

> There is something unspeakable in these outposts. They are like nothing else in the world, and a glimpse of them makes the breath catch. They rise abruptly, insanely, without the proportion that is kept by the wildest hills elsewhere, they bear no relation to anything dreamt or seen. To call them "uncanny" suggests ghosts, and they are older than all spirit. . . .
>
> The caves are readily described. A tunnel eight feet long, five feet high, three feet wide, leads to a circular chamber about twenty feet in diameter. This ar-

> rangement occurs again and again throughout the group of hills, and this is all, this is a Marabar Cave. Having seen one such cave, having seen two, having seen three, four, fourteen, twenty-four, the visitor returns to Chandrapore uncertain whether he has had an interesting experience or a dull one or any experience at all. He finds it difficult to discuss the caves, or to keep them apart in his mind, for the pattern never varies. . . . Nothing, nothing attaches to them, and their reputation—for they have one—does not depend upon human speech.
>
> (136–137)

"Unspeakable" and "readily described," all too ordinary and completely extraordinary, purely symbolic and marking the failure of the symbolic, the caves embody an interpretive impasse in the novel. The interpretive impasse described here and registered in the previous scene's formal treatment of the caves prefigures the interpretative impasse that occurs during Adela and Aziz's visit to the caves. Whether a rape happens during that visit is left indeterminate. The allegation calls forth the law in the form of a trial. The trial's response to this indeterminate event has in turn obstructed scholars' efforts to determine whether this work supports or challenges the ideals of imperial law and its distribution of justice.[51]

The scene in the caves that treats the inability to grasp India as an inability to witness an alleged transgression perpetrated by an Indian man against an English woman generates legal action whose presentation collocates formal practices of witnessing with historical problems of witnessing anticolonial resistance. Although this alleged transgression seems an act unconnected to the political sphere of national protest, as Jenny Sharpe has argued, it references the colonial discourse surrounding an earlier anticolonial revolt, the Indian Mutiny of 1857.[52] But Forster's text is arguably also haunted by the recent protest at Amritsar and the emergence of an anticolonial movement more sustained and organized than that during the mutiny. In light of these recent developments, the motivations for grasping an unknown, incomprehensible India extend beyond that of the apparently innocuous colonial curiosity parodied through Adela's "quest." Indeterminacy in India has become more threatening in the postwar years because it is now associated with the possible presence of subversives and because to manage such indeterminacy Britain must compromise what Conrad's Marlowe calls empire's "noble cause."[53] The protest at Amritsar revealed the brutality of British colonialism in its effort to control indeterminacies in order to prevent subversion. The extension of emergency powers during peacetime in the colony is part of a wider series of tactics through which English law compromises its claims to operate as a vehicle of universal justice. By choreographing a trial, the novel provides an occasion to redeem English law and reassert the colonizer's supposed imperial benevolence. Rather than do so, however, *A Passage to India* shows that law includes within itself the capacity to subvert itself as well as the capacity to generate further subversions by those it seeks to control when it endeavors to maintain a political status quo. The novel relates that law does so because it relies upon testimony.

The trial is enlisted to provide justice and knowledge of what transpired in the caves, but the orchestration of time and space in that scene famously prohibits both characters and readers from determining whether or not a rape occurs.[54] It is impossible to pinpoint where different characters are located in relation to each other at each moment in the caves. The trial, by contrast, appears to be a distinct episode with a beginning, middle, and end. It is set in a space that organizes its various participants and audience into specific compartments that reflect their roles during the proceedings. Like the contested event it attempts to capture and adjudicate, however, the trial's temporal and spatial boundaries are not so neatly defined. An "uncanny" force is summoned that disrupts the time and space of the trial, disturbing chronology and eroding the walls of the courtroom and the lines that divide witnesses on the basis of gender, race, class, caste, and national and colonial identifications. As the trial commences, witness for the prosecution Adela summons her prospective mother-in-law, Mrs. Moore, through an apostrophe: "In virtue of what had she collected this roomful of people together? . . . by what right did they claim so much importance in the world, and assume the title of civilization? Mrs. Moore—she looked round, but Mrs. Moore was far away on the sea" (242). Just as the episode in the caves confuses time and clear significations of what has and what has not been experienced, of characters' presences and absences, the trial scene does, too. The novel relates that "while thinking of Mrs. Moore she heard sounds, which gradually grew more distinct. The epoch-making trial had started" (242). The summoning of Mrs. Moore obscures the beginning of the trial, which "had started" by the time we read this passage and by the time Adela turns her attention to the proceedings. The apostrophe to Mrs. Moore minimally muddles the beginning, but a different summoning of her by others disrupts the middle spectacularly. Despite the fact that the elder English woman has already departed India for England, and despite her insistence before she left that she would remain firmly outside of the institutions of colonial law—"'I have nothing to do with your ludicrous law courts,' she said, angry. 'I will not be dragged in at all'" (222)—she is brought within the system only to disrupt it again.

This second summoning of Mrs. Moore causes the law's delegates to lose control at the hands, or voices, of witnesses situated both within and outside the institutional space of the trial. When the prosecutor makes reference to, without naming, Mrs. Moore, his words "brought on another storm, and suddenly a new name, Mrs. Moore, burst on the court like a whirlwind" (248–249). The court becomes disordered, the defense storms out, "the tumult increased, the invocation of Mrs. Moore continued, and people who did not know what the syllables meant repeated them like a charm. They became Indianized into Esmiss Esmoor, they were taken up in the street outside. In vain the Magistrate threatened and expelled. Until the magic exhausted itself, he was powerless" (250). It so happens that while this occurs, as we later learn, Mrs. Moore dies en route to England. No one is aware of this at the time, however. The depiction of this central character's death is both strikingly laconic and uninterested in attaining conclusiveness: "'She died at sea.' 'The heat, I suppose.' 'Presumably'" (274). This depiction of her death, coupled with the temporal logic that coordinates her death with the Indians' calling of her name, invites an interpretation that seems outrageous when we consider that the novel, and the modernist novel in particular, is a secular narrative form.[55] This interpretation is that the Indians' apostrophe conjures a specter. It is around the time that she dies that Mrs. Moore returns as a liminal figure in the courtroom, situated between the poles of material and immaterial. (By having her die between India and England, the novel figures her liminality in cultural and national terms also.) The effects of the Indians' testimony during the trial, its "magic" (250), therefore interrupts legal reason as well as modernist secular reason in the novel.

Conjured through apostrophe, Mrs. Moore returns as a specter because she does not return as herself but as one disappropriated from her body and proper name. At the moment Mrs. Moore's proper name is called, it is stripped of property and, her son will maintain, of propriety. It is translated from the colonizer's English into the colonized's English as "Esmiss

Esmoor." The incantation spectralizes her because it materializes her in the courtroom, but as a "Hindu goddess" rather than in her own material form. The chant thus gives face to the dead woman while de-facing or giving her a different face at the same time.[56] The spectralization of Mrs. Moore temporarily dissolves the law's potency and dismantles the boundaries between the inside of the institution and its outside as the chant carries into the street. Those excluded from the legal machinery, neither judge, jury, nor witnesses for defense or prosecution, become unauthorized participants in the trial by summoning and insisting, against the proscription of the court, that the specter bears witness. "'An extraneous element is being introduced into the case,' said the Magistrate. 'I must repeat that as a witness Mrs. Moore does not exist. . . . She is not here, and consequently she can say nothing'" (252), he warns the defense and prosecution.

The conjuring of the specter in the voices of those subject to the British legal system but without power to determine how it dispenses justice rehearses an aberrant sexuality and an errant witnessing that clarifies that the goal of the trial is tied to broader interests of the colonial state. That goal is to police the relations between and desires of colonized and colonizers and thereby to maintain separations between Indians of various castes and classes and English and Anglo-Indian subjects. The apostrophic translation that conjures the excluded witness as specter, rendering her "sensuous-nonsensuous,"[57] is an act of subversion as well as perversion. It subverts the authority of the court but also perverts the lines of racial and sexual identification and desire the court enforces. The possibility of perversion of colonially regulated desires and identifications, which reaches its apotheosis in "Esmiss Esmoor," is signaled in the opening of the trial scene through Adela's focalization of the only subaltern in the room mentioned, the punkah wallah, whom the narrative connects to Mrs. Moore.

> Almost naked, and splendidly formed, he sat on a raised platform near the back, in the middle of the central gangway, and he caught her attention as she came in, and he seemed to control the proceedings. He had the strength and beauty that sometimes come to flower in Indians of low birth. When that strange race nears the dust and is condemned as untouchable, then nature remembers the physical perfection that she accomplished elsewhere, and throws out a god—not many, but one here and there, to prove to society how little its categories impress her. . . . Opposite him, also on a platform, sat the little assistant magistrate,

> cultivated, self-conscious, and conscientious. The punkah wallah was none of these things: he scarcely knew that he existed and did not understand why the Court was fuller than usual, indeed he did not know that it was fuller than usual, didn't even know he worked a fan, though he thought he pulled a rope. Something in his aloofness impressed the girl from middle-class England, and rebuked the narrowness of her sufferings.
>
> (241–242)

This consideration of the subaltern leads Adela to summon Mrs. Moore, for how the English justify assuming the "title of civilization . . . was the kind of question they might have discussed on the voyage out before the old lady had turned disagreeable and queer" (242). Structural links emerge between the two figures of different genders, national, colonial, and class and caste status. The "queer," spectral Mrs. Moore and the untouchable are both outside and inside the proceedings simultaneously and are bestowed with an agency that exposes the limits of juridical power. The subaltern "seemed to control the proceedings" without consciousness, as does the specter who suspends the Magistrate's power without intention, and not as her proper self; however, both witnesses possess no institutional agency. The punkahwallah "had no bearing officially upon the trial" (241)—indeed, is presented as unconscious of its meaning as a political, "epoch-making" event entirely. This remark underlines that he figures a subalternity that is not yet in crisis or on the way to institutional resistance. Mrs. Moore, the court has ruled, "as a witness cannot exist." Both characters are also eroticized by others whose social, economic, and political standing is dissymmetrical with their own. Adela's gaze eroticizes the subaltern "god," and the translation of the English woman into "goddess" reads as another instance of eroticism condemned by Mrs. Moore's son as a sexual violation: "It was revolting to hear his mother travestied into Esmiss Esmoor, a Hindu goddess" (250).

When Adela asks "Isn't it all queer" (251) after the courtroom and street erupt in chants, "queer" reads in at least two ways. First, summoning the specter through translation is an act of illicit love. The summons highlights the etymology of the word translation, a carrying over and across, and literalizes it in both narrow and broad senses. In the narrow sense, the summons crosses linguistic codes (from Anglo-English into Indian English), and in the broader sense the summons carries the witness from death into an after-life or sur-vival. This double-crossing queers colonial law's policing of heteronormative desire as a prohibition on crossing national, racial, and colonially circumscribed limits of desire. Second, the summons queers a legal and institution-bound understanding of witnessing based on the categories of the evidentiary and the verifiable and on ontologies of presence and absence. Testimony here does not provide evidence. Rather, it connects subjects that the trial endeavors to divide.

The summons subverts because it illustrates that testimony cannot be entirely contained by institutions in which it emerges; by subverting containment, it insubordinately generates a proscribed, unstable cross-cultural alliance, a strange, catachrestic friendship between colonizer and colonized. While the novel relates that institutions cannot fully control the agency of testimony, its treatment of friendship also rejects the notion that legal forums are simply mechanisms of repression and silencing: it is the trial that occasions this friendship. By occasioning the perverting of law through the misdirections of testimony, the trial enacts a futurity in the here and now that controverts the novel's last words on friendship. The work's concluding paragraphs deny the capacity for friendship between Indians and English in the present and disavow its possibility in the future by dismissing the stated necessary condition for this friendship: India as sovereign nation. In the exchange between Aziz and Fielding, characters whose gender, religion, and class identifications the novel has established—the novel, by contrast, does not establish those of the Indians who summon the English woman during the trial—the possibility of friendship is foreclosed.

> India a nation! What an apotheosis! Last comer to the drab nineteenth-century sisterhood! . . . Fielding mocked again. And Aziz in an awful rage danced this way and that, not knowing what to do, and cried: "Down with the English anyhow. . . . Clear out, you fellows. . . . We may hate one another, but we hate you most. . . . we shall drive every blasted English to the sea . . . and then," he concluded, half kissing him, "you and I shall be friends."
>
> "Why can't we be friends now?" said the other, holding him affectionately. "It's what I want. It's what you want."
>
> But the horses didn't want it—they swerved apart; the earth didn't want it, sending up rocks through which riders must pass single file; the temples, the tank, the jail, the palace, the birds, the carrion, the Guest House, that came into view as they issued from the gap and saw Mau beneath: they didn't want it, they said in their hundred voices, "No, not yet," and the sky said, "No, not there."
>
> (361–362)

The trial operates as a forum for law's interruption through an act of witnessing that also interrupts the narrative's closure and defies laws of nature (the horses, the earth, the birds, the carrion, the sky) and culture, both Indian and British (the temples, the tanks, the jail, the palace, the Guest House). Testimony dispatched during the trial does not describe the status quo and solidify its divisions of class, caste, religion, gender, and colonial status under the dominant structuring, "in other words, literary and cultural forms (like legal forms) do not simply reflect the social world."[58] It calls forth a transcultural, -class, and -caste friendship among men and women that cannot exist in the novel's present. This alliance that perverts and subverts the law, however, is not plotted as one that either party intentionally enters into. Mrs. Moore is summoned, it seems, while she dies and enters into the alliance as a specter. The Indians do not know who it is they summon, "did not know what the syllables meant" (250) with which they call her. "Alliance" and "friendship" are therefore catachreses when used to describe the relationships the summons engenders. We would have to question Kieran Dolin's contention that while "the trial may be conducted along 'imperial' lines . . . the result affirms Mrs. Moore's faith in and sympathetic understanding of her friend."[59]

For although the defense insists that the prosecution has smuggled Mrs. Moore out of the country because she would "have proved his [Aziz's] innocence . . . she was poor Indians' friend" (249), there is no guarantee here or elsewhere that this determinate type of friendship either existed or exists. The defense calculates that by claiming Mrs. Moore as Indians' friend it could claim her as Aziz's alibi. The friendship testimony invokes does not operate according to calculation, however. It does not provide evidence or help prove Aziz's "innocence." We know why the defense would summon Mrs. Moore, but we never discover why the Indians summon her; it is not even clear that they know why since they are presented as not knowing the meaning or referent of the words they chant. Because the novel never verifies whether this summons occurs with the hopes of exonerating Aziz—whether the Indians rally around Aziz in a show of support of a fellow national—it leaves uncertain whether this summoning serves political ends. The text suggests that this testimony might stage friendship instead as an ethical encounter, a relation between others that is not motivated by calculation.

We might read as an historical index the fact that the trial is what occasions this subversive, perverting, nonidentitarian friendship emerging through a translation that creates an excess, an "extraneous element," as the Magistrate refers to the spectral Mrs. Moore. By articulating that colonial legal institutions can facilitate the eruption of alliances they would police but cannot entirely control, the novel registers threats to imperial power in its time. By convoking the strange friendship it does between members of different races, classes, sexes, castes, and nations, insurgent testimony indicates that the novel also imagines a future in which social structures imposed under imperialism have eroded. The trial scene intimates that colonial rule will eventually end, therefore; however, it does not do so by acknowledging that an anticolonial nationalist movement exists in the colony at the time. Said argued that Forster's text is restricted by the imagination of the England of his time because it cannot take seriously the coherence of such a movement in India, except, the critic maintains, for a brief moment. That moment is the eruption of the chant during the trial in which "the Indians [are] roused momentarily to a sort of nationalist coherence."[60] The "sort of" is significant. Only by ignoring a host of details in the choreography of this insurgent testimony—the aberrant sexuality and errant witnessing; the structural suturing of Mrs. Moore to the subaltern, who, as such, is necessarily *not* captured by a popular nationalist movement;[61]and the translation that generates a "community" whose members are not shown to be consciously resisting imperial power or even conscious of the meaning of their speech—can this chant be termed nationalist or coherent. Instead, this insurgent testimony and the alliance it convokes operate below the level of the national *and* cross national (and cultural-linguistic) borders.

The trial scene configures a mode of anticolonial subversion distinct from, and both less and more threatening than, the organized nationalist movement coincident with the novel's composition and publication. The disordered, spontaneous subversion, queer and unconscious, is less threatening than the nationalist movement that consciously and systematically resists because the latter proved strong enough to articulate a program that made explicit the implicit suspension of democratic principles of British law during the Amritsar Massacre and successfully prevented the implementation of a permanent state of exception in the form of the Rowlatt Acts. By contrast, the novel's alliance suspends the trial only briefly. The proceedings continue until Adela withdraws her charge. Insurgent testimony also does not recover the "truth" of the occluded event at the trial's center and does not resolve questions about culpability and innocence. The novel will not verify that justice has been served with the acquittal of Aziz. However, this mode of witnessing is more threatening than the extant nationalist movement because it discloses what cannot be represented in any direct way: the threat of a state of exception to the colonial government that will norm it as a governmental tactic. Insurgent testimony lays bare law's capacity to produce subversions that reveal law's internal interruptions. Moreover, the agents of subversion are no longer immediately recognizable by race, gender, class, or caste or identifiable by the logic of presence and the present or by the conditions of status quo the novel's conclusion countersigns. As we have seen, the courtroom draws together subjects the law hopes to separate and unintentionally creates the possibility of uncontrolled desire and collectivities that cross borders. Finally, because the alliance is disorganized and spontaneous, it is more difficult to anticipate or control, and it carries the possibility that the exposure of English law's suspension of liberal principles and claims to provide universal justice can occur at any time.

A Passage to India gestures toward a more just future through the insurgent conjuring of spectral witnesses, but without detaching itself entirely from the limits of its own present. The future testimony imagines is certainly not one defined by normative selves who transcend differences and historicities, the "utopia" articulated by R. Radhakrishnan in his examination of Forster's novel. Considering the depiction of flames that approach in the Marabar Caves, Radhakrishnan regrets that the novel forecloses the "ideal world"[62] it provokes, one structured by reciprocity rather than asymmetry: "Why can't each flame perform both as mirror and as window to the other so that transcendence into the utopian Real may be effected in radical transgression of the colonialist mode of recognition?"[63] The rearrangement of community testimony conjures does not resemble this "ideal world" in which unevenness and alterity have disappeared. Both more realistic and less teleological and problematically humanist than Radhakrishnan's formulation of the future, the collectivity insurgent testimony enacts through linguistic and cultural translation is not as divided as that of 1924, but it remains shaped by the unevenness of that time. For the trial's mise-en-scène reveals what must be given up in order for Forster to imagine a new community. After all, the alliance emerges through a disappropriation of its subjects, the divestment of selfhood and volition, as well as the erasure of markers of historicity and embodiment. Each "friend" is not a "normative Self . . . willing to be rendered vulnerable by the gaze of the 'Other' within the coordinates of a level playing field."[64] Testimony ensures that to become "poor Indians' friend," Mrs. Moore must die and be translated into an Indian deity, prosopoetically detached from a face, voice, and body produced by the contingencies of history. The Indians cannot even be rendered conscious that they might be engaging in an act of friendship. The novel cannot create a situation in which English women and Indian men and women become friends "in themselves" or as selves during the colonial era.

Thus, while the friendship that emerges during the trial inclines toward the ethical because it is not subject centered and is discontinuous with calculation, this friendship remains parabolic to the ethical that such theorists as Georges Bataille, Maurice Blanchot, and Jean-Luc Nancy articulate because it demands the effacement of all historical differences and perhaps even demands the transcendence of finitude, the transformation of friends into "gods" or "goddesses."[65] We thus cannot verify whether an "ethics" of witnessing has occurred. The alliance testimony conjures is already a perjury of the ethical because it is constituted out of the political-historical situations of modernity that structure the novel.

Radhakrishnan's reading of *A Passage to India* prompts Laura Winkiel to raise significant questions about modernism, utopia, and historicity as she reflects on how comparative methodologies might access global modernisms' varied relationships to modernity. "Modernism is rife with failed utopias," she reports, "but," she asks,

> is there a possibility for comparative modernisms that might allow us a glimpse of that utopian and potentially transformative space? I'm concerned most with keeping in play both colonial historicity and the utopian realm of transcendent temporality. . . . How does the novel as a global form signify modernity and enact that modernity by negotiating with other forms at the state and local levels? How does the novel negotiate those disparate spaces and temporalities, cultural otherness and sameness, especially at the level of literary genre?[66]

Insurgent Testimonies endeavors to respond to some of these questions. The book understands modernity as "by definition uneven, divided as it is between capital and labor, overdevelopment and underdevelopment,"[67] yet at the same time, as testimony to these particular historical traumas insist, as rife with the imaginative potential to disrupt unevenness.

The events the writings collected here address entailed enormous suffering and loss, but also, as the example of *A Passage to India* conveys, they conditioned possibilities for imagining new social, political, and economic arrangements. These works' testimonies to trauma therefore challenge any definition of modernity as the ready acquiescence to the singular and decisive triumph of capitalism and imperialism. To explore such imaginations, I rely on close reading, an increasingly anachronistic method in an era of "distanced reading" and "surface reading." Close reading, at its best, allows one to draw connections in a way that prevents universalizing ahistoricism, on the one hand, and, on the other, impedes the tendency to reduce literarity on the basis of preprogrammed historical knowledge. Jane Gallop asserts, "It is precisely my opposition to timeless universals that make me value close reading," and she makes a compelling case for the necessity of it in the midst of literary studies' return to historicism and the archive.[68] Here, close reading attempts to follow the shifting hyphens between the ethical and political, the literary and historical that testimony enacts. At this contemporary moment in which techniques of power these works elaborate and scrutinize are being restaged in new as well as old ways—from indefinite detention, to capital punishment, to racial profiling, to arguments for imminent threat and deterrence as bases for policy decisions in the ongoing war on terror—these writings might become, themselves, dialectical images. They might enable us "to seize hold of a memory as it flashes up at a moment of danger" so as to reexamine oppressive pasts that form a constellation with the present.

ONE

Compelled Confessions and Forced Attachments in Joseph Conrad's *Under Western Eyes* and "Poland Revisited"

Through the framing narrative of an English witness, Conrad's 1911 novel, *Under Western Eyes*, depicts the underground dealings of administrators and challengers of the Russian state as they travel across various geopolitical, cultural, and linguistic terrains of Europe. Suggesting the central role testimony will play in this text, Conrad places readers before the law in the first sentence. The novel commences with the flourish of a paraph, a confession sealed by the novel's narrator, an English teacher of languages: "To begin with I wish to disclaim the possession of those high gifts of imagination and expression which would have enabled my pen to create for the reader the personality of the man who called himself, after the Russian custom, Cyril son of Isidor—Kirylo Sidorovitch—Razumov."[1] By disclaiming possession of these gifts, the narrator confesses that he cannot take responsibility for the narrative that follows. He cannot claim authority for the events about to unfold and therefore cannot guarantee that the story will be a truthful or accurate account of the personality on which it centers or a faithful rendering of the common nouns to which that man's proper name refers: the Russian language, particularly writing (Kirylo, or Cyrillic), and reason (Razumov, or son of reason). Confessions of this sort repeat throughout the novel, insisting that the work we are reading is not an original text but a transcription of one that already exists. The English work, recites the narrator, "is based on a document; all I have brought to it is my knowledge of the Russian language" (3). The document that forms the novel's central embedded narrative is another confession, composed by the Russian student-turned-spy-turned–double agent, Razumov.

That confession would play such a prominent role in one of the most autobiographically inflected of Conrad's novels is intriguing, given the distaste Conrad expressed for this act in his actual autobiography, *A Personal Record*. Conrad associates confession with excessive self-exposure and revolutionary ideologies, which are embodied in the corpus of Jean-Jacques Rousseau. Conrad worries that confession will overtake his autobiography; "the matter in hand is to keep these reminiscences from turning into confessions, a form of literary activity discredited by Jean-Jacques Rousseau on account of the extreme thoroughness he brought to the work of justifying his own existence."[2] Rousseau uses this debased form to justify himself because he was "not a writer of fiction" but rather an "artless moralist, as is clearly demonstrated by his anniversaries being celebrated with marked emphasis by the heirs of the French Revolution."[3] Despite its association with assaults on established authority and literary artfulness—or because of them—confession drives not one but two of Conrad's most personal pieces, *Under Western Eyes* and the 1915 essay "Poland Revisited." It links these later works focused on Europe to Conrad's earlier fictions, whose plots are located in colonial peripheries and whose topics are the vicissitudes of colonial encounter: the crystallization of compelled communities. The emergence of these disturbing and unwilled connections to others is dramatized in narratives of "going native."

Conrad's later works, however, are typically read in light of his shift away from conflicts attending imperial-national and colonial consolidation, charted across such fictions as *Almayer's Folly*, *Heart of Darkness*, *Lord Jim*, and *Nostromo*. In 1905, Conrad's subject turns "from the map of Empire to the map of Europe,"[4] as his fiction enters metropolitan spaces populated with cosmopolitan characters whose identities are hybrid and who speak a globalized English detached from a national origin: London in the 1890s in *The Secret Agent*, St. Petersburg and Geneva during the Russian revolution of 1905 in *Under Western Eyes*. In recent years, these later "political novels,"[5] and even some earlier ones, have elicited a more generous account of their author's response to imperial modernity than previously. Critical tenets following Chinua Achebe's famous takedown of *Heart of Darkness* that identify in Conrad's oeuvre "complicity with (at best) or perpetuation of (at worst) racist, sexist, and classist," nationalist, and imperialist ideologies have been revised and even reversed.[6] Such readings argue that his works' rhetorical tactics challenge the foundations of categories "East" and "West,"[7] that his characters' performances denaturalize the national as the primary mode of subjective identification,[8] and that his cast of English speakers reflect a diffused, internally split language that interpellates a global imagined community of readers while undoing the hierarchy between metropolitan center and colonial periphery.[9]

Confession in *Under Western Eyes* and "Poland Revisited" complicates this critical refashioning of Conrad from an author guided by romantic, organicist principles of political community, whose fiction rehearses imperial-national epistemologies, into one whose worldly perspective suspends or contests imperial-nationalist determinations of subjects, languages, and collectivities. Of course, *Under Western Eyes*—a "Russian novel" written in English by a Polish subject–turned–British citizen, framed as a translation composed by a multilingual teacher of languages, and addressed to a supranational community of readers, the West—appears to embody just this perspective. And indeed, through its handling of confession, the novel registers the deteriorating boundaries of the nation-state, decline of imperialism, and the eruption of revolution by articulating subjectivity, language, and "East" and "West" as constructed and contingent rather than grounded. But it is precisely because it illuminates these instabilities that the work undercuts the critical valence critics impute to their disclosure. Shifting linguistic, geopolitical, and social formations of the first decades of the twentieth century are presented as a crisis because they threaten intolerable kinships. The conflict animating the novels of empire does not disappear when Conrad's plots travel from colonial contact zones to revolutionary and pre-War Europe, therefore. It is redirected onto the form of confession, which is propelled by traumas of anticolonial resistance and revolution.

Bearing witness to intertwined revolutionary and colonial histories in Poland and Russia in which alliances are ambivalent and collectivities amorphous and contested, confession in Conrad's works creates unintended binds and commitments to others. It elaborates a structure of responsibility that departs from and unsettles not only conservative organicist models of community based in race or nation but also a humanist ethic of conviviality and cosmopolitanism. This ethic is conceived as a conscious obligation to those beyond one's ethnic, religious, and national affiliations, a "recognition of our responsibility for every human being."[10] It constitutes willed efforts "to act morally and justly . . . in the face of otherness" by citizen-subjects "dissatisfied by the prospect of being forcibly attached by patriotism and nationalism to cultural and political formations that are wrong, unjust, evil, or misguided."[11] The crossing of borders and mixing of cultures that defines modernity is often thought to encourage cultivation of this pacifist ethic.[12] In "Poland Revisited" and *Under Western Eyes*, borders are crossed, cultures mixed, and obligations to others made; however, because they are orchestrated through confession, these commitments are neither the result of consciousness or choice, nor peaceful. As *A Personal Record* warns, confession can operate without witnesses' consent. Responding to political violence, it forces attachments and regulates the formal staging of revolution and resistance, topics connected to personal and collective pasts Conrad has been reluctant to address. *Under Western Eyes*'s story "had long haunted me," he confides; "now it must come out." The book aims to "capture the Russian soul" but also hopes to "make peace with [his] Polish shades." Written four years after its publication, "Poland Revisited" indicates that the novel has failed to exorcise these specters, that its confessional mode cannot bring things to an end. The essay serves as a lens through which to view *Under Western Eyes* not only because Conrad "treated the problems of Russia from a Polish perspective"[13] but because it both employs and enacts an autocritique of the earlier work's central mode of expression, providing instructions for reading the formal predicament of confession the novel relates.

Double Thought in "Poland Revisited"

Launched with a condemnation of revolutionary violence, "Poland Revisited" recounts the author's return to Poland with his family a year earlier on the eve of the Great War. That it is his first visit to Poland in twenty years and Cracow in forty evinces his ambivalence toward his Polish past, itself rife with revolutionary conflict. The son of Polish anticolonial revolutionaries who died when he was very young, Conrad was raised by an uncle who was critical of their political views. The divided perspectives on empire and resistance that resulted inhabit many of Conrad's works, including "Poland Revisited."[14] While it would seem that the contours of this travel narrative are determined by external factors, the journey Conrad undertakes, this is not the case. More psychobiography than documentary, it is nevertheless not an accurate account of the personal experiences it relates. It mistakes dates and chronologies, sentiments and so-called facts about emotional states are contradicted by Conrad's letters, and its management of time dilates certain periods and truncates others. These inconsistencies, along with other elements, suggest that the confessional form, rather than the trip itself, directs the narrative's unfolding. This form is spurred by events that have yet to settle into the past, namely, Polish revolutionary struggle and Conrad's family's participation in it.

The essay, however, repeatedly insists on separating personal from political realms and the present conditions of world war from Poland's long history of colonization, partitions, and insurrections, which are barely noted. When it does acknowledge this history it is in spiritual, nearly Messianic nationalist terms, describing a Poland that stubbornly remains despite being effaced by geohistorical inscriptions: "Poland then, if erased from the map, yet existed in reality; it was not a mere *pays du rêve* where you can travel only in imagination. For no man . . . would push the love of the novelist's art of make-believe to the point of burdening himself with real trunks for a voyage *au pays du rêve*."[15] Condemning the attack on dynastic rule, the assassination of Archduke Ferdinand, and observing the rise of imperial and anti-imperial nationalisms throughout Europe and the Balkans, the essay takes care to distinguish these political tensions from "private" matters, using the latter—whether a "conjuncture which, in a most private sense, was somewhat trying" (114), or thoughts of Conrad's imminent Poland trip, "the simplest sort of Continental holiday" (119)—to explain neglect of the former in the days leading up to war. Conrad implies that cries of "race, liberation, justice" (115) of the time are located mainly in "these Eastern nations [that] were not far removed from a savage state" (116), and he derides their "trivial demonstrations. One could not take today a ticket for Petersburg.

'You mean Petrograd' would say the booking clerk. Shortly after the fall of Adrianople a friend of mine passing through Sophia asked for some '*café turc*' at the end of his lunch. 'Monsieur veut dire *café balkanique*,' the patriotic waiter corrected him austerely" (115–116). Until the very end, the essay seems to ignore the fervor for national independence that has captured contemporary Poland, as it had the Poland of Conrad's youth. Escaping to a Polish health resort on the last train out of Cracow after war is declared, the family is surrounded by Poles from all over the country also unable to travel. Claiming "it was a wonderful, poignant two months" (135), Conrad immediately writes the contemporaneous crisis and long history of partitions, failed uprisings, and repressions out of the text while differentiating himself from this "whole people" and "its last illusions" (136) about the possibility of an independent Poland:

> This is not the time and perhaps not the place, to enlarge upon the tragic character of the situation: a whole people seeing the culmination of its misfortune in a final catastrophe. . . . I am glad I have not so many years left to me to remember that appalling feeling of inexorable Fate . . . come after so many cruel years, a figure of dread murmuring with iron lips the final words: Ruin—and Extinction.
>
> But enough of this.
>
> (135–136)

Yet the history of Polish insurgency is not so easily expelled from the piece. Displaced across the entire work, it troubles the author's aims by activating the confessional mode he wants to avoid and attaches him to this people he asserts are without a future.

Confession dissolves the limits between personal and political that Conrad attempts to establish, and it fortifies the filial and political bonds it endeavors break. *Under Western Eyes* has not made peace once and for all with those "Polish shades." They haunt "Poland Revisited" too, especially the specter of his father, Apollo Korzeniowski. Conrad's image of his father was shaped by his childhood memories but also largely by his maternal uncle and guardian, Tadeusz Bobrowski, who represented Korzeniowski in a less than flattering light. Bobrowski painted a picture of a privileged member of the *szlachta*, or ruling class in Ukraine, whose opinions were naïve and incoherent. While agreeing that Korzeniowski's program was not always well defined, Zdzislaw Najder has also corrected Bobrowski's interpretation.[16] After leaving Ukraine for Warsaw in 1861, Korzeniowski became a leading member of the Reds, the most radical revolutionary faction of anti-Russian Polish nationalists of the time. They pushed for broad social reforms across classes and the abolition of serfdom. They advocated liberation from Russian rule in the Congress Kingdom, Ruthenia, and Lithuania but were not chauvinistic or expansionist. They hoped to achieve a formation that could accommodate the existence of other nations from the old Polish Commonwealth within a single state, if necessary. The Korzeniowskis' home in Warsaw became the headquarters for the movement in 1861, and Korzeniowski was eventually imprisoned and then exiled with his wife, Ewalina, and young son. Geoffrey Galt Harpham argues that "Conrad registered not just the *similarity* of family and nation, father and Fatherland, but their near *identity*, and he did so at the moment of his father's funeral."[17] "Poland Revisited" leads to the site of his father's funeral and supports Harpham's point that the subject of Poland produces disruptive effects in his writing. Here, it generates confessions while interrupting them, inducing the predicament of "double thought." Disrupting the essay's itinerary and proving, just as *A Personal Record* fears, that confession can overtake reminiscences, the essay's ironic detours disclose a process of witnessing compelled by a confrontation with anticolonial revolt concentrated in the figure of the unmourned father.

This ironic mode is theorized by J. M. Coetzee in an exploration of the confessional discourse of Dostoevsky, a writer whose literary practices and politics, like Rousseau's, Conrad criticized. The essay's oscillating resistance and capitulation to confession enacts what Dostoevsky names and Coetzee analyzes as double thought, "a potentially infinite regression" driven by contradictory desires: "the doubling back of thought that undermines the integrity of the will to confess by detecting behind it a will to deceive, and behind the detection of this second motive a third motive (a wish to be admired for one's candor), and so on."[18] This process threatens the project of confession in the secular literary tradition, which is to achieve absolution and closure, "liberation from the oppression" of a known truth as well as one not known to the confessant. Double thought thwarts the confessant's efforts to reveal the unknown truth, which emerges through irony as a discrepancy between a confession's statement and performance. It slips out "in strange associations, false rationalizations, gaps, contradictions."[19] In "Poland Revisited," the known truth is that Conrad has entirely separated himself from his early life in Poland, and the unknown truth is twofold—that this life has not separated itself from him and that instead of enabling him to make peace with and disconnect from those Polish shades, confession only binds him to them more tightly.

The essay announces itself as a search for a hidden truth sealed away in Poland and as an attempt to resolve a discontinuity within the self created by a break with the past. Conrad describes the journey, and by extension the essay, as an archaeological expedition, a recovery of a moment sedimented into an internal archive that has become foreign to him. The instituting and sealing of this archive from conscious memory is tied to the life and death of the father, for it was in Cracow, he tells us, "where I spent with my father the last eighteen months of his life" that "I began to understand things, form affections, lay up a store of memories and a fund of sensations with which I was to break violently by throwing myself into an unrelated existence. It was like the experience of another world" (117). Conrad hopes to discover whether imagination is betraying "shadows in my youth" and to test "the reality of my past" (117). This truth-seeking mission is more a matter of war than peace. The journey is metaphorized as "the invasion of a tribe" (117), a phrase that identifies Conrad with colonizers rather than colonized. The ironic metaphor highlights the essay's ambivalence toward his native land and the return to it and signals the challenges confession will face in making known the essay's unknown truths.

A stronger signal that confession struggles to establish knowledge and accomplish ethical and narrative closure is registered by the essay's structure and sequencing, which imply that, as the narrator of *Heart of Darkness* describes Marlowe's methods, "the meaning of an episode was not inside like a kernel but outside, enveloping the tale which brought it out only as a glow brings out a haze."[20] Divided into four parts, the piece breaks its title's promise; despite the announced subject, it does not revisit Poland until part 4. Its circuitous forays into an ever-retreating past through a slow regression in time as readers move forward in narrative space mirrors the voyage itself, which "would have something of a migratory character" ("Poland Revisited," 117). This is quite an understatement: The Conrads embark on a route that makes the journey *thirty-six times* longer than necessary. Foregoing an expedient passage seems especially odd because Conrad declares his desire to begin this long-awaited journey so intense that it blinds him to the danger brewing throughout Europe. He explains the current deferral of "this Polish journey which for so many years had been before us in a state of a project full of colour and promise but always retreating, elusive, like an enticing mirage" (119) by placing responsibility on his wife, who chooses this passage. Conrad agrees to her request because it offers an "air of adventure in better keeping with the romantic feeling of this Polish journey" (119).

This rationale of manufacturing narrative tension in the name of romance notwithstanding, other aspects of the piece hint at why both journey and essay possess a migratory character. The sequencing not only betrays the expectations the title establishes but mimics the anxieties of betrayal that organize this work as well as *Under Western Eyes*, along with so many others, as Ian Watt has demonstrated.[21] In part 1, Conrad unwittingly intimates why the essay delays reaching its destination by recounting that the journey will land him "in a country house in the neighborhood of Cracow, but within the Russian frontier" (117). He does not mention that this topos condenses the tension structuring his early life, the opposing allegiances of his father and uncle to the Russian state. Instead, he inexplicably relates that his initial reaction to the journey is "dismay" (117). While this dismay would be understandable given his conflicted family history, this is not the reason Conrad gives. Instead, he explains his dismay in terms of betrayal, a betrayal twice displaced: "Since leaving the sea to which I have been faithful for so many years, I have discovered that there is in my composition very little stuff from which travelers are made," he confides. "I confess that my first impulse about a projected journey is to leave it alone" (117). Betrayal is indicated via its antonym, "faithfulness," to an entity that signifies an alternative genealogy. His faithfulness to the "sea" is a displacement of his fidelity to another set of parents, not Polish but British. Britain's Merchant Shipping Act gives birth to his life on the sea; it had been "in a manner of speaking a father and mother to me" (123). The essay's architecture belies what remains unstated, a crisis of memory caused by contradictory attitudes toward a different set of parents and their role in antistate rebellion.

Although both journey and essay hope to gain possession over Conrad's Polish past, the mission is compromised by double thought, which is initiated by a transposition from confession to excuse. Conrad is detained in Poland as a consequence of war, and he is detained in the essay by the confessional form. In addition to deferring the trip and the projected redemption of the past, narrative strategies disrupt the work in another way. The text slides continuously from confession, a mode directed toward truth revelation, to excuse, a mode directed toward self-exculpation.[22] Indeed, "Poland Revisited" originates with an excuse: "I have never believed in political assassination as a means to an end, and least of all in assassination of the dynastic order" (114). The sentence seeks to justify the events the memoir recalls, namely, Conrad's decision to allow himself and his family to travel into Eastern Europe on the brink of World War I. Increasing references to guilt and innocence code this statement as excuse rather than mere explanation. Echoing sentiments uttered by *Under Western Eyes*'s English narrator, Conrad claims that "it fitted with my ethical sense that an act cruel and absurd should be also useless" (115). He excuses himself by citing ideological presuppositions, which prevent him from reading the signs of future disturbances in Europe's political stability, but only a few sentences later, he excuses himself for an entirely unrelated reason. "There was no man capable of forming a judgment who attended so little to the march of events as I did at that time," he asserts, because "my mind was fixed on my own affairs, not because they were in a bad posture, but because of their fascinating, holiday-promising aspect" (115). Leaving aside why he mentions the negative, "bad posture" when he hopes to underline the positive aspects of his affairs, the need to exculpate himself for leading his family into Poland on the verge of war is made clear when soon after this statement Conrad describes his desires to revisit Poland as "innocent" redundantly, insisting that "whatever sinister passions were heaving under its splendid and complex surface, I was too agitated by a simple and innocent desire of my own to notice the signs, or interpret them correctly. The most innocent of passions will take the edge off one's judgment" (116).

The piece suggests that summoning confession to take responsibility for the past and unify a divided self is a losing game, for it demonstrates the failure of the excuses to exculpate the confessant. This failure is disclosed through the ironic articulation of the hidden truth as contradictions and false rationalizations that are the symptoms of double thought. These occur when Conrad protests his innocence excessively. Comparing the past framed as excuse to the past represented elsewhere illustrates the weakness of these protestations and the memoir's contradictions. In his excuse, Conrad states he overlooks the violence of the present and future because he turns toward a past absent of violence, "the past that one can not suspect and mistrust, the shadowy and unquestionable moral possession, the darkest struggles of which wear a halo of glory and peace"(116). The depiction of the past Conrad goes forth hesitantly and circuitously to encounter in Poland troubles this statement. Although the "holiday-promising" aspect of the journey allegedly diverts his attention from the imminent geopolitical conflict, his description of the journey's commencement implies a different cause for distraction. His companions were

> looking forward to a voyage in space whereas I felt more and more plainly that what I had started on was a journey in time, into the past; a fearful enough prospect for the most consistent, but to him who had not known how to preserve against his impulses the order and continuity of his life—so that at times it presented itself to his conscience as a series of betrayals—still more dreadful. (120)

The memoir expands and consolidates the evidence that an underlying ambivalence slows its pacing by formally negating Conrad's encomiums to a peaceful, hallowed Polish past and anticipation of this "enticing" journey. When Conrad finally arrives in Poland, the essay orchestrates a shameful conscience that prompts him to relive a time marked by revolution led by his father, painful memories of witnessing his father's death, and a homeland from which Conrad has violently "thrown" himself. The excuses offered throughout therefore paradoxically fold back on themselves, inculpating more than exculpating their confessant, indicating double thought.

"Poland Revisited" enacts double thought as an abyssal structure animated by shame, a crucial element in the choreography of any confession, according to Coetzee. The essay, however, also departs from the dominant understanding of shame as self-consciousness, which Coetzee also voices. Double thought operates through the concealing of truth, which generates shame, which generates more confession, which generates shame, which generates more confession, ad infinitum.

> Either the confessant was aware of the deeper truth but was concealing it, in which case he was deceiving his confessor; or, he was not aware of the deeper truth (though now he acknowledges it), in which case his competence as a confessant is in question: what was being offered as his secret, the coin of his

> confession, was not the real secret, was false coin, and a de facto deception has occurred, which is fresh cause for confession.[23]

Coetzee's explication contains an inconsistency, however, that Conrad's text illuminates. The testimony's form shows that in question is not simply whether the confessant acknowledges the "deeper truth" about his desire to return to Poland and endanger his family or conceals it and thereby deceives his readers. Rather, in question is whether the confession acknowledges this truth without its author's knowledge.[24] "Poland Revisited" indicates that an unknown truth can be acknowledged to the confessor—or reader—without the confessant's awareness of this acknowledgment. The distinction between truth and lie, acknowledgment and concealment, is undone by what Coetzee himself calls the "ironic confession," the confession that says more than or other than what it intends to say, for example, though elisions. An acknowledgment emerges, indirectly, through the narrative production of this other truth, or truth of the other within the self, constituted as much by absences as by what the confession states.

Shame toward what remains unknown results in a proliferation of confessions that never own up to a "deeper truth" except obliquely, impeding the essay's successful end through narrative evasions and a tropological movement by which Conrad at once refuses to take responsibility for his actions while simultaneously taking responsibility for them as an other. He ironically admits shame without acknowledging the truth of his motives both to return to Poland and to confess his desires in this piece. The *OED* defines shame as a result of consciousness: "The painful emotion arising from the consciousness of something dishonouring, ridiculous, or indecorous in one's own conduct or circumstances (or in those of others whose honour or disgrace one regards as one's own), or of being in a situation which offends one's sense of modesty or decency." "Shame" in Conrad's text, therefore, becomes a term without a proper referent. It cannot be understood as a reaction to an act of the conscious self. Desire to return to Poland to gain absolution and respite from ghosts of those he has betrayed might be "selfish" because it endangers others, but it is also "selfless" because it seems to operate outside the limits of the conscious self. By separating "thought" from consciousness, Conrad's text offers a new reading of double thoughts. An instance of such double thought appears when the text collapses the two moments, revelation of truth and suppression of truth, in one sentence in which responsibility is enfolded in its concealment and vice versa. The essay expresses a desire while repudiating it through the contradictory meanings of "unconscious." "All unconscious of going towards the very scenes of war," Conrad confides, "I carried off in my eye this tiny fragment of Great Britain" (119). This passage supports Paul de Man's claim that "excuse occurs within an epistemological twilight zone between knowing and not knowing."[25]

This staging of shame through double thought culminates in a frustration of the goals of both journey and essay. The final section does not conquer the distance between the two Conrads but rather concludes in an act of doubling and expropriation that returns once again to the spectral revolutionary father haunting the piece. In terms of narrative plotting, this section proves anticlimactic: it spends a total of three pages recounting Conrad's past in Cracow. In those three pages, Conrad discusses witnessing his father's death in terms that transmit a desire for absolution difficult to achieve. About to enter Poland, he comments, "Each of us is a fascinating spectacle to himself, and I had to watch my own personality returning from another world, as it were, to revisit the glimpses of old moons" (131). In Cracow, the uncanny doubling continues when the writing identifies Conrad as specter or spectacle by oscillating between first- and third-person narration. Perspectival shifts situate him as an other to both the Polish language and national identity, as when the essay details a police officer who "turned his head to look at the grizzled foreigner holding forth in a strange tongue" (131).

The memoir's final attempts to achieve absolution and closure are blocked, also, by the simultaneous exposure and denial of shame. In Poland, Conrad shamefully reproduces his lack of shame, inducing the need for more excuses. Discussing his father's death, he writes,

> I looked forward to what was coming with an incredulous terror. I turned my eyes from it, sometimes with success; and yet all the time I had an awful sensation of the inevitable. I had also movements of *revolt* which stripped off of me some of my simple trust in the *government of the universe*. But when the inevitable entered the sick room and the white door was thrown wide open I don't think I found a single tear to shed. I have a suspicion that the Canon's housekeeper looked upon me as the most callous little wretch on earth.
>
> (134, my emphasis)

Shame is confessed and not confessed at once; the essay's assertion that he did not feel shame for his lack of tears is at odds with his repeated exposure of reputed shamelessness. After this first exposure, Conrad once again exposes and condemns himself in a mitigated manner by examining himself from the point of view of others, presenting his refusal to mourn the father in the third person: "The day of the funeral came in due course. And all the generous 'Youth of the Schools,' the grave Senate of the University, the delegations of the Trade-guilds might have obtained (if they cared) de visu evidence of the callousness of the little wretch" (134). The desire to put shame on display is made clearer when we consider that he invents this shameful scene—he did, in fact, shed tears for his father. The repetition of this fiction suggests that like Rousseau, who spectacularizes his shameful behavior in the famous stolen ribbon episode of *The Confessions*, Conrad finds pleasure in theatricalizing shame, a pleasure that cannot be directly confessed but only displaced.[26] This relentless logic of shame and exposure heralds confession's endlessness, its failure to provide absolution.

"Poland Revisited" demonstrates that confession cannot accomplish the two goals set forth and that it produces unintended consequences. It neither makes known a truth unknown nor does it solve the discontinuity within the self; in failing to bring things to an end, it interminably binds one to others so that Conrad becomes "the helpless prey of the Shades [he] had called up" (135). For the passages cited above also fail to suture the gap between the Conrad of the past and present for another reason—not his announced conscious refusal but rather an unannounced, unconscious failure to mourn. When Conrad depicts his reaction to his father's death in the language of politics, not sentiment, his phrases convey a failed mourning, a melancholic identification, the swallowing of an exquisite corpse.[27] Rather than separating him from this specter, his words identify him with the revolutionary. Conrad incorporates the father through his metaphors of political resistance: The father's death effects "revolt" and a loss of "trust in the government" of the universe. Thus, the piece does not conclude with the coming to consciousness of the loss of the father, who is also a metonym for Polish revolutionary aspirations and hence an avowal of what these losses mean. Rather than providing a cure to self-splitting, confession "ends" without ending, with a melancholic identification that is at the same time a self-othering, an unconscious insertion of the other within the self who can haunt indefinitely. This conclusion supports Harpham's point, although in a way different from his own reading, that the case of Conrad evades psychoanalytic and political-theoretical distinctions; "Conrad's personal experience seems to be graspable by theory but in fact falls on both sides of distinctions—family and nation, mourning and melancholia—that theoreticians (Anderson and Freud) wish to maintain."[28]

Prompted by unrest in Europe that results in the redrawing of national, regional, and colonial boundaries, confession pathologically attaches the confessant to a "family and nation" whose history of rebellion he criticizes while nevertheless championing one aspect of it: its nationalist spirit. Only this spirit can redeem revolt against the state. In spite of the wry dismissals of those calls for "race, liberation, justice" ringing across Eastern Europe, Conrad asserts that spiritual nationalism—not the materialist demands that comprised the Reds' program such as class equality, democratic representation, and a state that would accommodate ethnic pluralism—is what saves Poland's unsuccessful insurrections. The difference between revolutionaries and Polish rebels, specifically his father, is that the former work "for the subversion of any social or political scheme of existence" while the latter are "patriots" who, "believing in the spirituality of a national existence could not bear to see that spirit enslaved."[29] Nationalism can even redeem confession itself, the essay suggests.

The piece naturalizes national community by remarking on the effects of the father's confession of faith, and it opposes these to the dissolution of national community and perverse attachments Conrad's own confessions engender. It insists that both Korzeniowski and the crowd of mourners who flood the street for his funeral "were victims alike of an unrelenting destiny which cut them off from every path of merit and glory. They had come only to render homage to the ardent fidelity of the man whose life had been a fearless confession in word and deed of a creed which the simplest heart in that crowd could feel and understand" (134). Korzeniowski's confession is generative rather than destructive because it is not that of a revolutionary like Rousseau but that of a patriot. It is faithful to and constellates a living social form, a bond of hearts and minds—an organic, spiritual nation. Conrad also shares kinship with Poles, but not through a natural/national organic bond. Because he betrays and deserts his birthplace, his confessions crystallize pathological attachments and manifest a death drive, chaining him to a horde of specters and a country without a future. His confessions transform the collective of mourners from a national community into a mob of ghosts. He flees Korzeniowski's funeral site because the "shades" he summons are "crowding upon me, enigmatic and insistent, in their own clinging air of the grave that tasted of dust and ashes and the bitter vanity of all hopes" (135).

By contrasting confessions of Polish nationalists to those of revolutionaries and betrayers, Conrad separates the topic of "Poland Revisited" from that of *Under Western Eyes*. Historically, however, there were parallels between dispositifs of state power, insurgencies, and counterinsurgencies in Poland and Russia as well as alliances forged between Polish and Russian revolutionaries. Korzeniowski himself argued that the conduct of Polish resistance should serve as a model for Russian revolt against autocracy.[30] From 1893 through 1914, the main political debate in Poland occurred between the Polish Socialist Party, whose agenda was defined almost solely with the aim of national self-determination, and the Social Democratic Party, who were Marxist internationalists, including Rosa Luxemburg, who opposed the other party's program and allied themselves with the Russian workers when the revolution began in 1905. Moreover, the repressive situation in Russia resembled that of the peripheries, including Poland.[31] "The boundary between 'colony' and 'metropole' (as well as between the correspondingly different attitudes and methods of rule) was much less clear" in the Russian empire than in the transoceanic empires, and "the 1905 Revolution had gone some way toward eroding this boundary between a colonial realm of militarized 'extraordinary rule' and a domestic civil realm."[32] Conrad obscures and even denies any connections between Poland and Russian insurgencies throughout his writings, implicitly distinguishing his novel of Russian revolution from the Polish question.[33] But confession is also the organizing mode of *Under Western Eyes*, and the novel shares the problems of witnessing that the essay enacts. As "Poland Revisited" demonstrates, confession eludes the grasp of those who employ it, and in the novel, too, it threatens nationalist and organicist models of community while creating unwanted responsibilities and attachments to others.

Contaminating Confessions

The narrative effects of broaching the subject of revolution, and thus returning to divided allegiances, have been discussed by critics who read *Un-*

der Western Eyes using a biographical approach[34] and by others who examine its methods of witnessing from a legal standpoint.[35] Largely overlooked, however, is the central role confession plays in the novel. Among the few critics who have addressed confession at length is Keith Carabine, who argues that confession, as practiced by Razumov, a double for the author, represents Conrad's attempt to manage a traumatic past. Carabine correctly maintains that confession in the novel does not "promise conversion" as does confession in the Augustinian tradition, can remain "incoherent," and cannot guarantee refuge from Conrad's Polish shades.[36] His analysis, however, considers only those moments explicitly circumscribed as confessions while focusing tightly on Conrad's individual past. But in *Under Western Eyes*, confession fragments, multiplies, and takes over the entire novel, driving the narrative and generating effects that exceed the biographical, which have gone unrecognized in criticism on the text.[37]

The propulsion of confession and its articulation of attachments to others are the result of its structure—key aspects of which "Poland Revisited" illuminated—as well as the novel's reaction to wider geopolitical transformations of the time: resistance to imperial and autocratic techniques of governance in Russia and beyond and shifting alliances between nations and empires across Europe in the first decade of the twentieth century. Responding to these changes but also subject to internal exigencies of form, confession in *Under Western Eyes* reminds us that confession occurs between an addressor and addressee, something "Poland Revisited," detailing only the confessant's position, does not emphasize. Dwelling on the vexed relation it materializes between confessants and confessors, the novel foregrounds that confession not only demands interpretation but also attaches one to others beyond one's national, linguistic, and cultural milieu. In his study of confession, Peter Brooks advises that "we need to ask, in all cases, what purpose is served by confession, what response it solicits, and what the person or persons who receive the confession are supposed to do with it."[38] Examining the purposes and effects of the novel's confessions—those of the student-revolutionary Victor Victorovich Haldin, then of the English language teacher's translation of Razumov's diary, and, finally, Razumov's confessions described within the diary—indicates that the erosion of borders occurring during the revolutionary era and incipient globalization, and the attendant denaturalizing of categories of race and nation, does not lead to a tolerance, much less a welcoming, of others and otherness.[39]

Confession is precipitated in the diegetic narrative—the story of Razumov's betrayal of Haldin—by the student revolutionary's assassination of an authority based on Interior Minister V. K. de Plehve, an act that encapsulates what the novel depicts as the irrational and unconscious nature of Russian politics. Haldin confesses the assassination to Razumov, setting off other confessions reported in Razumov's diary. The frame narrative is also initiated by confession: the language teacher receives Razumov's confessional text from Haldin's sister, Natalia, and translates it for Western eyes. The minister Haldin kills is a despot "invested with extraordinary powers" whose own "mystic acceptance of the principle of autocracy" aims at the "destruction of the very hope of liberty itself" (6). That mysticism is innate to Russia and infuses every aspect of Russian life is insinuated in figurations of the land. In terms similar to *A Passage to India*, which presents India as excess, too immense and muddled to be comprehended, *Under Western Eyes* makes Russia resistant to all manner of cognitive and sociohistorical mapping. Referring to the "endless space and countless millions" of which Razumov received an "*almost* physical impression" (my emphasis), the novel goes on to describe how "under the sumptuous immensity of the sky, the snow covered the endless forests, the frozen rivers, the plains of an immense country, obliterating the landmarks, the accidents of the ground, leveling everything under its uniform whiteness, like a monstrous blank page awaiting the record of an inconceivable history" (25). Just as it refuses attempts to record impressions of it, as "the land of spectral ideas and disembodied aspirations" (25) revolutionaries endeavor to realize, Russia refuses the imprint of material processes of development, or "modernity."

The purpose of Haldin's confession is to enlist help from Razumov in arranging his escape. Like the "mystic" act of assassination, Haldin's confession is mystical: it is delivered by a ghost, an uninvited guest whose entry into and exit from Razumov's rooms are not witnessed. When Razumov returns home, he is startled by "a strange figure" who "loomed lithe and martial" (11). Haldin had entered unnoticed: "Your dvornik was away from the gate and talking to a sleigh driver on the other side of the street. I met no one on the stairs, not a soul. As I came up to your door I caught sight of your landlady coming out of your rooms. But she did not see me. . . . I slipped in" (12). The passage notes clock time repeatedly and highlights that Haldin's escape takes place in an interval rather than an instant of a present or presence. Razumov listens to "the faint sounds of some town clock tolling the hour. Haldin, already at the door . . . might have posed for the statue of a daring youth listening to an inner voice. Razumov mechanically glanced down at his watch. When he looked towards the door again Haldin had vanished" (47). This anachronous, spectral Haldin, who might return a second time, as the revolution itself would, is another metonym for this "land of spectral ideas and disembodied aspirations" (25).

As "Poland Revisited" indicates, Conrad uses the language of ghosts and specters when addressing revolution as it pertains to his personal past; however, the novel's deployment of the rhetoric of mysticism extends beyond the personal. This deployment mirrors historiographic approaches to the Russian revolution of 1905, which viewed it as mystical explicitly or implicitly, wittingly or unwittingly. One dominant approach argues that the revolution was both inevitable or compelled, and prophetic. This teleological view, once Marxist orthodoxy, is summarized in V. I. Lenin's metaphor of the revolution as a "dress rehearsal" for the Revolution of 1917. It was also long doxa that the Revolution of 1905 was characterized by spontaneous and chaotic revolt rather than by conscious, rational, and programmed action. Other interpretations, which, as Peter Holquist points out, correspond to a strain of Holocaust historiography that sees the Shoah as the effect of a pathology inherent in the German "psycho-social type," locates the inevitability of the revolution in the Russian "character." This character is a cultural backwardness thought to be either the result of years of autocratic rule or an innate Russian "special way."[40]

In recent decades, historians, sociologists, and political theorists have demystified the revolution by challenging these interpretations. Against the teleological understanding, scholars assert that the revolution was shaped by contingencies of the revolutionary era, whose years have also been recalibrated so they begin both earlier than 1905 and later than 1917.[41] Rather than prophecy or fulfillment, "an event that made any one path of development inevitable," the revolution was "a critical juncture that opened up several alternative paths" of social and political transformation.[42] Correcting its representation as a chaotic and spontaneous event undertaken by a peasantry lacking class consciousness, some have shown that a reciprocal radicalization between the rural peasantry and urban proletariat took place so that both were further politicized during this time.[43] Others refute, as well, the portraits of a revolution with its roots in Russian backwardness and cultural and economic stagnation, contending that it actually occurred during a period of rapid industrial and social change.[44] Theorists have, in addition, disputed arguments based on notions of Russian exceptionalism and "character" by situating the revolution in the context of global processes of capitalism and arguing that it was comparable to other insurgencies. As Theodor Shanin writes, "the events in Russia were part of a radical wave which in those years swept the world at large. . . . important were the substantive similarities [between these insurgencies] rooted in the underlying social structures which have later come to be known as the 'developing societies.'"[45]

Under Western Eyes, though, airs the interpretations of its time as well as those that would follow in the wake of the October revolution of 1917. Such interpretations are often voiced through the narrator's commentaries on Razumov's diary. Readers have argued that the language teacher's attribution of an irrational Russian nature that underlies both the revolutionaries' use of violence and autocracy's systemic depredations—what Conrad calls in his author's note a shared "moral anarchism"[46] that the language teacher opposes to the morality of an enlightened West—is subverted by Conrad's stylistic strategies.[47] But to treat the rhetoric of Russian mysticism as ironic is to detach the novel from contemporaneous debates about the meaning and causes of revolution. Conrad himself points to the relationship between text and context in the author's note to the 1920 edition, confiding that although he hoped "to render not so much the political state as the psychology of Russia itself," he has been gratified to discover that in many "articles on Russian affairs of the present day reference is made to certain sayings and opinions uttered in the pages" of the novel.[48] Throughout the note he repeats the mystical interpretations of events that envision them as mystical. He states that inevitability and compelled outcomes defined the revolution, and, homologically, his novel of it: "It was only after I had finished writing the first part that the whole story revealed itself to me in its tragic character and in the march of its events as unavoidable and sufficiently ample in its outline."[49] Having already become "a sort of historical novel dealing with the past," *Under Western Eyes*, like the historical event itself, was prophetic too, the current political analyses of Russian affairs "testifying to the clearness of my vision and the correctness of my judgment."[50] The note's final words stress the teleological view of the revolution and, by way of a metaphor taken from nature, describe an innate Russian character destined to perpetuate itself: "These people are unable to see that all they can effect is merely a change of names. The oppressor and the oppressed are all Russians together; and the world is brought once more face to face with the truth of the saying that the tiger cannot change his stripes nor the leopard his spots."[51]

If the author's note provides extratextual reasons for considering the novel's rhetoric of mysticism as serious, confession in the novel invites us to refine and reformulate the thesis that the work subverts the narrator's naturalizing of differences between the West and Russia on the basis of the latter's "moral corruption" (6) and irrationality. The structural logic of confession operates independently from the language teacher's perspective and challenges ideals he espouses. Resonating with historical portrayals of the revolutionary period in which it emerges, confession is a mystical force that creates outcomes that are not programmed or conscious, and it also disturbs models of identity and community the translator insists upon. In doing so, however, it engenders a crisis of contamination that the novel endeavors to resolve.

The revolutionary's confession initiates the conflict that drives the narrative: Razumov's reputed betrayal of Haldin and the intolerable haunting by the other that propels Razumov's confessions. Haldin's confession takes Razumov prisoner, making the home unhomely. Harboring the revolutionary's confession is "harboring a pestilential disease . . . a subtle pest that would convert earth into a hell" (24). To cure this contamination and fight against parasitism, incorporation of a foreign body, what is needed is yet another confession; "the corpse hanging round his neck would be nearly as fatal as the living man. Nothing short of complete annihilation would do. And that was impossible" (24). This leads to the question, "What then? Must one kill oneself to escape this visitation?"(24). Aside from death, escaping the visitation demands that Razumov confess to Haldin's confession, but this is as impossible as it is necessary because "Razumov had not even a refuge of confidence. To whom could he go with this tale—in all this great, great land?" (24). Confession is as oppressive as the immense Russian land: "Razumov, who amongst eighty millions of his kith and kin, had no heart to which he could open himself" (29). Haldin's confession sets into motion Razumov's encounters with Haldin's mother and sister, the revolutionaries, and state authorities, which form the substance of the confessional work that the language teacher translates.

As in "Poland Revisited," in the novel, confession induces a self-othering and exposes the fragile and vertiginous character of national identity. In doing so, it undermines the narrator's sharp delineations of Russia and the West. Ironizing the teacher's assurance that "it is unthinkable than any young Englishman should find himself in Razumov's situation" (19), the confessional scene between Haldin and Razumov identifies the latter with that very figure. After confessing, Haldin exclaims, "You say nothing, Kirylo Sidorovitch! . . . To be sure, I cannot expect you with your frigid English manner to embrace me" (12), and a short while later he observes: "Ah! You are a fellow. Collected—cool as a cucumber. A regular Englishman" (16). The effects of Haldin's confession contradict the narrator's definitions of national character as enduring and stable. The confession exposes the fragility of Russianness by summoning an Englishman in the heart of the Russian, and the moment it does so, it simultaneously exposes the fragility of Englishness. The confession dissolves the rational manner that prompts the confessant to describe him as English, making Razumov embark on a frantic quest for a confessor to exorcise the haunting "pest" : "It is really a wonder he managed to keep going as he did," the narrator comments; "no rational determination had any part in his exertions" (20). The dramatization of confession suggests that if there is no firm ground to national identity, it is that much easier to become contaminated by, even turned into, an other.

The purpose of Razumov's diary to the text as a whole, therefore, as handled by the language teacher, is to contain the contaminating effects of this confessional work by showing how it proves that an unbridgeable gap exists between East and West. The teacher translates it, paradoxically, to prove its untranslatability, to demonstrate to the novel's implied audience—"Western" readers—that, like Russian autocracy, revolution, and land, this confession is excessive to understanding, even to language itself. Feeling "the difficulty of the task" (49) of translation and intimating that the English language is totally incompatible with the Russian experience, the translator claims he must shape the material by using a key term that best approximates these incomprehensible details: "cynicism" (50). He warns that "If to the Western reader" the details of Razumov's confession "appear shocking, inappropriate, or even improper . . . this is not a story of the West of Europe" (19). The diary allegedly remains unreadable to Western readers in part because governments and nations determine character, worldview, and the limits of imagination, for "nations it may be have fashioned their governments, but Governments have paid them back in the same coin" (19). Insisting that national character protects one from being expropriated, prohibits one from occupying empathetically the place of the other in acts of writing, translating, or reading, he proclaims, "it is unthinkable that any young Englishman should find himself in Razumov's situation. This being so it would be a vain enterprise to imagine what he would think. The only safe surmise to make is that he would not think as Mr. Razumov thought at this crisis of his fate" (19).

Rather than evidence of a critical "cosmopolitan style,"[52] then, the exposure of the foreign within the home and destabilization of national and racial identities confession performs is coded as a crisis of contamination. The anxiety toward contamination elaborated both in Razumov's response to Haldin's confession and the teacher's handling of Razumov's diary also organizes the novel's central intertext, Conrad's 1905 essay "Autocracy and War." Reading this piece alongside the novel further complicates arguments that Conrad's works enact cosmopolitan critiques of imperialist models of national belonging, language, and race.[53] It also suggests that substituting an exploration of the novel's relationship to a philosophical tradition of cosmopolitanism for a culturist approach helps better explain the novel's depictions of identity and community. *Under Western Eyes* and "Autocracy and War" express a legacy of cosmopolitical thought associated with Immanuel Kant's "Toward Perpetual Peace." This work's vision of cosmopolitanism does not question groundings of race or national belonging or posit a "beyond" or end of the nation—and certainly not of nationalism[54]—as telos. Kant describes a federation of nation-states that weigh the rights of each in relation to one another and insists that nations must not be fused and that boundaries must be maintained. Though he prescribes "universal hospitality" as a duty of all nations to one another's inhabitants, he actually limits the universal to those who can claim national citizenship. The stateless are not owed hospitality. Although it is written over a century later, "Autocracy and War" echoes arguments of Kant's influential work and offers another context with which to read the novel's articulations of national, regional, and linguistic community. Discussing the community of postmonarchic nation-states emerging in Europe, it uses the language of mysticism employed throughout the novel and laments the dissolving of national borders by war, trade, commerce, and journalism during an era of incipient globalization.

"Autocracy and War" suggests why the porous boundaries between the rational and irrational that the narrator aligns with the West and Russia respectively is treated as a crisis in *Under Western Eyes*. Written after the defeat of Russia in the Russo-Japanese War, this piece deploys the revolutionary period's interpretive discourse of Russian mysticism, exceptionalism, and cultural backwardness. It also reconfigures nineteenth-century discourses of orientalism. Rather than setting the "East" as other to Europe, it poses an internalized orientalism within Europe; East and West are aligned through their radical heterogeneity to Russia. Conrad modifies well-known Hegelian formulations by treating Russia as the introduction to the *Philosophy of History* treats Africa, writing it out of world history: "By no industry of investigation, by no fantastic stretch of benevolence, can it be presented as a phase of development through which a society, a state, must pass on the way to the full consciousness of its destiny. It lies outside the stream of progress."[55] He composes Russian autocracy's epitaph in the first sentence, but by the end of the essay he still cannot exorcise this "specter." Russia is mysticism itself, "part Ghoul, part Djinn," both ana-chrony—"curse" (78), "visitation" (82)—and anarchy: it lacks "a law giver with the wisdom of a Lycurgus or a Solon" (85). Conrad announces the death of Russian "might" to look toward Europe's future as a "brotherhood" (87) of nation-states but continues to disavow that this guest, this "visitation," still haunts Europe.

The rhetoric of autochthony, heredity, and tellury, which underwrites imperial-nationalist models of community, molds Conrad's criticism of a world increasingly defined by transnational economic and political relations. The cosmopolitan community of postmonarchic democracies, the "brotherhood likely to be established between the rival nations of this continent, which, we are assured . . . is the heritage of democracy" (87), is doomed by the scission of democracies from their fathers and heirs. Conrad's text is inscribed within a history of thought in which "brotherhood" among polities is contingent not on a shared paternity but a sharing of paternity, and genealogy.[56] "No leader of a democracy without other ancestry but the sudden shout of a multitude and debarred by the very condition of power from ever thinking of a direct heir, will have any interest in calling brother the leader of another democracy—a chief as fatherless and heirless as himself" (87), writes Conrad. Russia, however, is the extreme example of an orphan. It lacks and can never give rise to a genealogy; it is depicted not merely as a foreigner but as entirely other—irrational, illegitimate, and barbaric.[57] It is without "rational origin in the vices, the misfortunes, the necessities or the aspirations of mankind," "has neither a European nor an Oriental parentage," "no root either in the institutions or the follies of this earth" (81). It comes from the sky, "like a curse from heaven falling in the darkness of ages upon the plains of forest and steppe" (82). There will be no heirs, no future for its people. The revolution "can never be a revolution fruitful of moral consequences to mankind" (84).

The essay repeats ideological premises underlying the historical processes of nation and continent building that excluded "rootless" elements in Europe during the nineteenth century and into the twentieth. It also responds to the remapping of the West as both greater than but also smaller than Europe, its "Western" part, the result of Russia's defeat in the Russo-Japanese war; however, it imagines this new community, the West, in the exclusionary terms that consolidated Europe.[58] Classifying its people as nationless and rootless, the essay expels both an autocratic and a postrevolutionary Russia from its vision of the cosmopolitan community of nations. Although Conrad claims that any democracy that results from revolution and is detached from heirs and fathers must also be excluded, he treats Russia as *inherently* outside of genealogy, disconnected from a past and future. The essay expresses what Étienne Balibar calls "theoretical racism," which isolates, expels, or eliminates those who are claimed to lack a genealogy. This expulsion of "'false,' 'exogenous,' 'cross-bred' 'cosmopolitan' elements,"[59] and "stateless others" helped forge Europe as a community of modern nation-states, through official policies of anti-Semitism and imperialism.[60] Russia, of course, consolidated its empire through anti-Semitism while also denying colonized peoples their own claims to genealogy, their own fathers and heirs. But Conrad's criticism of Russia uses these same terms, reflecting imperial modernity's intolerance of rootlessness, imaginations of nationhood based on blood and soil, and visions of cosmopolitan community propped on these values.[61]

The essay argues that testimonial writing is the medium through which Russia contaminates the West. Russia defies logic and truth, "hence arises her impenetrability to whatever is true in Western thought . . . when [the latter] crosses her frontier [it] falls under the spell of her autocracy and becomes a noxious parody of itself" (82). Western journalism gives hospitality to that illegitimate stranger by examining Russia's political affairs and pondering its future. The materiality of the journalistic letter lodges the parasite within the Western reader, making its host as irrational and "morally corrupt" as Russia's autocrats and revolutionaries:

> All these speculations . . . have appeared gravely in print; and if they have been gravely considered by only one reader out of each hundred, there must be something subtly noxious to the human brain in the composition of newspaper ink; or else it is that the large page, the columns of words, the leaded heading exalt the mind into a state of feverish credulity. The printed voice of the press makes a sort of still uproar taking from men both the power to reflect and the faculty of genuine feeling.
>
> (76)

Writing that documents and speculates about Russian current events—exactly what the language teacher's writing does in *Under Western Eyes*—contaminates. The West becomes as mystical and delusional as Russia, "a fascination . . . a hallucination" (76). Compounding things is that "*Il n'ya plus d'Europe*—there is only an armed and trading continent, the home of slowly maturing economical contests for life and death and of loudly proclaimed worldwide ambitions" (92). The beginnings of globalization, the shift from nation-based imperialism to "empire," has collapsed borders, rendering Europe unhomely, permeable to the "moral anarchy" and mysticism of that which lies "on the border of two continents" (87).

"Autocracy and War" indicates why *Under Western Eyes* conveys an anxiety that its readers will become hostage to the Russian story it hosts through its central narrative conceit, translation. The frame narrative tries to immunize readers from the "noxious" contamination caused by documenting events in the Russian confession: the narrator draws a border between his own and the Russian text from the very beginning and throughout, but this border, as many have noted, erodes regularly.[62] As theorists have argued, the act of translation carries with it the potential to activate nationalistic responses. Lawrence Venuti remarks, although "translation is seen as the practice that overcomes the boundaries between national languages and cultures to communicate the universal spirit," a universalist theory of language poses a threat. "Nationalism . . . goes hand in hand with a literary xenophobia, a fear that foreign literatures might contaminate native traditions"[63] through translation. Whether translation agendas attempt to emphasize or to erase cultural and linguistic differences, they "depend on the same circularity: the national status of a language and a culture is simultaneously presupposed and created through translation. Insofar as such agendas implicitly reveal the incompleteness of the nation, translation is a scandal to nationalist thinking, providing yet another motive for indignation and offense, for perceiving a translated text as an international act of violence."[64] In the novel, the nationalist thinking that poses distinctions between Russia and the West is threatened by a universalist theory of language inhabiting the premises of translation the novel articulates.

Under Western Eyes orchestrates translation of the Russian confession to prove the impossibility of culturally translating between Russia and the West while linguistically contesting this impossibility by rehearsing the simulacrum of a seamless translation. The translated language is never seen to disturb, interrupt, nor, as Walter Benjamin famously theorized, "expand" the limits of the translating language[65] through idiomatics or straining of syntax. There is no inclusion of Russian words, phrases, or Cyrillic graphematics. English is protected from the influence of a language of a deracinated people, an "heirless" and "fatherless" nation. In *A Personal Record*, Conrad considers the relationship between language and national genealogy. He rejects the claim that he "had exercised a deliberate choice" to write in English rather than French:

> I have a strange and overpowering feeling that [the faculty to write in English] had always been an inherent part of myself. English for me was neither a matter of choice nor adoption. The merest idea of choice never entered my head. And as to adoption—well, yes, there was adoption; but it was I who was adopted by the genius of the language, which directly I came out of the stammering stage made me its own so completely that its very idioms I truly believe had a direct action on my temperament and fashioned my still plastic character.[66]

Even before English law, in the form of the merchant shipping act, helps naturalize Conrad as English by serving as a "mother and father" to him (as "Poland Revisited" related), he had a preternatural capacity to write in the language, which then further molded his character. English, then, is a language that produces heirs. It inscribes him into a genealogy. The exclusion of the Russian language in the novel, therefore, might signal another instance of Conrad's unwillingness to contaminate the rooted with the rootless, a hypothesis that seems more likely given that another language does appear in text—French. But exclusion of Russian could function as an autobiographical cipher in another way: as a sign of anticolonial resistance. As a Polish subject, Conrad was sensitive to Russia's imperial policy of the 1880s, which replaced Polish with Russian as the official language of education as well as of social, cultural, and governmental institutions. The burying of the national language in a novel that purports to render "the essence of things Russian" could be a response to the imperial state's interment of the Polish language.

Whatever the case, the performative contradiction of seamless linguistic translation undermines the cultural distinction on which the use of English is predicated *and* by which it is to be produced, tautologically. The consequences are xenophobic disavowals that the Russian story is incomprehensible to Western readers as well as an ironic literary xenophobia. It is ironic because the narrative, itself structured by confession, denegates the very Russian texts that *Under Western Eyes* resembles. These include *Crime and Punishment*, the confessional work of a Russian female aristocrat and sympathizer to revolutionary assassins, the haunted writing of a "political confession of faith" produced by Razumov, and even the central intratext, Razumov's diary.[67]

Offering hospitality to a "noxious" force in the form of Razumov's diary, the novel proves incapable of resolving the haunting effects of the Russian parasite within. The diary is replete with troubling confessions that, like "Poland Revisited," composed years later, cannot bring things to an end. Just as the frame narrative struggles against the contaminating effects of Razumov's diary, Razumov's confessions detailed within the diary, and those that spill outside it, struggle against the contaminating effects of Haldin's confession. Hoping to reestablish the "reason" for which Razumov is named and that Haldin's confession suspends, Razumov confesses Haldin's confession to an autocrat. As "Poland Revisited" made clear, however, confession escapes confessants' control. In the novel, it generates the need for yet more confessions that endeavor to resecure borders between the West and Russia. Instead of providing closure and relief from shades and specters, however, confession mobilizes a struggle between competing models of responsibility. The ethics that emerges from this struggle is not that of a rational, self-aware cultivation of obligations to others but rather one that locates these obligations prior to and as discontinuous with decision and choice and that originates with and is sustained by confession.

In/conclusion: Other Obligations

A "sort of political confession of faith" (73) attributed to Razumov summarizes an impasse readers encounter in Razumov's confessions throughout the diary. This document simultaneously illustrates both the task of confession—to stabilize identities, to (re)establish differences between Razumov and revolutionaries, and the rational and irrational—and the failure to accomplish it. The document is intended to dispel any ambiguity on where its signatory's sympathies lie, but the formal staging of the signature only amplifies uncertainties. Composing it after confessing to having heard Haldin's confession, Razumov then pins the document to the wall above his bed, where a confession of faith would conventionally appear in the image of one's god.

> He flung the book away and took a square sheet of paper. It was like the pile of sheets covered with his neat minute handwriting, only blank. He took a pen brusquely and dipped it with the vague notion of going on with the writing of his essay—but his pen remained poised over the sheet. It hung there for some time before it came down and formed long scrawly letters.
>
> Still-faced and his lips set hard, Razumov began to write. When he wrote in a large hand his neat writing lost its character altogether—became unsteady, almost childish. He wrote five lines one under the other.
>
> History not Theory.
> Patriotism not Internationalism.
> Evolution not Revolution.
> Direction not Destruction.
> Unity not Disruption.
> He gazed at them dully.
>
> (49)

The passage's formal elements immediately raise questions: Who confesses here? Is the writer the source of the confession? Is the confession an intentional act? Is this even a confession? For the document appears as a literal interruption of an intended writing—logically, but grammatically as well, as the dash in the fourth sentence relates—and is presented as an interrupted and doubled writing. The pen begins writing; then, in the next sentence, the passage relates that "Razumov began to write." Composing it results in the loss of the confessant's distinguishing features, his "character"—textual persona as well as linguistic mark. Without determining that it is false, other narrative devices render the document's truth status unverifiable. In the previous scene, the novel relates that Razumov fears arrest, since Haldin had escaped Razumov's room before the police arrived to arrest him. This fear might motivate him to write the confession as a way of protecting himself from suspicion. Thus, rather than a cognitive act whose truth status can be determined by recourse to an extraverbal referent, this "confession of faith" might function as an excuse. These disruptions of the source and status of confession recur throughout the novel.

Under Western Eyes prefigures the disturbances of confession that "Poland Revisited" enacts when that confession addresses colonial and revolutionary unrest. In the novel, however, such disturbances elaborate a staging of responsibility that defies Conrad's proclamations of the "moral anarchy" of revolutionary Russia while also denying that obligations to others are derived from the state, legally regulated, or a matter of moral decision. Counterposing the effects of the revolutionary's confession with those of legal and religious traditions, the novel puts into confrontation competing theories of responsibility. Traditions of Western secular and religious thought rely on the autonomous, intending subject as the basis of definitions of moral decision, dissimulating the aporia of responsibility that haunts them.[68] That aporia is that the subject must, but cannot, ground moral decision and responsibility, in part because these acts occur through language. Language, as testimony, separates the subject from herself and leaves her words (or gestures) open to effects that cannot be calculated. Testimony discloses that "decision and responsibility are always of the other[.] They always come back or come down to the other, from the other, even if it is the other in me."[69] *Under Western Eyes* brings this impasse to the fore and, in a deployment of mysticism unintended by its author, makes the effects of the revolutionary Haldin's confession the vehicle that elucidates it.

Razumov's confessions are attempts to relieve the haunting aggravated by Razumov's supposed betrayal of Haldin when he confesses Haldin's confession to the authorities. Yet the novel simultaneously and ironically questions the very reason for Razumov's confessions, leading readers to wonder why they occur at all. The language of legal reasoning asks whether the "betrayal" that induces Razumov's subsequent confessions occurs in the first place. Razumov's first act after suffering the silencing caused by Haldin's confession is to confess to the police, but his next act is to rationalize why such a confession will not constitute a betrayal. Razumov puts himself on trial and applies techniques of logical argumentation. The text spotlights the organizing term of "Poland Revisited": "Betray. A great word. What is betrayal? They talk of a man betraying his country, his friends, his sweetheart. There must be a moral bond first" (28). Razumov casts himself as witness on the stand while playing prosecution and defense also, as he examines and cross-examines himself by delivering a series of syllogistic questions and answers:

> All a man can betray is his conscience. And how is my conscience engaged here; by what bond of common faith, of common conviction, am I obliged to let that fanatical idiot drag me down with him? On the contrary. . . . What can the prejudice of the world reproach me with? Have I provoked his confidence? No! Have I by a single word, look, or gesture given him reason to suppose that I accepted his trust in me? No!
>
> (28)

The passage rules that betrayal has not occurred by positing that no bond existed before the confession. Haldin's confession cannot institute a bond; thus no responsibility to Haldin exists.

By indicating that Razumov has not necessarily truly given Haldin his word when he enters into what seems like a verbal contract, the novel supports this rational argument and legal conceptualization of responsibility. After Haldin confesses the assassination to Razumov, he makes a request to his reluctant host: "Confidence" (14). Despite an exchange between the two that suggests Razumov agrees, the novel never determines that he promises to honor this request because it never establishes the conditions that make a promise a promise: the commitment to tell the truth. After Haldin asks Razumov to help him vanish by keeping his secret and carrying a message to the peasant Ziemianitch, a digression into Razumov's mental theater follows that details the punitive consequences and misery to befall him if caught. This concludes with Razumov's summation that "he hated the man

[Haldin]" (16). When immediately after this interior monologue Razumov assures Haldin, "Yes, of course I will go. You must give me precise directions, and for the rest—depend on me" (16), the novel refuses to verify that this is a promise to keep Haldin's confession in confidence. Indeed, the passages preceding this imply that Razumov's acquiescence to sending the message seems motivated by the desire to detain Haldin in his rooms should he decide to hand him over to the authorities. By leaving the status of the promise unclear, the novel apparently underwrites the model of responsibility grounded in reason Razumov's quasi-trial scene relates.

Paradoxically, however, by portraying Razumov's reasoning as sound, confirming that he is not morally bound to and therefore cannot logically betray Haldin, the text accords the revolutionary's confession all the more power, given its narrative effects: the compulsive repetitions of confessions that endeavor to exorcise the haunting within. The irrational, mystical force of the revolutionary's confession challenges the rational, legal notion of responsibility espoused. Because it is never determined whether Razumov promises and it is even implied that Razumov's response is actually composed of empty words, it is irrational that Razumov can neither keep Haldin's confession to himself nor give it up. More irrational is that the confession holds him captive even after he decides to turn Haldin in, for example, by compelling him to confess this betrayal/nonbetrayal to Haldin himself, "to pour out a full confession in passionate words that would stir the whole being of that man to its innermost depths; that would end in embraces and tears" (29). The revolutionary confession produces unintended results. It creates a bond that compels Razumov to make endless confessions.

Haldin's confession's irrational power manifests through the multiple confessions it incites. These attempt to eradicate the pest and make good on Razumov's statement that "I am reasonable. I am even—permit me to say—a thinker, though to be sure, this name nowadays seems the monopoly of hawkers of revolutionary wares, the slaves of some French or German thought—devil knows what foreign notions" (66). His confessions, however, only continue to erode boundaries between the reasonable self and the foreign, mystical revolutionary, and they do so often while eroding boundaries between secular and sacred speech. It would seem that Conrad's modernist novel includes a language associated with the sacred and mystic only to criticize its naiveté, just as the narrator criticizes Russian mysticism's naiveté. For, "If the novel is indeed the characteristic art form of secularization, in Lukács's words, 'the representative art form of our age,' and if modernity is indeed a secular age, we might expect the modernist novel to be doubly secular."[70] Pericles Lewis rejects this secularization thesis, however, arguing that novelists such as Kafka, Joyce, and Woolf went on a "quest for a modern form of the 'secular sacred,'" which inspired the formal experiments we identify as modernist.[71] *Under Western Eyes* also takes the sacred seriously. The formal conduct of Razumov's confessions maps the Christian ritual onto the legal tradition. Because juridical confession's stated goal is to reveal a truth but Christian confession's goal is expiation, this mapping disrupts Razumov's speech. It generates a shift from confession to excuse, which, as "Poland Revisited" showed, will only prevent the closure and unification of the self that confession sets out to accomplish.

The choreography of Razumov's confession to the state implies that its aim is exculpation rather than the revelation of truth. When Razumov first confesses to harboring Haldin, he confesses to a godlike figure rather than an ordinary police officer or bureaucrat, whom the novel dismisses as inadequate. Bestowing a transcendent power in a patriarch of the state, the closest thing to (and unbeknownst to him, in actuality) Razumov's own father—"There were no Razumovs belonging to him anywhere. His closest parentage was defined in the statement that he was a Russian" (8)—a sentence depicts the confessor through appositions that move increasingly toward a higher power, "a senator, a dignitary, a great personage, the very man—He!" (30). Although the novel spends pages building tension as Razumov searches for a confessor with the potency to provide redemption from the haunting "pest," when it finally describes him entering the palace of Prince K, then being admitted into his room, then on the verge of delivering his statement, it abruptly enacts a lapse where the confessional scene should appear. "Though he saw the Prince looking at him with black displeasure," the narrative tells us that "the lucidity of his mind, of which he was very conscious, gave him an extraordinary assurance. He was not asked to sit down. Half an hour later they appeared in the hall together" (31). The confession is never narrated but occurs "offstage," behind closed doors in a time and space from which readers are barred. This scenography invokes the religious sacrament: Confession "occurs" in the self-enclosed, shadowy enclave that marks and separates private communion and communication from public. This mise-en-scène indicates that Razumov confesses to right wrongs and neutralize guilt through expiation by the all-powerful. Instead of God, the all-powerful is the state.

The mystical authority attached to the state here seems to support the narrator's characterization of Russian autocratic power as exceptional, transcendent, total, and nothing like power in the West. Such representations, like those of revolution, reflect widely held beliefs of the time. That Conrad chooses Plehve as the victim of revolutionary assassination is especially symptomatic of these beliefs. This interior minister was the symbol of Russia's "mystique," the figurehead of an apparently centrally coordinated police state with a surveillance system extending to every corner of the empire and that was thought to wield brutal counterinsurgency tactics. This mystique was more imaginary than real, however. Jonathan Daly argues that the picture of an "autocracy which transformed legislation, administration, scholarship, church, school, and family into police [organs]"[72] was exaggerated, and he shows that "the uncoordinated, disjointed nature of the civil administration continued to facilitate revolutionary action throughout 1905."[73] Revising one revolutionary's judgment that in Plehve's death "the autocracy lost not only a most faithful servant: it lost its terrible mystique of power," Daly instead asserts that "Plehve, by fulminating against sedition without vigorously rooting it out, had himself eroded much of that mystique."[74] Despite changes in the laws regulating state crimes and a new criminal code that made it easier to punish instigators in the court, "at a time when more and more public activists were castigating the regime as a 'police state,' when revolutionary conspirators were growing more numerous and bold, and when a relatively broad-based coalition of educated opponents of absolutism was maturing, a relatively modest number of people were being punished for political activism."[75] Moreover, the argument that Russian tactics were exceptional requires that one overlook the parallels and even collaborations between Western European nations and Russia throughout the nineteenth and into the twentieth centuries in methods of surveillance and policing and the means used to contain and suppress colonial and revolutionary unrest.[76] In Conrad's novel, though, Haldin's strike against Plehve is presented as strike against an omnipotent state.

Yet it is not Haldin's assassination of Plehve but rather his confession of it to Razumov that actually threatens autocratic power, and it does so as a result of its own mystical force. While the choreography of the confession to Prince K ratifies the narrator's portrayal of state power as mystical and transcendent, the narrative logic of confession contradicts it: Prince K is not all-powerful because he cannot exorcise the irrational haunting produced by Haldin's confession. Razumov's confession to the Prince, which operates as an excuse, only tightens his attachment to the revolutionary other. By retrospectively relating that Razumov strategically edits his confession, the novel highlights that it operates within the Christian logic of expiation. Because it occurs offstage, readers are not made aware of what exactly or how much Razumov revealed. Did he reveal to Prince K that Haldin confessed *and* that he is complicit in Haldin's attempted escape? Or did he censor these parts of the story, as the narrative censors the confession by omitting it? Only later do we learn that Razumov has not admitted complicity, and this retrospective revelation signals that the confession does not aim toward disinterested truth production but rather exoneration. By accusing Haldin, Razumov excuses himself. Consequently, the need to confess to attain relief from the haunting only gains strength as the narrative progresses.

When Razumov confesses to another representative of the state, the effects of Haldin's confession once again bring to the surface connections between secular and Christian discourses and the limits of reason as well as the limits of autocratic power. The same textual choreography that shapes the confession to Prince K occurs in part 4, when Razumov is called before Councilor Mikulin. Initially, Razumov rejects the possibility of confessing to Mikulin that he has withheld information pertaining to de P's assassination, namely, that he served as Haldin's envoy and then killed the peasant. Razumov's rationalizing converts counterfactuality to truth: "Confess! To what? 'I have been speaking to him with the greatest openness,' he said to himself with perfect truth. 'What else could I tell him? That I have undertaken to carry a message to that brute Ziemianitch? Establish a false complicity and destroy what chance of safety I have won for nothing?—what folly'!" (219). But immediately following this reasonable refusal to wager against safety, the haunting becomes intolerable. "Nothing but Haldin—everywhere Haldin: a moral spectre infinitely more effective than any visible apparition of the dead" (220–221). When the Councilor summons him, Razumov therefore responds with "eagerness," for "Mikulin was the only person on earth to whom Razumov could talk, taking the Haldin adventure for granted"

(224). The novel primes readers for Razumov's confession of complicity and murder—"Mr. Razumov, certain of relief, went to meet Councilor Mikulin with the eagerness of a pursued person welcoming any sort of shelter" (224)—only to frustrate expectations in the next sentence: "This much said, there is no need to tell anything more of that first interview and of the several others" (224). The withdrawal of confession from representation indexes the Christological tradition and conveys that it is delivered with the hopes of exculpation.

But autocracy is not omnipotent, the confessant is not absolved, and the haunting continues. Razumov is forced to confess again, then yet again. Like Razumov's confession of faith and his confessions to Prince K and Mikulin, and Conrad's confessions in "Poland Revisited," disruptions prevent these final confessions from achieving closure. They exacerbate self-othering rather than detaching Razumov from the other. After his confessions to the state, Razumov seeks out Haldin's sister because "there is no one anywhere in the whole great world I could go to . . . Do you conceive the desolation of the thought—no one—to—go—to?" (259). The irony of Razumov's confession to Natalia is that it never takes place all the while it appears to occur. Through interruptions of sentences, clauses, ideas, and voice, the novel frames Razumov's confession in the mode of fiction, a "tale" and "story" that only *might* have happened. Like Conrad at the end of "Poland Revisited," Razumov does not identify himself as the subject or agent of the events but refers to himself as another, speaking in the third person. "Suppose that the real betrayer of your brother," Razumov proposes, "—suppose that he was a young man, educated, an intellectual worker, thoughtful, a man your brother might have trusted lightly, perhaps. . . . But there's a whole story there" (259). When Natalia demands to know this story, the text continues to double and split Razumov, positioning him as the confessor of the tale he presents rather than confessant. "I have heard it," he tells her. "There is a staircase in it, and even phantoms, but that does not matter if a man always serves something greater than himself—the idea. I wonder who is the greatest victim in that tale?" (259). After Natalia demands "the story!" a lapse follows that would be extraordinary if this device did not appear so regularly whenever a confession is about to emerge. "'There is no more to tell! . . . It ends here—on this very spot.' He pressed a denunciatory finger to his breast with force, and became perfectly still" (260). Razumov's confession ends without having begun. Not only is the story, the events that have occurred, excised, but the framing and pronouns displace responsibility. Situated as the climactic revelation, this "confession" culminates in frustrated expectation. As if to underline that confession has not unveiled the truth, the novel has Razumov leave the scene veiled from sight, literally and figuratively. "Something, extreme astonishment perhaps, dimmed my eyes, so that he seemed to vanish before he moved" (261), the English language teacher, who witnesses this scene, relates, and then he expresses with shock to Natalia, "That miserable wretch has carried off your veil!" (261).[77]

This confession fails to produce truth or to exculpate Razumov. After he confesses to Natalia, Razumov confesses to the revolutionaries. The novel underlines that what follows is not a choice: "he stopped, thinking over the form of his confession, and found it suddenly, unavoidably suggested by the fateful evening of his life" (267). As in the previous confessional scene, the same use of third-person narration and of the self-positioning of confessant as confessor while in the midst of confessing appears in this scene. "Am I to tell you of the feelings of that student, sought out in his obscure solitude, and menaced by the complicity forced upon him?" (268) he asks the crowd of revolutionaries, thus excusing himself as the victim of "forced complicity," without, however, naming himself as that student victim. After he recounts that "the student went to General T——— himself, and said, 'I have the man who killed de P——— locked up in my room, Victor Haldin, a student like myself'" (268), the crowd's response clarifies that the testimony has not been received as confession. It demands that Razumov "name him!"(268). As in the case of the "confession of faith" and his "confession" to Natalia, the grammatical staging makes the source of this discourse unclear and its status as testimonial act uncertain. Here, Razumov does not follow the basic rule required to make a speech act a confession: using the first-person pronoun and inhabiting the subject position in a declarative sentence. He describes the actions for which he would confess in the third person, and then, when he responds to the revolutionaries' demand to name the perpetrator, his response is an interrogative: "haven't you all understood that I am that man?" (268). It is no surprise that even after this moment, the revolutionaries wonder whether or not a confession has occurred: "'But this is a confession!' [was] uttered by somebody in a desperate shriek" (269).

This supposedly "closing" confession should serve as a narrative triumph of secular and religious discourses of responsibility. Razumov claims to uncover the truth and take responsibility for betraying Haldin, thus exorcizing the revolutionary "moral specter." After confessing to the revolutionaries, he declares himself "free." "'I beg you to observe,' he said, already on the landing, 'that I had only to hold my tongue. Today, of all days since I came amongst you, I was made safe, and today I made myself free from falsehood, from remorse—independent of every single human being on this earth'" (270). The effects of the confession ironize this statement, however. The revolutionaries beat him, he loses his hearing, and then he is hit by a tram-car. At the end of the novel, he is "crippled, ill, getting weaker every day" (278), and is not independent but relies on a caretaker, the peasant woman Tekla, to live.

The novel ironizes Razumov's claims to freedom in another, perhaps more important way, however. It relates that confession is a double bind: it obligates one to others, but it is also the condition of possibility of community. Rendered deaf as a result of the revolutionaries' blows, Razumov is without use of an organ that mediates between inner and outer world, self and other, language and silence. That organ opened him to Haldin's confession in the first place. Left without the alterity that haunts within, Razumov is no longer in danger of receiving such dangerous confessions. He is, as he claims, "safe" (270). But he is also henceforth separated from the rest of the world in crucial ways. His "freedom" emerges at the cost of a loss of the possibility of community.

Under Western Eyes contests concepts of ethical agency founded on rationalism, autonomy, or moral decision, all of which the novel aligns with the West. The itinerary of confession rejects Razumov's claim that in order to betray an other, there must be a "moral bond first," a bond that arises from one's choice to commit to another. Irrational revolutionary confession as the language of the other—the other of reason and of the autonomous subject—is the medium through which responsibility emerges. The functioning of Haldin's confession separates ethics from volition and responsibility from conscious decision by severing language from authorial control and intent while revealing the aporia of responsibility that juridico-legal discourses dissimulate. The revolutionary's confession commits Razumov without waiting for him to countersign, except through a language that works beyond his control and exceeds, even thwarts, intention.[78] Readers have often addressed Razumov's actions in terms of "moral character," but the staging of responsibility as incalculable effects of revolutionary confession renders the question of moral character moot.[79] According to *Under Western Eyes*, the ethical is not a matter of ego psychology, rational choice, or utility but an obligation to others beyond self-knowledge and intent.

In its elaboration of confession, Conrad's work departs from articulations of community based on genealogy, ethnicity, or race that find historical form in nationalisms and imperialisms as well as from articulations of community often expressed in culturalist theories of cosmopolitanism. Relating that "Western" and "Russian" are precarious markers of identification and fragile subject positions, confession demonstrates that commitments to others do not proceed from the basis of shared blood or soil. Neither, however, are these commitments formed on the basis of shared behaviors, consumer practices, affects, or ideals. They emerge through a testimonial language that repudiates the premise that subjective choice and free will determine one's responsibility to others. It is necessary to point out, however, that although the novel subverts imperial and nationalist models of identity and belonging and attendant subject-centered models of responsibility, it also struggles against this subversion. If Christian and legal models of confession ultimately do not call an end to self-splitting induced by the revolutionary confession and therefore fail to consolidate an ethics founded on rationality, selfhood, and legal models of responsibility, it is not for lack of trying. The multiplication of these confessions, which is driven by unresolved attitudes toward anticolonial insurgency and revolution, warns that an age of increasingly permeable borders in which transnational alliances multiply and shift as they travel through new economic and political circuits does not necessarily herald a postracial, postethnic, or postnational ethics or politics. It is the very porousness of borders that can activate a resurgence of racialized, nationalist circumscriptions of community, a rejection of responsibility to others that confession demands.

TWO

Traumas of Nation and Narrative: Legal and Literary Witnessing in Rebecca West's Wartime Writings

Rebecca West was a prolific Anglo-Irish writer whose work appeared in diverse venues across the twentieth century, from books brought out by the Hogarth Press, to the Vorticist magazine *Blast*, to the *New York Herald Tribune*. Her novels, short stories, literary criticism, travelogues, reviews, and trial reports form an impressive body of transdisciplinary literature that often features an interdisciplinary approach to the topic at hand. Several of West's pieces center on events frequently viewed as the most extreme, and exemplary, ruptures of modernity—the two world wars. Among these are the novel *The Return of the Soldier*, which was composed during the first, and trial reports collected in *The Meaning of Treason*, composed in the aftermath of the second. The testimony to trauma that each work enacts demonstrates, as Bernard Schweizer argues, that "West cuts across traditional ideological categories, being neither wholly a conservative nor entirely a progressive thinker."[1] But testimony in each writing also challenges Schweizer's assertion, echoed by other scholars, that West's oeuvre displays "a syncretic blend of political ideals emphasizing stability, tradition, loyalty, and nationalism, as well as anti-imperialism."[2] In distinct, even contrasting ways, *The Return of the Soldier* and *The Meaning of Treason* relate that anti-imperialism cannot be syncretically blended with stability, tradition, loyalty, and nationalism. In both works, anti-imperialism disrupts narratives that enable and sustain these ideals.

Like Conrad's essay "Poland Revisited" and novel *Under Western Eyes*, which Chapter 1 examined, West's novel about a shell-shocked English soldier and her coverage of the trials of the "Irish revolutionary" William Joyce encourage us to expand and revise critical understandings of British modernism as a literature that imagines a transnational ethics and politics of community and that arises out of historical traumas of modernity. As is the case with Conrad's writing, West's is often associated with modernism but not considered the most canonical example of it. West employed some of modernism's stylistic techniques and broached modernist subjects in her works but also became increasingly wary of forms of leftist internationalism shared by Bloomsbury and other modernist vanguards. West's commitment to feminist and socialist principles early in her career did make her critical of patriarchal, bourgeois ideologies that writers such as Virginia Woolf argued were of a piece with imperialist and nationalist discourses. As decades passed, however, West's politics separated her ever further from modernist peers. One reason for this is that by the 1940s, as Marina MacKay points out, West found the literary left's critiques of nationalism generally an expression of Western privilege. She developed this position in part through encounters with the history of imperialist repressions of diverse nationalities and nationalisms in her trip to the Balkans during the 1930s. West documented these encounters in the magisterial 1941 travelogue *Black Lamb and Grey Falcon: A Journey Through Yugoslavia*. Like Conrad's, however, West's perspectives on imperialism and resistance to it are not consistent across her oeuvre, or even within a single work. Responding to a shifting global order of the present and to colonial traumas of the past, Conrad attacks Russian imperialism throughout his writing but does not subject British imperialism to this same assault; similarly uneven treatments of imperialism occur in West's fictional and nonfictional responses to wartime presents and colonial pasts. Testimony in her World War I novel subtly nudges readers toward a critique of narratives of modernity that underwrite British imperial nationalism and that its plot, characters, and narrator express. The deployment of such narratives in *The Meaning of Treason* indicates that by the end of World War II, West is more capable of criticizing Eastern imperialism than British imperialism and that her sympathy for nationalist movements in the Balkans does not extend to those in British colonies. Although their perspectives on imperialism and nationalism diverge more than converge, both wartime writings' modes of witnessing help dislocate Eurocentric responses to trauma in literary and cultural studies that focus on the two world wars.

Testimony in *The Return of the Soldier* and *The Meaning of Treason* suggests that because the wars threaten the stability of empire, state, and nation, they elicit narratives of modernity that obscure structural violence shaping high and late imperial eras. By elucidating how the grammar of connectivity and rhetoric of continuity molding such cultural, socio-scientific, politico-economic, and legal narratives—and critical models that consolidate them—conceal forms of repression that contour and drive them, these works dispute representations of the European wars as ruptures of otherwise stable and peaceable eras. I explore, first, how *The Return of the Soldier* asks readers to situate World War I trauma writing in wider contexts than that of the nation and European continent and within a longer historical trajectory than that of the twentieth century. I then analyze how the report entitled "The Revolutionary" in *The Meaning of Treason* obliges—rather than asks—us to situate the writing of West's middle period in the context of two co-implicated processes often treated separately in literary studies, World War II and imperial retrenchment.

Conflicting Scenes of Trauma

The Return of the Soldier, first published in 1918, tells the story of a soldier who returns home an amnesiac as the result of shell shock. This work has attracted renewed interest in recent years in part because it centers on trauma and memory loss, issues of concern in contemporary criticism, but also because it explores the war's effects on women as well as men. The novel therefore supplements, by adding to and exposing a lack within, the literary and literary-critical canon on World War I trauma, which has long been dominated by a focus on masculinity, often through masculinist interpretations such as those of Paul Fussell and Samuel Hynes.[3] Although the novel features a wounded soldier, the domestic sphere and not the military theater takes center stage. It relates how amnesia prompts the male protagonist, his wife, cousin, and former lover to return to the past and reexamine love affairs and filial attachments from before the war, and, moreover, it employs a female witness to tell this story. For these reasons, the novel might contribute to what Margaret Higonnet calls an "alternate history of World War I traumas" that would restore voice to female witnesses of the period 1914–1918, who were silenced by modernist literature and criticism alike.[4] Testimony in this novel does articulate an alternate perspective of a period, but more than World War I, that period is what Eric Hobsbawm calls the "age of empire."[5] This is the era in which England's economic and political power as a nation is sustained through imperial and quasi-imperial exploitation and uneven gender and class arrangements.

This claim contradicts the novel's plotting, characters' statements, and critical interpretations, which identify the war, and war wounds, as the text's organizing traumas. Attending to the novel's formal staging of testimony reveals a more diffuse conceptualization of trauma, one that locates its sources beyond French and British soil and battle wounds. To trace the indirect articulation of historical trauma by concentrating on the rhetorical itinerary of testimony is to break with contemporary approaches to trauma that analyze it as a clinical affliction of character and an explicit focus of war narratives. A conflation of trauma with battle wounds has dominated writings that reference the war, such as Hemingway's, Lewis's, Woolf's, and Brittain's, and the category of post-traumatic stress disorder (PTSD) is sometimes invoked to understand literature of this period.[6] Fragmented language and other modernist formal devices become legible as reflections of a clinical condition of war rather than self-conscious strategies that emerge in response to wider literary and cultural histories. In *The Return of the Soldier*, it is these devices, which elaborate a crisis of memory through testimony, that challenge interpretations of trauma as an individualized affliction with a single cause—war—and trouble claims that the work mourns an idyllic Victorian past.

Because it is written under the pressures of a nation rendered vulnerable by war and imperial unrest, however, West's novel presents conflicting articulations of trauma and incompatible stagings of collective memory. On the one hand, it plots trauma as an illness suffered by a soldier in battle that causes him to yearn for a reputedly stable Victorian past. This plotting consolidates entrenched approaches to trauma in modernist studies that envision the twentieth century as a rupture in former national and historical stability. On the other hand, the formal enactments of testimony situate origins of trauma beyond a war fought on European terrain, and they trouble the narrative of historical rupture the novel plots. Testimony indicates that in a climate of national anxiety, vulnerability, and retrenchment coincident with war, nationalist and metropolitan focalizations become resolute, and other traumatic histories both within and without the boundaries of the nation-state become impossible to witness and archive. This warning remains pertinent today, because literary criticism continues to center the European war as the site of trauma in modernist literature, neglecting Anglophone modernism's imbrication in the economic and cultural imperialism from which it emerged and includes within itself, Fredric Jameson famously contended, as a structuring absence.[7] By foregrounding testimony's unverifiability, its literarity, the novel invites readers to become active witnesses to—by becoming facilitators of—the precarious emergence of a counter-representation of England's past. This counter-representation problematizes critical narratives that posit the war as the central crisis of modernity, the event that constitutes a break from earlier historical moments, and retroactively define the prewar past as static and stable.[8]

The Return of the Soldier is a novel about mourning. The losses in the novel seem to accumulate or "condense," but they also appear to substitute or displace one another, making an original loss difficult to identify. The text calls to mind Freud's observations regarding mourning, and pathological mourning particularly. "Mourning is regularly the reaction to the loss of a loved person, or to the loss of some abstraction which has taken the place of one, such as fatherland, liberty, an ideal."[9] Freud points to the conundrum that a loss generating pathological mourning, or melancholia, poses. In these "other cases," he writes, "one feels justified in concluding that a loss of the kind has been experienced, but one cannot see clearly what has been lost, and may the more readily suppose that the patient too cannot consciously perceive what it is he has lost."[10] Thus, pathological mourning produces an interpretative crisis not only for the analysand, the witness who "experiences" the loss without knowing who or "what it is he has lost," but also for the analyst, a witness whose task it is to facilitate the analysand's negotiation of this unconscious loss.[11] In its articulation of British modernity through a vexed narrative of loss it depicts as characterologically *and* textually unconscious, the novel produces a crisis of interpretation for both its internal witnesses and external witnesses, or readers.

The theater in which this crisis unfolds confounds the divide between fiction and history, signaling to readers a rift in historical claims the novel will locate there. That locus is Monkey Island, the site of an idyllic interlude in the plot in which the story of the male protagonist's past, before he has suffered shell shock, is related. The portrayal of Monkey Island illustrates the modern novel's attempts to consolidate fragments of space, as landscape, into a unified whole and figure the nation as a cohesive topos. Depictions of landscape convey completeness and tranquility: "The whole world seemed melting into light. Cumulus clouds floated very high, like lumps of white light against a deep, glowing sky, and dropped dazzling reflections on the beaming Thames. The trees moved not like timber shocked by wind, but floatingly, like weeds at the bottom of a well of sunshine."[12] The oxymoron "well of sunshine" is representative of the island. Oppositions dissipate into specular identification; from the height of the heavens to the subterranean depths of the Thames, everything there neutralizes its other, coinciding with itself. It is a spatial figuration of a time of pure unity, Victorian England bathed in the master trope of light, untouched by the "shock" of later years.

Monkey Island is part of the novel's fabula, but it is also real, an actual place whose idyllic surface covers over personal and collective unrest, even trauma. West visited the small island in the Thames with her lover H. G. Wells, claiming it as a favorite place, but it might have functioned as an ambivalent site also, the locus of escape, refuge, perhaps even exile. When West became pregnant with the married Wells's child, Wells requested she avoid their social circle. She retreated there, where Wells would join her, and Monkey Island allowed the lovers to avoid the pressures of London society, for which, however, West's letters suggest she yearned.[13] Monkey Island is also a site whose history and topology are thickly layered. According to records, the island was first used by monks fishing on the Thames. By the fourteenth century it had become property of Canonesses of Burnham Abbey, a mile north. In 1723 it was purchased by Charles Spencer, Third Duke of Marlborough, who erected its first buildings, a pavilion and temple. Commissioning a French artist to paint the pavilion with figures of fully dressed monkeys engaged in human activities—shooting, fishing, and boating—he gave Monkey Island its most famous feature, which, as the aleatory effects of language's materiality would have it, obscured the origin of the island's name. "Monkey Island" derives not from the paintings in the pavilion, now the inn, but from the earlier, old English *Monks Eyot*, or Monk's Island. The Monkey Island of the duke's day, West's day, and today owes its existence to a catastrophic event in history, the Great Fire of London in 1666. The island was employed as a dumping ground for the rubble carried away from the burned city. This waste provided a solid foundation for building and the elevation necessary to prevent flooding.[14] Monkey Island's literal foundations are the ashes of England's capital, the future metropolitan center of the empire. The traces of the dead and a national traumatic past lie buried beneath its charming inn, manicured lawns, and temple.

The novel appears to contrast England's long period of national and imperial peace in the nineteenth century it figures through Monkey Island with ruptures and violence that emerge in the twentieth and to mourn the loss of this peace.[15] The present is 1916, and Chris Baldry returns home with amnesia, the consequence of an exploding shell. He remembers nothing after 1901, neither his marriage to upper-middle-class Kitty, nor the death of their son Oliver, but only his love affair with working-class Margaret, which in fact ended in 1901. Samuel Hynes notes that Chris's amnesia eclipses not only this affair's end but the dawn of the Edwardian age, a tumultuous time. Increasingly powerful pressure was exerted on Britain in the decade before the war, as social, economic, and political unrest grew at home and abroad. In England, the agitation of mass labor movements coincided with the growing popularity of the Women's Social and Political Movement, the suffragists, and, after the return to power of the Liberal Party in 1906, with violent public demonstrations by its radical factions up to 1914. Indian nationalist demands for self-rule strengthened with the outcry against the colonial partitioning of Bengal in 1906. Demand for home rule in Ireland regained momentum even after its attempted quashing through the Irish Land Acts, the latest implemented in 1903. And in another "peripheral" nation that the novel specifically references, Mexico, nationalist unrest over foreign control of land had culminated in revolution by 1910. Although Mexico was not a British colony, longstanding British commercial interests were threatened by revolution. The text, we will see, underlines this.

The Return seems to join the many modernist works that critically register the transformative effects of the long nineteenth century on English topography and culture through its protagonist's reaction to this period of unrest. "Chris's amnesia has taken him back to the time before change," Hynes contends. "Other Englishmen yearned back, too, to an innocent, unspoiled England that had been lost, not because of the war alone, but because of the whole disfiguring process of modern change."[16] Expressed here is the dominant narrative of the transition from the Victorian to Edwardian eras. According to this view, the former, reputedly belle époque was a time before rupture in the longue durée of English stability, before "modernity" and its attendant modifications, or "disfigurations," of English landscape and social life. Allegedly responsible are not only civil, labor, and colonial agitation but also the decline of an agrarian economy, the rise of industrialism, and the ecological violence accompanying technologies of industrialization, warfare, urbanization, and suburbanization.

There are biographical as well as textual reasons to suspect the novel's endorsement of this narrative of a fall from stability and pastoral plenitude into twentieth-century trauma, however. A feminist, suffragist, and socialist with Anglo-Irish parentage, West also attacked British imperialism, denying the distinction between Britain's benevolent imperialism and malevolent imperialism.[17] In her monograph on Henry James, published in 1916, West criticized James for mythologizing a national past shaped by historical struggles. In *The Passionate Pilgrim*

> you have the first statement of the persistent illusion, to which he was helped by his odd lack of the historic sense and which confused his estimate of modern life, that the past would have been a happier home for those who like himself loved fastidious living. . . . He was always being misled by such lovely shells of the past as Hampton Court into the belief that the past which inhabited them was as lovely. The calm of Canterbury Close appeared to him as a remnant of a time when all England, bowed before the Church, was as calm; whereas the calm is really a modern condition brought about when the church ceased to have anything to do with England. He never perceived that life is always a little painful at the moment, not only at this moment, but at all moments.[18]

By claiming that a lack of "historic sense" misreads conflict as a peculiarly modern condition, this passage illustrates that appropriating a single moment as the origin of trauma generates fiction as history. It also suggests that, as Dominick LaCapra points out, if "one assumes that there was . . . some original unity, wholeness, security, or identity that others have ruined, polluted, or contaminated and thus made 'us' lose . . . to regain it one must somehow get rid of or eliminate those others."[19] West's words indicate that fictional representations of idyllic national pasts entail the violence of erasure.

The Return attacks the normative narrative of a "fall" into modernity that Hynes's introduction conveys and that her criticism of James would seem to reject, but it also expresses it. In the episode recounting Chris's affair with Margaret on Monkey Island fifteen years earlier, the novel converts the absence of an Edenic, prewar era into a loss while concealing the effacement of those who threaten this idyllic image. *The Return* appears to ratify the narrative of loss most intently in the interlude recounting Chris's affair with Margaret on the island fifteen years earlier. The text presents this time that escapes Chris's amnesia as memory. Later, when familial, social, and economic obligations arise, their love will be thwarted, but in 1901, on Monkey Island, no such conflicts exist, and division and discord are declared absent. Even the island's name, which West opens to interpretation by forgoing mention of the monkey paintings, figures a "prehistorical" moment, before humans acquire language, marking their fall into separation and their perpetual attempts to bridge the distance that language opens between them. However, the novel also disturbs this image of an uncontaminated Victorian nation through testimony, which operates as a vehicle of aesthetic contestations over national histories.

The framing of the section on Monkey Island in terms of psychoanalytic treatment throws into relief the conflicting interpretations of trauma the work elaborates while troubling the coherence, unity, and reality of the supposedly prelapsarian national past.[20] This framing operates in friction with the novel's critical assessments of psychoanalysis in its concluding pages—the plotting of trauma ends by rejecting the possibility of a talking cure. A cure is found not through methods advocated by the doctor loosely modeled on Freud but through Margaret, whom the doctor approaches "as though she were the nurse in charge of the case" (73). After the doctor searches into Chris's Oedipal past for the cause of amnesia, the text dismisses the value of testimony while mocking the analyst for his "glib assurance, his knowingness about the pathways of the soul" (81). "What's the use of talking? You can't cure him" (81), Margaret tells the analyst, and then she brings Chris's memory back not by listening to him speak but by showing him an object that recalls to him the death of his son. The introduction of the episode on Monkey Island, however, pushes against Margaret's dismissal of testimony as talking cure. Here we find another nurse and the miming of a psychoanalytic scene that both suggests that the novel attempts to bring something beside the son's death to consciousness and that doing so requires the facilitation of a witness, a listener, a reader. Chris's cousin Jenny, the novel's narrator, is cast as analyst to Chris's analysand. The narrator recognizes that in returning to Baldry Court in 1916, Chris enters what for him is a fantasy world, because his reality is 1901. "He was like a patient when tiring visitors have gone and he is left alone with his trusted nurse; . . . I watched him vigilantly and was ready at that moment when thought intruded into his drowsings and his face began to twitch" (32). The medical attendant, "nurse," reads the language written on the "patient's" body, interpreting physical symptoms as signs of inner conflict. She then intervenes by promoting the talking cure and establishing herself as listener: "'Tell me what seems real to you,' I begged" (33). Chris responds, "Why, Monkey Island's real. But you don't know old Monkey. Let me tell you—" (33). The narrator interrupts where Chris's speech cuts off, claiming, "I have lived so long with the story which he told me that I cannot now remember his shy phrases. But this is how I have visualized his meeting with love on his secret island. I think it is the truth" (33).

The choreography of this scene does not pinpoint the source of amnesia in either war or shell shock, or where the doctor, Margaret, or the cure locate it—in Chris's relationships with a cold mother and jealous father and the death of his son. Neither, however, does it situate trauma entirely outside of history and representation. The scene's structure disputes what Jenny and Chris declare. The past on Monkey Island is not "real" but a belated invention through narrative of a moment that can never be grasped as itself. Because it formally configures the episode on Monkey Island as an unverifiable testimony to trauma, or, in Freud's words, *Nachträglichkeit*, the novel presents this episode as an event that calls for representation and clarifies that such representation can only occur through an interaction between text and reader, a witness who will help translate it.[21] In *Beyond the Pleasure Principle* we find the most oft-cited definition of *Nachträglichkeit*, literally "carrying-afterness," translated as "aftereffect." The traumatic neurotic [*traumatisch Neurotiker*] suffers from a paradoxical aftereffect, a compulsive return from the past of a self-differing event. The event differs from itself because its origin is unavailable, and it returns only through displacements, interruptions, or transfigurations.[22] In the novel, the story of Monkey Island is never supported by an omniscient or third-person narration but instead undergoes multiple translations, from Chris's memory, to language, to Jenny's memory, to Jenny's visualization, and, finally, to the words on the page framed with an oath: "I think it is the truth." Because the oath is a performative utterance it is heterogeneous to either truth or falsity. The past it dispatches to readers is therefore necessarily discontinuous with verification. This testimonial framing of Monkey Island hence disrupts the narrative of modernity that locates loss and rupture with the turn of the century and the war while placing readers in the role of facilitating this disruption.

The significance of testimony in the novel, then, is not that it recovers historical truth or that it fails to because it is "false." It is, first, that as an unverifiable mode that is (also) literary, testimony provides the lineaments of a collective past that cannot emerge through the discourse of psychoanalysis that the text parodies as a science of family romance, or through the clinical discourse of PTSD that would explain Chris's trauma as the effect of battle wounds. Second, testimony foregrounds the need for reader-witnesses to enable the submerged past to surface. Finally, this abyssal framing highlights that because testimony remains disconnected from both source and destination, author and receiver, it "must allow itself to be parasitized by precisely what it excludes from its inner depths, the *possibility*, at least, of literature."[23] Indeed, to portray the so-called real past the novel paradoxically deploys testimony's parasites, literature, even fiction. Although West includes elements of the historical Monkey Island—Lord Marlborough, the pavilion-turned-inn, and the temple—she replaces its most famous feature, the monkey paintings, with literary works that share its own concerns: Proust's *In Search of Lost Time* and Wordsworth's "Lines Composed a Few Miles Above Tintern Abbey." Both question the capacity of memory to access the past. The engagement with these literary works suggests that the national anxiety coincident with war produces collective amnesia. Inviting readers to trace the indirect emergence of trauma through interruptions, displacements, and transfigurations, the novel conveys that the rhetorical details that compose

Monkey Island provide clues about what other histories must be obscured for the normative narrative of loss to cohere.

The White Hawthorn and the Magic State

The first reference *The Return* makes to another literary work, one published just five years before the novel, is through the white hawthorn. The white hawthorn, like the madeleine, is an important element in *Swann's Way*, authored by the only modern writer whose "greatness," West declared, "cannot [be] exaggerated."[24] I would argue, however, that Proust's white hawthorn is important to the novel not because it functions as a symbol that provides access to *memoire involontaire* but, on the contrary, because it frustrates the act of symbolization and memory, troubling attempts to attain a correspondence between nature as object and the mind of the subject contemplating it.

In West's and Proust's novels, the relationships between art and artifice on the one hand and nature and reality on the other coalesce around the figure of the white hawthorn, which both texts inscribe into a literary history of the symbol. In both novels, the rhetorical mode of symbol is also deposed by allegory. Allegory, Paul de Man demonstrated, operates in aesthetic and ideological struggle with symbol throughout literary history.[25] Through symbol, the poetic subject claims to exceed finite limits and attain mastery over himself and the objective world. Symbol's materiality evanesces, providing unmediated access to truth or the real. In contrast, allegory is a debased mode that forces unbridgeable distance between subject and world, because allegory is pure mediation and figuration. Symbolic achievements are illusory, however, and allegory persistently displaces this valorized mode by exposing its reliance on mediation. These displacements are often instances of intertextuality that arise at the point at which symbolic truth is purported to occur. Through the allegory of the white hawthorn, West's and Proust's writings challenge symbol's mastery while betraying anxieties of memory peculiar to twentieth-century history and literary history.

The recurring mention of the white hawthorn implies its "immense significance" (35), as well as the significance of tracking rhetorical figurations outside of the main plot or action, for the hawthorn plays no part in these.

First, after describing the pathway leading toward Monkey Island, West writes, "between the two [poplars]—he [Chris] described it meticulously as though it were of immense significance—there stood a white hawthorn" (35). The second mention of the plant provides more direct reference to Proust's novel. When the hawthorn appears again, so does the titular figure of *Swann's Way*, his proper name transformed into a common noun, highlighted through an alliteration that makes it difficult not to stutter over, or at least notice, the word.

> Past the spit of sand at the far end of the island, where a great *swan swanked* to the empty reach that it would protect its mate against all comers, the river opened to a silver breadth between flat meadows stretching back to far rows of pin-thick black poplars, until it wound away to Windsor behind a line of trees whose heads were bronze with unopened buds and whose flanks were hidden by a hedge of copper-beech and crimson and white hawthorn.
>
> (39, my emphasis)

Invoking another fiction, West's novel challenges, by ironizing, claims that Monkey Island is real. More ironic, or rather allegorical, is that this particular allusion directs us to passages that refute Monkey Island's past unity. Proust's novel portrays the white hawthorn as a figure of disunification, as what creates distance within and between self and world. Marcel is frustrated by his inability to get beyond unsignifying nature in order to turn it into a symbol, as Chris Baldry says of the white hawthorn, of "immense significance."

> But it was in vain that I lingered beside the hawthorns—inhaling, trying to fix in my mind . . . , losing and recapturing their invisible and unchanging odor, absorbing myself in the rhythm which disposed their flowers here and there with the lightheartedness of youth and at intervals as unexpected as certain intervals in music—they went on offering me the same charm in inexhaustible profusion, but without letting me delve any more deeply, like those melodies which one can play a hundred times in succession without coming any nearer to their secret. I turned away from them for a moment so as to be able to return to them afresh.[26]

Marcel turns back to them but again is frustrated by their inability to enlighten. His turning is also a troping, which, in the passage that follows, is disclosed as irreducible. For the hawthorns will not reveal their "inner essence," "offer no enlightenment."[27] The problem cannot be resolved, for the white hawthorn alone holds the secret of truth Marcel pursues: "I could not call upon any other flowers to satisfy this mysterious longing."[28]

These passages enact a thwarting of symbolic by allegorical discourse. They illustrate the white hawthorn's refusal to submit to the self that contemplates it as if symbolic, preventing the male protagonist from identifying with the real, or natural, world. Marcel takes recourse to metaphors of artistic production at moments he seems to describe its opposite, nature. The flowers' refusal to reveal their secret is likened to "melodies" one plays to solicit their inner meaning, but without success. Later, he frames them as art, a "masterpiece," metaphorically and literally.[29] Still, they fail to signify other than themselves, nor do they allow unification of feeling and object. Employing a rhetoric of artifice to portray the real manifests the figurative deposing of nature by art and underscores the overcoming of symbolic by allegorical diction.

This intertextuality projects an allegorical structure to the white hawthorn in West's novel. The blossom can no more bridge a distance within the self and between the self and the natural world for Chris on Monkey Island, where he attempts to transcend his distance from the "real" past through the white hawthorn as symbol, than it can for Marcel. Proust's text indicates that the unity of the national past Monkey Island figures is illusory, that it is *already* marked by separation and loss. Allegory intimates the gap between history and memory, the past and its belated reinvention.

The third mention of the plant reveals how the dominant narrative of loss obscures uneven gendering and class formations in England's past. The struggle between allegory and symbol questions whether the hawthorn can overcome the distance not only between memory and history but also between men and women of different classes. Jenny finds it "strange" (49) that both Margaret and Chris "should describe meticulously the one white hawthorn that stood among the poplars by the ferryside" (49) but then surmises, "I suppose that a thing that one has looked at with somebody one loves acquires for ever after a special significance" (49), which suggests the blossom's reality *and* symbolic force, its capacity to bind Chris and Margaret. However, because the white hawthorn is located on Monkey Island, it is situated outside of reality, and thus its binding of these two is predicated on illusion. "It was strange that both Chris and she spoke of it [Monkey Island] as though it were not a place, but a magic state which largely explained the actions performed in it" (49). If Monkey Island is a "magic state," a fantasy, as is the white hawthorn within it, the latter can bridge the distance between Chris and Margaret only through fiction. "State" doubles its referent here; in addition to a quality of feeling, it designates a sociopolitical entity. Magical Monkey Island is a figure for England before 1901, a phantasmatic geopolitical topos.

Allegory's deconstruction of symbol in passages that present Margaret as an aesthetic object illustrate that the narrative of loss is marked by fiction and that it censors heteronormative and patriarchal policing of masculinity and femininity, classes, and sexualities. These passages parody late nineteenth-century academic art, which revived neoclassical motifs to figure the female body in painting and sculpture, as well as aesthetic discourses that emerge in the 1870s and become more reactionary in relation to social purity movements of the 1880s and 1890s.[30] Just as this testimony misreads the white hawthorn's significance as symbolic, a dematerialized and transcendent access to truth, so it treats Margaret as a symbol, dematerializing and disfiguring her. Symbol is exposed as allegory again, however, revealing that this Margaret is created from textuality and artifice. Recycled fictions and art of the past shape her as a reactionary, patriarchal ideal of the late Victorian period, the epitome of feminine modesty and chastity. The imagery of classical Greece and the language of the medieval chivalric code, whose intimacy with the religious practice of object worship is ironized, portray Margaret as divine symbol, beyond the reach of everything human and "base"—beyond figure, figuration, and thus allegory.

> He drew her out into the darkness . . . to a circle of smooth turf. . . . On this stood a small Greek temple. . . . He had never brought Margaret here before because Mr. Allington had once told him . . . it had been built by the Dook for his excesses, and it was in the quality of his love for her that he could not bear to think of her in connection with anything base. . . . He lifted her in his arms and carried her within the columns and made her stand in a niche above the altar. . . . He could not tell if her hair was white as silver or yellow as gold. . . . His love was changeless. Lifting her down from the niche, he told her so.
>
> (41)

The lower-middle-class female body operates as the site of a fetishistic reaction, the production of the upper-middle-class male's erotic investment and denegation at once. The realist conventions persistently used to portray Margaret as utterly material, *too* material, throughout the novel indicate the need for this effacement of the body. She enters Baldry Court with a "deplorable umbrella, her unpardonable raincoat" (14), "muddy boots," and "a seamed red hand" (10). A "stain" (16) on the English drawing room and the English garden, both metonymic of the English nation, Margaret possesses "the gift of animals and those of peasant stock" (14), the "heaviness of the draught-ox or the big trusted dog . . . repulsively furred with neglect and poverty" (10). A belated invention of an unmarked Margaret, a lack of "historic sense" that positions the working-class woman as an immutable symbol of a masculinist ideal of femininity, divesting her of materiality and historicity, enables Margaret and Chris's relationship to form in 1901. The doubled articulation of Margaret—she is all too material, historical, and "scarred" on the one hand, and not material at all, lacking a relation to time, history, and sensuousness—is paradigmatic of many philosophical and literary representations of women in Western modernity.[31]

This allegory of Margaret can also be read as West's indictment of the discursive management of the laboring female body in the last decades of the nineteenth century. A host of phenomena contributed to variegated social purity movements: the perceived but by no means actually widespread liberation of women from monogamous, patriarchal, reproductive, and heteronormative constraints, for example in the form of "free love" practiced by women and men in socialist and intellectual circles; the rise in popularity of neo-Malthusian justifications for contraception; the change in legal statutes granting unmarried women property rights and protecting married women against marital rape; and calls for the protection of lower-class and working-class women and prostitutes, whose regular, even organized sexual exploitation by middle- and upper-class males was journalistically decried.[32] A biopolitics devoted to regulating the desires of middle- and upper-middle-class young men like Chris Baldry by inculcating self-discipline or "manly purity" through a language of chivalry in educational and religio-medical tracts was one dominant strain of these. The social discourses of chivalry of the 1880s and 1890s also affected aesthetic deployments of the female body, and specifically working-class female bodies, such as artist's models', dancers', and performers' bodies. As one art historian explains, "the association made by purists between vice and upper-class morals did much to discredit the nude in the domain of high art. . . . In the 1880s the artistic nude was denounced, alongside *tableaux vivants* and billboards advertising dancers, actresses, and acrobats, as a demoralizing influence."[33] West's own politics and behavior, her affair with the married Wells, and the highly eroticized exchanges with him as "Jaguar" and "Panther" arguably place her on the other side of this biopolitics and aesthetics of male chivalry and its accompanying effacement of female desire and sexuality. West's essay "1900" also castigates the hypocrisy of the era in which middle-class men regularly engaged prostitutes while women of all classes were denied sex outside of marriage. She points out that most of the art and literature of the time was "restrained by formal manners and religious practice" while in fact "the pudency of the age was . . . absurd."[34]

When the aesthetic ideology of symbol betrays anxieties toward the female body, allegory indicates that Margaret and this past are fictions taken for history. The ironic portrayal of the episode in the temple conveys that Chris, like Henry James, is "always being misled by such lovely shells of the past . . . into the belief that the past which inhabited them was as lovely."[35] Only by misreading fiction as history and effect as cause can Chris believe that Monkey Island, a shell of loveliness containing another shell, the Greek temple, held a past as lovely. His scene of religious worship obfuscates its history. It was never employed for physical denial and spiritual purification, only for sensual indulgences, those "excesses" of the aristocratic male that social purity campaigns targeted by regulating the impulses of young men. That Margaret scandalizes Kitty and Jenny at the end of the novel by remarking on Chris's pronounced sexual drive when they were together at this earlier time gives the lie to this symbolic staging as well.

The novel suggests that the narrative of loss articulated through these aesthetic practices, and the drive to symbolize, results not only in failure but in the disappearance of women as witnesses to history. By literally and figuratively "exulting" as a mythic object and by metaphorically freezing, or "friezing," Margaret by lifting and making her "stand in a niche above the altar" like a *statue* of a goddess in this Greek temple, Chris evacuates her of her human, material form, her gendered and classed subjecthood, to render her transcendent and inanimate. The testimony concludes with Margaret's literal disappearance: "And as he spoke her warm body melted to nothingness in his arms. The columns that stood so hard and black against the quivering tide of moonlight and starlight tottered and dissolved" (41). Margaret dissolves "as he speaks" twice—testifies to and through his proxy—because this speech turns her into a symbol. The testimony implies that women can be included in the master narrative of the Victorian era only in objectified, dematerialized, and fictional form.

"Tintern Abbey" and Colonial Trauma

If the intertextuality of Proust's white hawthorn illuminates that the narrative of Victorian stasis that the war inspires relies on the occlusion of struggles over gender, sexuality, and class relations, the deployment of Wordworth's "Lines Composed a Few Miles Above Tintern Abbey" illuminates how the stability of England's past is constituted through the instabilities generated by imperialism and anti-imperialism, which the narrative of loss marginalizes. *The Return* enacts what Edward Said identifies as the European novel's consolidation of imperialism. Analyzing its deployment of "Tintern Abbey" also enables a "contrapuntal reading"[36] demonstrating how the novel resists the imperialist logic it apparently underwrites. The text implies that colonial space is the supporting but excluded structure of the metropole, what Fredric Jameson contends remains unconscious in English modernism. Modernism will "always have . . . a privation that can never be restored . . . an outside . . . it constitutively lacks, and which can never be made up or made good."[37] West's novel departs from literary examples that fit neatly into Jameson and Said's models, however. Rather than (dis)articulating a dependency of metropole on official colony, this work encodes a space with a more complex politico-economic connection to Britain: Mexico. Perhaps because Mexico did not have a formal colonial relationship to the British state, Britain's imbrication in the trauma of land relations there is even less represented in British modernism than that of official colonies, histories already displaced. Situating Mexico at an oblique but pivotal point in the narrative construction of trauma indicates its limited visibility textually as well as historically. The novel's reappropriation of "Tintern Abbey" attempts to bring this constitutive lack to consciousness, paradoxically by manifesting it as unconscious.

Like the staging of the white hawthorn, that of "Tintern Abbey" also disturbs the narrative of loss and illustrates an alternative vision of the collective past. The novel guides readers toward the poem, not the abbey itself, by framing memory as Wordsworth does: as a work of art. The artwork in the novel is even oriented from the same vantage point as in the poem, which is "Composed a Few Miles Above Tintern Abbey." The painting *The Views Overlooking Tintern Abbey* appears twice. It hangs on the otherwise unadorned walls of Monkey Island Inn in 1901 and in Margaret's terraced house in 1916. The recurring mention of a temporal interval also points to the poem, specifically the incipit, which details the time since the poet's return to Tintern Abbey: "Five years have passed; five summers, with the length / Of five long winters!"[38] In the novel, five years have passed since Chris's son Oliver's death, but five years also separates every date in the novel, moments significant, and dated, because each figures a transformative event: 1901 is when Chris's memory ends; in 1906, he marries Kitty; in 1911, his son dies; and in 1916, Chris suffers shell shock.

Although their publications are separated by over a century, both novel and poem are written in the midst or recent aftermath of an event of great interruptive force that called into question the future of Europe and the conventions, traditions, and philosophical premises of the past on which its polities and cultural formations were structured: the French Revolution and the First World War. One might expect their historical contexts to induce them to enact what LaCapra diagnoses as a compensatory movement caused by a traumatic event. Faced with radical uncertainty of the future and the crises in witnessing posed by such events, they might manifest a desire to escape the instabilities of the present by retreating into a past of their author's invention, one that offers an illusory stability. But even if such authorial desires were operative in these texts' composition, both works' articulations of memory expose such a compensatory movement as ultimately insupportable.

Through their memories, both the poetic persona of "Tintern Abbey" and Chris Baldry revisit a space unmarked by modernity. The "I" of the poem returns to the pastoral scene on the banks of the Wye after five years, although he has often returned before, through the faculty of memory. The poem represents this return as an escape from the tumult of contemporary life. The poetic voice relates that "'mid the din / Of towns and cities" (66, lines 25–26) and "when the fretful stir / Unprofitable, and the fever of the world, / Have hung upon the beatings of my heart— / How oft, in spirit, have I turned to thee,/O Sylvan Wye!" (67, lines 52–56), in order to recall the "beauteous forms" of the Wye valley (66, line 23). Both the poetic subject and Chris seek to take refuge in the idyllic space-time of memory when modernity, or the "fever of the world," becomes too great.

The poem's orchestration of this past and the subject's relation to it reveal, however, that this space-time is more likely a belated invention, an instance of *Nachträglichkeit*, than reality. By bracketing the natural world from the subject's conscious experience, or cognition in the Kantian sense, Wordsworth intimates that this past self had an inauthentic relation to the place and time "Tintern Abbey" describes. Then, nature "To [him] was all in all" (68, line 75). Consequently, he could not experience nature as it was because he failed to employ the faculties of mind that come later, with maturity, when he has "learned/To look on nature, not as in the hour/Of thoughtless youth" (68, lines 88–90). Toward the end of these lines, one might hear the influence of Coleridge, and his debt to Schelling, when Wordsworth writes: "Therefore am I still/A lover of the meadows and the woods,/And mountains; and of all that we behold/From this green earth; of all the mighty world/Of eye, and ear,—both what they half create,/And what perceive" (68, lines 102–107). Earlier, nature was only what the subject could see absent the intervention of cognition, thought, or understanding. Later, he recognizes what he sees in nature is not the world as it is, without mediation, but the product of an interaction between mind and external phenomena. The senses, "eye and ear," do not passively receive images, "perceive," but also "half create." By making this distinction between childhood and adulthood, Wordsworth suggests this subject will always remain barred from the world of his youth because his experience of nature was not comprehended. It escaped the mind's cognitive faculties, was shaped by a "thoughtless" youth, and therefore is without foundation in reality.

Moreover, while this earlier time purportedly lacks the anxieties coterminous with modernity, the poem renders untenable this temporal opposition. Even in the past, nature functioned as refuge from reality. The poem relates that the feeling that prompts the subject to return to this pastoral scene in his memory also occurred in the past. Then, too, he sought to escape from "the burthen of the mystery,/In which the heavy and the weary weight/Of all this unintelligible world" (67, lines 38–40) cannot be lifted without the "gift" of a "blessed mood," by taking flight into nature. "Like a roe/I bounded . . . /Wherever nature led: more like a man/Flying from something he dreads than one/Who sought the thing he loved" (67–68, lines 67–72). The subject confesses he has entered this pastoral scene not to search for what he loved but to flee from what he feared—the end of childhood, mortality, death, an anxiety without an object that can be posited: "dread."

The novel intimates that for Chris, too, the natural world operated as an escape from reality even before 1916. In his youth, a retreat into nature was an escape into the imagination. Chris has always projected his desires onto natural objects, evading life's mundanities, anxieties, and disappointments. Jenny remarks, "he had always shown great faith in the imminence of the improbable. He thought that the birch tree would really stir and shrink and quicken into an enchanted princess, that he really was a Red Indian . . . with a stronger motion of the imagination than the ordinary child's make-believe" (7). Like Wordsworth's poetic persona, Chris also has limited access to the natural landscapes of his past. That he treated the woods in his childhood as a supernatural place through imagination suggests that soon he would treat Monkey Island similarly. It will become the site of his fears transformed by fictions created to avoid the dread confronted as a young man, which eventually become sedimented as truths. Reading the novel's and poem's articulation of returns as homological, we can infer that Chris goes to Monkey Island *not* to seek out "what he loves" (Margaret), as he attests, but more "like a man flying from something he dreads." The fears that drive him to a fictional world are similar to those from which the voice of "Tintern Abbey" fled, the end of childhood and transition to adulthood.

Unlike Wordsworth's poem, however, West's novel ties this transition directly to economic and political vicissitudes; intertextuality stages capitalism and imperialism as traumas, interrupting the plot's substitutive designations of trauma. Adulthood means becoming an English patriarch, "gentleman," and capitalist, the inheritor of an overseas mining firm. This is a transition to which Chris cannot bear witness, an impasse—a trauma. The day he leaves to embark on this new life is where his memory abruptly ends. Attempting to learn why she is "barred out" (38) of the last day in Chris's memory, Jenny thinks back to a spring "fifteen years ago . . . Chris had lingered with Uncle Ambrose in his Thamesside rectory as he had never lingered before, and old Mr. Baldry was filling the house with a sense of hot, apoplectic misery" (52).

Eventually Mr. Baldry does send for Chris, who has retreated from reality to Monkey Island. Jenny announces, "I had got the key at last":

> That night he talked til late with his father and in the morning he had started for Mexico, to keep the mines going through the revolution, to keep the firm's head above water and Baldry Court sleek and hospitable, to keep everything bright and splendid save only his youth, which after that was dulled by care.
>
> (52–53)

Through its homologies with "Tintern Abbey," the novel opens onto a politicohistorical situation outside the plot and diegetic space of England. Becoming the English gentleman means exploiting the resources of a comprador state and functioning as stopgap to the effects of a revolution against a dictatorship.[39]

Chris participates in the counterrevolutionary movement, expanding English wealth by exploiting the resources of foreign soil while helping render its people landless and indigent. The novel makes the causal logic clear while undermining the image of the healthy English soldier who heads into battle in the European War. This quasi-imperialism has already damaged Chris Baldry *before* the war. British firms benefited from Porfirio Diaz's dictatorship in the latter half of the nineteenth century and had much to lose in a revolution that would overthrow him. By giving enormous land concessions to foreign speculators who greatly increased gold and silver production in Mexico, Diaz bankrupted a majority of rural farmers by 1910. The Mining Law of 1884 was particularly significant, producing long-term effects, such as the growth of the foreign-owned oil industry and the removal of lands from common ownership by Mexicans. As Peter Calvert writes,

> Common rights in the subsoil, including vital water supplies, were replaced in the Mining Law of 1884 by the concept of private ownership of irreplaceable minerals being vested in the ownership of the surface. In the poorest parts of the country, rich foreign colonies suddenly appeared, offering high wages which might cease at any time when the deposits ran out.[40]

British investment was concentrated not only in mining but in industry and railways, which also contributed to the traumatic effects of land enclosures in Mexico at the end of the nineteenth century. Land held by village communities in common ownership since precolonial times was opened by the government to enclosure by plantation owners and foreign corporations, and as a result "more than a quarter of the land surface of Mexico passed into the hands of not more than 834 men. . . . Of all these factors in the growth of pre-revolutionary discontent, it was agrarian revolt against enclosures that was to have the most significance for the internal history of Mexico."[41]

By suggesting this historicopolitical situation is what Chris flees, what drives him to an invented world and to inventing this world, the novel indicates that England's economic dependence on foreign soil and labor generates a phantasmatic pastoral nation-state: Monkey Island, a figure for England itself. The textual site mirrors the historical site. Undergirding both idyllic places are traumas. Although the Mexican conflict induces Chris to escape the "misery" of the law of the father as (neo)imperialist by retreating to Monkey Island, this "retreat" is actually a running toward "what he dreads"—the trauma of imperialism appears excessively displaced across the island. We see this through associations that repeatedly recall the Mexican mines, the whiteness of silver and references to gold and copper: Margaret, "a girl in white who lifted a white face or drooped a dull gold head" (38), a "white figure" (38) whose "white dress shone like silver" (39), her hair "white as silver or yellow as gold" (41); the poplars' "silver spires" (35); the clouds, lumps of "white light" (38); chestnut candles, "no longer proud flowers, but just wet white lights" (37); Mr. Allington's boots, "white ducks" and his "copper-coloured hair" (37); the inn, a "low white house" (35); the "silver breadth" of the river (39); and the high trees "whose heads were bronze . . . whose flanks were hidden by a hedge of copper-beech" (39). And of course, the white hawthorn.[42] Monkey Island is the chronotope of the Victorian era as the age of a displaced colonial trauma.

By figuring Monkey Island as this chronotope, the novel sends a warning. Staged as a missed encounter with history, a "key" event that cannot be recalled, imperialism's effects are traumas in danger of succumbing to collective amnesia in twentieth-century wartime and postwar narratives of modernity as loss. The testimony relates that in the midst of the contemporaneous international crisis and reactionary nationalist retrenchment, England is in danger of forgetting past historical moments in which the suppression of others are enacted in the consolidation and perpetuation of British empire and wealth, which relied on the appropriation and exploitation of natural resources and labor power by the 1890s in Africa, India, the Caribbean, and

South America. By generating formal parallels with "Tintern Abbey," the novel recalls that colonialism and capitalism function as supporting structures of England's prewar peace and stability. Allegory and intertextuality reveal the violent underpinnings of "Pax Britannica."

Reading Beyond the Cure

Whether colonial complicity is the key to Chris's amnesia remains the site of narrative contestation, however. This uncertainty has enabled readers to locate the cause of trauma in war and shell shock, or outside of history and representation, or where the plot locates it by providing a cure to amnesia: the death of Chris's son. When Margaret returns memory to Chris by reminding him of Oliver's death, the novel contradicts the testimony's designation of colonial complicity as the key to amnesia. But by correlating the departure to Mexico with the end of Chris's memory, the final day in his recollection, the text produces a narrative manipulation of "consecution" into "consequence."[43] The departure to Mexico offers an explanatory power other diagnoses lack. Yet Margaret's is the last word on the matter because it resolves the organizing conflict, even though the doctor cannot explain why recalling the son's death should cure amnesia: "I don't know why [it matters so much]. But it does" (82), he tells Kitty. The cure suggests that the loss of the patronym's power, survival through the male heir, is what Chris mourns and is the trauma perpetuating his amnesia. By relating that Kitty cannot have another child, the novel supports this interpretation.

The testimony's interrogation of the narrative of loss seems subsumed by the cure's closure. The working-class woman and the upper-middle-class man become sutured not through an illusory white hawthorn that reveals political, economic, and social inequities and discontinuities concealed by a nostalgic image of Victorian stability but through their failure to secure through social and biological reproduction what is now imputed as England's former stability. Both Chris and Margaret have sons who die, and this represents the fragmentation of life in the Edwardian age, the disruption of national continuity and genealogical futurity. "It's as if . . . they each had half a life" (77), Margaret muses. If, as Freud contends, the melancholic may know who has been lost but not what he himself has lost thereby, Chris's cure relates that what is lost is the possibility of reproducing the name of the father and ensuring the nation's future. This resolution makes Margaret's role primarily reproductive, maternal (just as Jenny does throughout the novel). Although Margaret fails to secure the patronym and the nation's future through her own child, who dies, by curing Chris she enables the soldier to return and secure that future through war. The novel of course indicates that the cure is poison because it returns Chris to the traumas of the front; however, even if the cure ironically comments on the reality to which the soldier is made to return, by displacing colonial trauma, the closure it provides apparently supports Jameson's hypothesis that life in the colonies cannot be included consciously in the modernist novel and must remain part of the textual unconscious.

Yet the novel departs from this paradigm of modernism's relation to imperialism through its highlighting of the unverifiable and literary structure of testimony. Testimony persistently asks readers to bear witness to the textual unconscious, to address the incompatible staging of trauma the novel cannot resolve within itself. Although the exposure of colonial complicity and uneven class and gender arrangements shaping the nostalgic narrative of loss is jettisoned by the plotting of cure, testimony's intertextuality interrupts narrative closure by directing readers' attention to the lacks that enable that closure. By troubling the historical narrative of the fall into a fragmented Edwardian age and war-torn modernity, testimony does not merely invite but indeed requests that readers imagine alternative versions of England's past scripted by those who have been expelled from the Garden but cannot be banished from history.

West's other work that illustrates how war induces amnesia toward Britain's past is *The Meaning of Treason*. The differences between the novel and the report's negotiation of colonial trauma demonstrate the effects of changes that occur between their publications. The trial reports are written after the process of imperial contraction has greatly accelerated and after the conditions of warfare have dramatically shifted from a soldier's battle fought at the front to a "People's War" that brings death home in unprecedented ways. Like *The Return of the Soldier*, *The Meaning of Treason* also relates how dominant narratives obscure histories of violence, but the World War II text conveys a stronger desire to secure the nation than the World War I novel. It therefore mobilizes those narratives rather than calling attention to their coercive effects, which, in turn, interrupt its articulations of law and justice.

Blackout as Juridical Unconscious

The Meaning of Treason earned West the title of "The World's Number One Woman Writer," bestowed by the magazine *Time*. West began reporting on trials in 1945, a labor for which she professed little love but continued to perform. Over the next decade she would cover the Nuremburg trials, murder trials in Britain and the United States, and treason trials, which were collected in *The Meaning of Treason*, later developed and revised as *The New Meaning of Treason*. "The Revolutionary," the first part of *The Meaning of Treason*, initially published in the *New Yorker* in 1945, focuses largely on the trials of William Joyce. Joyce, or Lord Haw Haw, as he became known, traveled on a British passport to Germany, where he broadcast Nazi propaganda into England over the radio. The great interest the Joyce trials held for legal and lay communities alike was due to the technical question at their center. Joyce's English mother and Irish father traveled from Ireland to the United States and were naturalized before Joyce was born. The family returned to Ireland and eventually settled in England; Joyce learns during the trials he is an American citizen by birth. If Joyce is not legally a British subject, could he be guilty of committing treason against the British state? How will the court define treason in this case? Over the course of three trials, the court decides that because Joyce lived under the King's protection for thirty years and traveled on a British passport, he owed allegiance to the state. By becoming naturalized as a German citizen during the war, he commits high treason for which he is served the death penalty. By crafting the Joyce trials into something more and other than a documentary report, West attempts to dress the wounds England suffers as a result of World War II and imperial contraction. She shapes these legal events into a narrative of development and rehabilitation of a colonial subject who tries and fails to become an English citizen.

Recently, critics have sought to bridge the apparently oppositional forces of antifascism and anticommunism, nationalism and anti-imperialism at work in West's interwar, wartime, and later writings.[44] Not sufficiently examined, however, is how British imperialism particularly is implicated in the network in which her criticism of fascism and communism, and her support of national rather than transnational alliances, cross. West's political views shifted during the interwar period. West became a vocal antifascist but also an emphatic nationalist and intense critic of communism over the next decades, which separated her further from a modernist grouping to which she had never really belonged and also helped marginalize her postwar writing for decades. Reconsiderations of her work, however, have led critics to assert that West's writings that emerge on the cusp of the postcolonial era are prescient of postcolonial critiques and that they critique as well the rise of an English bureaucratic state that betrays the promises of the nation. Marina MacKay argues that in *Black Lamb and Grey Falcon*, West's most celebrated work of the interwar/wartime period, the author motivates nationalist ideals toward a "tentative post-colonial sensibility" that demonstrates, as West puts it in the travelogue, that "one empire is very like another." MacKay contends that West does not dwell on British imperialism because by the end of the 1930s it is no longer an issue; "she writes as if the empire were already thing of the past."[45] But *The Meaning of Treason*, published six years after the travelogue, shows that the affective force of empire has not yet settled into the past, that it is reactivated by war and the ramifications of imperial decline. The effects of these pressures on the report's form question Patricia E. Chu's compelling argument that West presents Joyce's story as an encapsulation of "the difficulty of defining the British subject . . . as national definitions were fitted to the needs of the bureaucratic welfare state" and that she lays bare the divide between national affect as imaginative and flexible and "a state that imposes 'durable' identities amenable to state administration."[46]

The report does expose a breach between nation and state and attests to the difficulty of defining the British subject. I contend, however, that rather than sympathetically portraying Joyce's desire to become English and criticizing the bureaucratic state for denying his national aspirations, as Chu argues, West condemns the state for potentially enabling Joyce to pose as English. Instead of countering the state's imposition of durable identities with a flexible model of national belonging, West deploys narratives that serve imperial and ethnonationalist aims to correct for what she perceives as the state's failure to secure national identity and community. She also attempts to correct for the state's increasing separation from the missions of an organic nation by reestablishing English law as the means for carrying out those missions. These textual strategies, I maintain, are reactions to co-implicated historical traumas of war and imperial retrenchment.

While trauma in West's reports on the Nuremburg trials has been examined, overlooked is how trauma deforms the treason trial reports.[47] In "The Revolutionary," trauma is translated into a problem of restricted vision, or "blackout." Blackout refers to material, epistemological, and political phenomena that together crystallize England's interrelated struggles with fascism and its colonies during World War II. On the most basic level, the report responds to the blackout of information caused by the wartime economy. In *The New Meaning of Treason*, West explains the origin of the first version: "I was encouraged to make a book about [Joyce, John Amery, and other World War II traitors] by an eminent lawyer who was concerned because the shortage of newsprint due to the war meant that these trials were either not reported, or were reported too briefly for the public to gain any real information regarding a significant tendency."[48] *The Meaning of Treason* centers on that significant tendency, a "force" that returns and refuses to settle into the past. "When I began my book I was under the impression that I was dealing with a spent force only interesting as part of the past," West writes, "but when I was halfway through it Alan Nunn May followed William Joyce into the dock of the Old Bailey, and I became aware that the force still lived, and that its significance was even more grave than had been supposed."[49] The report aims to fill in the gaps produced through the blackout of information by making the compulsive repetition of treason comprehensible, but struggles with other forms of blackout hamper its efforts.

Blackout structured life and literature during the war in at least three other ways. It was a literal phenomenon that harkened the arrival of bombings; it was an effect of propaganda, of which Joyce was a notorious wartime practitioner; and, finally, as Patrick Deer has shown, it was experienced as curtailed surveillance of geopolitical boundaries, a lack of *oversight* of a decentralized empire whose "fronts were everywhere," which made the English isle, and the British empire, vulnerable to enemy forces.[50] The trial report mentions the first sense of blackout only once and registers the after-effects of the other two through narrative strategies that (dis)avow England's limited sight and foresight during the war. These strategies react to the failure to oversee the empire's many fronts, but especially those within the English nation, whose porous boundaries, its airwaves, make it vulnerable to the invisible migrant William Joyce.

The opening pages of *The Meaning of Treason* relate that England confronts blackout in the form of Joyce's voice. According to the court, Joyce commits a crime against the British state, but according to West, he commits a crime against the English nation as a filial and cultural formation. Joyce's crime is a scandal to Englishness itself, "for throughout history treason has always been the crime most abhorred by the English, as parricide has been . . . by the French."[51] Joyce "sinned that sin which is the dark travesty of legitimate hatred because it is felt for kindred, just as incest is the dark travesty of legitimate love" (3). Likened to a violation not of just any law but the law on which law and culture is founded and exogamy secured, Joyce's crime threatens a regression to nature and lawlessness that undoes "England-as-family," a formulation West expressed in her letters.[52] Joyce incestuously penetrates the English body politic; his voice "climbed into the ears of frightened people" (28). The first sentence names the desire that drives the report, to *see* what has never been seen before and could not be "foreseen."

> Everybody in London wanted to see William Joyce when he was brought into trial as a radio traitor, for he was something new in the history of the world. Never before have people known the voice of one they had never seen as well as if he had been a husband or brother or close friend; and if they had foreseen such a miracle they would not have imagined that the familiar unknown would speak to them only to prophesy their death and ruin.
>
> (3)

The disembodied voice questions limits between the known and unknown, proximate and strange. A "dark travesty" (3) who evades surveillance and makes England the object of surveillance, Joyce is literally part of the family—a "familiar unknown" (3)—but also a *rupture*. Radio technology compounds blackout by compromising borders that would secure national community and makes Joyce into "something new in the history of the world," a "miracle," a "hideous novelty" (3).[53]

To confront these threats, "The Revolutionary" tries to establish a stable legal foundation by which to judge Joyce that would simultaneously differentiate the English state from (post)revolutionary, fascist, and anticolonial formations. In its elaboration of English law generally and the treason trials specifically, however, the report illuminates what Shoshana Felman calls the juridical unconscious. Felman argues that "despite its conscious frames and rational foundations, the law has quite conspicuously and remarkably its own structural (professional) unconscious."[54] Trials translate trauma into "legal-conscious terminology" to reduce its disruptive force, but trauma can recapture trials, revealing the law's unconscious. "The Revolutionary" discloses the problematic of the juridical unconscious as the ineluctable return of blackout. Law must contend not only with the unforeseeable and violent Joyce but must also wrestle with its own partial vision, even its own violence—a fact the text continually suppresses after regularly bringing it to light.

Joyce's exposure of the state's instability leads West to safeguard the *nation* from the masquerading "Irish revolutionary" by staging England as an impermeable cultural formation. The ethnographic strategies she uses to bolster England and Englishness illustrate the importance of examining how events often disaggregated in literary study—World War II and imperial decline—are in fact imbricated.[55] During the era of imperial retrenchment, West's contemporaries, such as Woolf, Eliot, and Forster, repurposed ethnographic discourses to restore national integrity in response to the "the over and under-determined nature of Englishness"[56] while rejecting the ideologies of race and ethnicity that characterized Nazi Germany. The over- and undetermined nature of Englishness to which West's report reacts, however, is as much the result of wartime treason by a subject who confused the distinction between Nazis and British citizens as it is imperial retrenchment. Consequently, although West employs ethnographic discourses to consolidate Englishness, she does not repurpose them to avoid ethnic absolutism but to insist on absolutes. She responds to the People's War by writing against the legal category of the traitor as intimate enemy, a man of and against the people. The report's ethnographic eye materializes the ephemeral and spectral by making Joyce's body visible and portraying his crime as a violent rupture orchestrated by a failed Englishman only English law can cure. But although the report strives over and again to fortify and protect both state and nation from blackout and violence, the juridical unconscious relentlessly returns and thwarts its efforts.

Law, Vision, and Violence

In a highly influential essay, the legal scholar Robert Cover writes, "Neither legal interpretation nor the violence it occasions may be properly understood apart from one another."[57] Cover explains that legal decisions on violence are authorized by and practice violence. "A judge articulates her understanding of a text, and as a result, somebody loses his freedom, his property, his children, even his life. Interpretations in law also constitute justifications for violence which has already occurred or which is about to occur."[58] Christopher Menke expands Cover's argument but also qualifies it, arguing that "every attempt at defining the relationship between law and violence must start with two tensely related, if not blatantly contradictory," premises:

> On the one hand there are the *discourses of the legitimation* of law, according to which legal verdicts are justified verdicts and thus, no matter how harsh they may be for those sentenced, they are not violent. For violence—in the relevant sense of the term—is not the same as restriction or even violation. Violence is a restraint or violation imposed by somebody on somebody against their will. But if the legal verdict is justified, it is valid also for the person sentenced, and insofar as it is not against her will, it is not violence. On the other hand, there are the *discourses of the critique* of law: legal verdicts are enforced by exerting or threatening violence. There is no law—and this holds also for post-sovereign law that has given up on the cruel celebrations of punishment and torture—that does without violence. Even the justification of the legal verdict does not change this: neither the legitimation by (just) purposes nor by (conventional or fair) procedures can free law from its violence.[59]

West's report runs together discourses of legitimation and critique of law. By highlighting law's belatedness and limited vision, "The Revolutionary" discloses that violence underpins the British state and empire as well as revolutionary regimes, entities she assiduously seeks to differentiate.

The report argues that partial sight accompanies and even enables the emergence and conservation of social and political formations, from the British state to African tribes to nomadic groups across Asia. As a foundational act of ordering and constituting the socius, law is both universal and universally lacking a fully rationalized foundation. No society can comprehend and envision the conditions of its emergence.

> The law is a force which has never yet been finally analyzed. To make laws is a human instinct that arises as soon as food and shelter have been ensured, among all peoples, everywhere. There have been yellow people who have flashed on horseback across continents, apparently too mobile to form customs, apparently preoccupied with slaughter and destruction; there have been black people who have squatted on their thin haunches unchangeably through the centuries, their customs drooling to superstition round them. These have been thought by men of other kinds to be without law, but it was an error. Both societies had reached a general agreement as to how to order their lives, and ordained penalties against its violation. But neither they nor any other society could define exactly what they were doing when they were making that agreement and ordaining those penalties.
>
> (62)

West employs Eurocentric axiomatics of race to contest Eurocentric axiomatics of race that claim that non-European societies lack law, while comparing the English nation-state with those formations. She then inverts the gesture that typically attends such imperialist formulations: Rather than cast these societies as enlightened because they found community through legislation as Europe does, she subjects Europe to darkness. European law mirrors other laws not because they are grounded in reason or natural justice—how English common law has always defined itself—but because all law is blind and lacks a firm foundation. No "society could define exactly what they were doing when they were making that agreement and ordaining those penalties."

Using metaphors that assert affinities between the seemingly disparate domains of law and art in "The Revolutionary" (affinities her other reports also assert),[60] West relates that the limited vision that accompanies the law that institutes the socius also accompanies the laws that conserve it, and she suggests that Joyce's case lays bare the imperative built into all law. The relationship between art and law "The Revolutionary" proposes complicates paradigms in critical legal and literature and law studies, which often treat art as the repressed of law that returns to interrupt it from the outside. Dismissing the intricate legal arguments about the nature of allegiance as "filigree work" (27), describing the trials as "an Irish drama" (6), "tragedy" (73), "cinema or concert" (29), and "three performances of the same piano concerto by the same conductor and the same soloist but by three separate orchestras" (43–44), West argues that legal and artistic interpretation alike endlessly confront an "inevitable time-lag" (63):

> The law, like art, is always vainly racing to catch up with experience. Life is always unpredictable. At every turn of history it presents the citizen with new obligations, and renders dangerous the exercise of his liberty in some sphere by suddenly rendering that exercise an affront to the liberty of others. It is the task of judges and legislators to alter the law that it may cope with these capers of time . . . they run as fast as the hands of the clock, reaching out to the present with one hand, that they may knot it to the past which they carry in their other hand. There are always lapses in time when the present and the past are not joined, and it is these which Englishmen such as wished Joyce to live loved to exploit.
>
> (63–64)

Art and law labor to make historical time continuous while remaining always provisional. Structured by limited vision and belatedness, racing "vainly" against the march of time, both demand persistent self-alteration. Art, including literature, thus does not expose law's bad conscience from the outside, therefore; rather, as Mark Sanders explains in his study of law and literature, "the self-othering that can be termed 'literary' (allegory, irony, for instance) does take place *within* the operations of the law, . . . is not separate from it."[61] Joyce's case seems exceptional but is actually exemplary. Both unique and general, it demands that law forge a passage across the interval between past and present by repeating while "altering" precedent.

This elucidation of the limited vision and internal irony of law creates an irreducible commonality between things West wants to keep separate: the English state and revolutionary and fascist regimes. For it is the limited sight and foresight of the French and Russian revolutions that led to their ironic interruptions. "The scaffolds of Paris took, in the end, all those that set them up; and of the actual engineers of the Russian Revolution, all but a handful were hoist by their own petard" (114). Joyce's trials threaten that English distribution of justice might come to resemble Nazi violence: "England was anxious to see Joyce suffer the just penalties of the law, but it was very anxious, too, that no penalty should be inflicted that was not just." To this end "people were asking themselves whether the trial was perfectly fair and whether we were being careful to be loyal to our tradition of impartial justice and to escape the Nazi contamination of our troubled times" (48). The report has shown, however, that it is not only these "troubled times" that raise the possibility of "contamination" of just by unjust dispensations of power. The potential for this contamination is ever present given the abyssal, blind, and repetitious structure of law at the root of all social and political formations. By disclosing this, "The Revolutionary" raises a question West would rather not: how does one distinguish between "the force of law of a legitimate power and the supposedly originary violence that must have established this authority and that could not itself have been authorized by any anterior legitimacy, so that, in this initial moment, it is neither legal nor illegal—or, as others would quickly say, neither just nor unjust"?[62]

West's descriptions of the origins of the state and law's potential for contamination resonates with Jacques Derrida's reading of the "contamination"[63] of state and revolutionary violence in his analysis of Walter Benjamin's *Critique of Violence* (*Kritik der Gewalt*). Derrida explores how violence not only attends revolutions but founds and preserves the polis and law, or *droit*. Pressing on the double meaning of the German term *Gewalt*—both "violence" and "sanctioned authority"—Derrida theorizes that the force or "violence" that founds a state and law erupts in an interval between past and future. States analeptically interpret this force of law as legitimate, but it is neither legitimate nor illegitimate in essence because this positional act generates the conditions for determining (il)legitimacy. Revolution projects a new order, proleptically legitimating its own destructive force, but because the order it seeks to institute does not yet exist, this force, too, is neither essentially legitimate nor illegitimate. Therefore, "the foundation of all states occurs in a situation that we can thus call revolutionary."[64] Yet the state fears revolutionary situations that threaten it through "founding violence, that is, violence able to justify, to legitimate (*begrunden*, to found, p. 283), or to transform the relations of law (*Rechtsverhaltness*), and so to present itself as having a right to law" ["*un droit au droit*"].[65] The foundations of authority are hence "mystical" and prohibit all nonviolent or neutral interpretation and justification. Benjamin wants to maintain a distinction between founding violence and conserving violence, violence that "ensures the permanence and enforceability of law," but this distinction cannot hold, Derrida argues. On the one hand, every positional act of ordering encodes within it the call to conserve. Its origin is divided, fissured by the promise of repetition and conservation. On the other hand, the force that conserves and enforces law always refounds it, because "the decision of a judge . . . must not only follow a rule of law or a general law, but must also assume it, approve it, confirm its value, by a reinstating act of interpretation, as if ultimately nothing previously existed of the law, as if the judge himself invented the law in every case."[66] Derrida concludes that a "différantielle contamination"[67] relates conserving and instituting violence.

Had West pursued the implications of her analysis of law, she might have glimpsed in the foundation and conservation of the English state the force she condemns, which is embodied in the French, the Russian, and what she calls the "Nazi Revolution" (114). Her description of the act instituting the social order implies that no interpretive metalanguage can rigorously justify either revolutionary violence or state authority because no society "could define exactly what they were doing when they were making that agreement and ordaining those penalties" (62) that constitute it and its law. She also rejects the distinction between founding violence and the laws that conserve the state, to which Benjamin imputes permanence, by proposing that historical change demands that law suspend, repeat, and alter itself. Because belatedness and necessary lack of foresight must underlie founding as well as conserving violence, states, like revolutions, cannot rigorously legitimate their orders through retrospective and projective justifications. According to her own analysis, therefore, England is not fundamentally different from postrevolutionary states such as France, whose "increases of liberty, equality, and fraternity [were] no greater than were won by other nations untouched by revolution" (114).

The Joyce case is disturbing because it continually illuminates uncanny resemblances. For example, in revealing the shifting ground and limited vision of English law, the case of this "familiar unknown" defamiliarizes the familiar, raising to the surface the revolutionary tendencies of a people "untouched by revolution." West derides the "vast number of English people" who cheer men like Joyce and Horatio Bottomley for exploiting the legal time lag, condemning their "winking admiration for the rogues" who "travel through life with a criminal purpose" yet maintain legal innocence (64). Versions of what Benjamin calls the "great criminal,"[68] they expose how the legal system falters. The mass pleasure at their "rogue" acts derives from these acts' exposure of law's belatedness and blindness. Both men "exploit

[an] unforeseen situation" and in doing so "opened to all of them [the English people] the prospect that one day they might find some such opportunity of gain easier than honest and unpunishable" (64).

West employs tenets of natural law to cover over the instabilities Joyce's case elucidates and to distinguish English law from revolutionary force. Countering her insight that the founding and conserving of the state is never entirely rational and that all law is subject to an "inevitable time-lag," West writes, "Pagan and Christian alike realized that the law should be at once the recognition of an eternal truth and the solution by a community of one of its temporal problems, for both conceived that the divine will was mirrored in nature, which man could study by the use of his reason" (62–63). English law has its source in "eternal truth," reason, and divine will, which are also "written into nature" and secular life in the form of "service of humanity, the rights of the state, the sovereignty of intelligence or moral sense" (63). Revolution assaults the order that supposedly endures even among those states not necessarily erected upon the pillars of reason, truth, and natural justice that support England. The revolutionary "wants to overthrow the existing order which exists and which may be the only order capable of existing. But he risks the annihilation of all order only because he believes he can evade that disaster and can substitute for an existing order another which he believes to be superior" (113). Repeating the root "exist" to the point of absurdity desperately (and paradoxically) endeavors to bestow duration and permanence upon the state, which the report has already argued relies instead upon instantaneity for its origin and persistent interruption and repetition for its conservation.

The other ways the report denies the abyssal foundation of English authority it exposes indicate that West responds to blackout and war's threats not only to the endurance but also the legitimacy of Britain's rule over a large swath of the world. West delegitimizes colonies' increasingly strident and powerful claims to self-rule by identifying anticolonial agitation with revolution rather than autonomy or nation building and by defining post-revolutionary states—and, by extension, future post-colonial states—as the product of unconscious, compulsive repetitions of violence. She maintains that English law repeatedly but consciously alters itself and, in doing so, foments historical change, whereas states "touched by" revolution lack rational necessity and testify to a death drive in European history:

> Perhaps the revolutionary is not really treating order as an end in itself but is using it as the means to an end. Perhaps he is really preoccupied with the establishment of a balance of forces within the sphere of his being: that balance which alone can restore nothingness to a world so obstinately created, so irretrievably stuffed with things. . . . In revolution there is a vast explosion of the creative powers, and nothing is created; nothing is even altered. So the appetite for death that is in us all is immensely gratified.
>
> (113)

Revolution in France and Russia initiates the blind, compulsive reenactment of the political violence/legitimate authority of a previous order, for "when the dust settled, France was ruled by a self-crowned emperor who wielded power more absolute than any French king had ever been given by the priests that crowned him," and Russia "slowly reconstituted the Tsardom it destroyed, identical in spirit, and reinforced in matter" (113–114). Revolutions not only repeat the orders they overthrow, but each other. Among the French, Russian, and "Nazi revolutions" the main difference is "the expenditure of blood" (114). Fearing "violence able to justify, legitimate . . . or to present itself as having a right to law,"[69] West suggests that anticolonial insurgency is the most recent manifestation of this death drive. Although she grants "the severance of England and Ireland as an historical necessity" and concedes that the counterinsurgency was of such violence that "even those who thought that England should not have relinquished Ireland were ashamed at this reminder of the impudicity of the conqueror's sword"(17), she portrays Irish anticolonialism as criminal, not entirely conscious, or even sane, thus without right to law: "the furtive slouching of a peasantry distracted with poverty and revolutionary fever" (16).

As the oscillating and contradictory depictions of English law and authority convey, however, the report is divided on the subject of imperial legitimacy. A writer ambivalent toward her own Irish ancestry,[70] West delivers her strongest and most disruptive claims about the violence inhabiting English authority when she diagnoses the root cause of Joyce's treason: British imperialism. West translates Joyce's trauma into the narrative of the alienated colonized intellectual. Like so many other historical cases, decolonization of the Irish state does not amount to decolonization of the heart and mind. Colonization persists as a wound well after Ireland gains home rule and Joyce commits his crimes against Britain. Raised as a loyalist by his father while Ireland was under British rule, both men, father and son, turned against "their own kind and worked with the alien oppressor" and were "passionately sincere" (16) in this. As a teenager Joyce fought with the counterinsurgency Black and Tans, professing not mere loyalty to but even love for England, and "it was this love, slanting across time, which made him a Fascist" (18). England betrayed Joyce by granting Ireland independence, and "this meant an actual, material betrayal. The family had to leave Ireland. . . . William Joyce found himself exiled from his real motherland, Ireland, which his blood must have loved, and confined in England, for love of which he had betrayed Ireland, and which showed no gratitude for that sacrifice" (18–19). As in the cases of the Russian and French revolutionaries, so too in the case of the Nazi revolutionary Joyce does the law fail to alter itself while repeating the violence of the (colonial) past; "inexorably the law that to him hath it shall be given would have come into operation again" (112). This law determines his "completely unnecessary death" at the hands of the British state, which results from the desire to identify with the colonizer, "his own and his father's lifelong determination to lie about their nationality" (28), to claim British citizenship. But it also results from the love of Ireland programmed into his blood, which makes Joyce hate the colonizer. West elucidates that the divided self created by colonialism causes his treason when she considers Joyce's reaction to the traitor John Amery, another propagandist during the war who was an English citizen by birth:

> When Amery was tried for high treason there were eight counts against him in the indictment. In Joyce's indictment against Amery there were four. First, Amery was an Englishman, and the conflict between England and Ireland had never quite resolved itself in Joyce's mind. He adored the English, he had fought for them as a boy, or had at least performed some services which he thought of as fighting for them, and he genuinely believed that as a Fascist he was laboring to confer benefits on England. All the same it was to England that he had come as a boy and had been sniggered at as a queer little bog-trotter with a brogue, it was in England that he had been denied the power and position which he felt to be his right by virtue of his intellect; and ancient hatreds, however much they be adulterated, often return under stress to their first purity. When William Joyce cursed the raiders who were bombing Berlin, he cursed them as an Irishman cursing the English.
>
> (139)

The return of the repressed "ancient hatreds" ultimately leads to the event that launches the trial report, the penetration of the English people. Like a boomerang, the force that returns to generate World War II trauma, therefore, is British imperialism, the source of crimes by the revolutionary—"the sublime example of this extreme type" (115).

By inserting Joyce's case into a narrative of imperial history, West depicts treason's assaults on English national integrity as the manifestation of Britain's death drive, imperialism's boomerang effect. Joyce's crime was not a rupture, this argument states, but prepared for by the long history of British control over social, political, and economic forces. In making this argument, West mobilizes narrative critically, illustrating the importance of story making not for clinical healing of individual trauma but for a postcolonial politics of historical memory. Trauma studies has long focused on how traumatic events resist discourse, and narrative in particular, while debating the politics of representing the unrepresentable. While some, perhaps most famously Theodor Adorno, argue that certain aesthetic modes cannot do justice to the traumatic event in its alterity because they give meaning to what evades meaning, make it consumable, and too neatly clear up the past,[71] others have emphasized the importance of narrativizing what denies sequential logic and sequencing and thus of breaking protocols of veridicality.[72] West breaks documentary protocol when she fabulates a narrative of trauma induced by imperialism—Joyce never testified that he suffered the wounds of the colonized intellectual and that this is what drove him to deliver Nazi propaganda during the war. This constructed psychobiography offers a counternarrative of British history that never appears in the court. Though it is not strictly "correct" or historically verifiable, it puts the state on trial.

But once the juridical unconscious returns in the form of West's statement that British imperialism developed the revolutionary whose voice makes it impossible to envision nation and empire as integrated wholes, it is buried again. Not only does West abandon the narrative of colonial trauma she invents; she also revives another narrative in order to refuse Joyce entry into it. Unable to secure the state from the boomerang effects of imperialism and the blindness of English law, both of which facilitate Joyce's crimes, she attempts to secure the nation by employing a narrative whose aim is to produce the citizen-subject while projecting the nation as the "highest and most natural form of human sociality"—that of *Bildung*.

Failed Bildung: *Mimicry, Physiognomy, and Resistance*

Whereas *The Return of the Soldier* challenged the continuity of the narrative of loss in World War I to reveal the imperial ideology of traumatic rupture, *The Meaning of Treason* institutes a narrative defined by continuity and harnessed by imperial ideology to stage as rupture the colonial subject's treason during World War II. The revolutionary's story is that of failed *Bildung*. As Joseph Slaughter explains, the *Bildung* narrative is both antirevolutionary and reformist, and, by formally emphasizing the values of continuity and development, has been used to justify colonialism as civilizing mission.[73] The narrative through which man is turned into "man," *Bildung*'s "historical social work was to patriate the once-politically marginal bourgeois subject as national citizen." In the eighteenth and nineteenth centuries, "the *Bildungsroman*'s progress narrative represents a German cultural nationalist counternarrative to the violent eruptions of the modern French nation-state,"[74] and to achieve its ends, the narrative uses a grammar of "amplification and expansion rather than . . . substitution."[75] This form is reactivated in cultural practices and throughout literary history and often in response to disturbances of the stability of the nation-state. "The Revolutionary" deploys the *Bildung* narrative to show how Joyce resists it, but in doing so, it disrupts its own formal continuity, its staging of amplification and expansion. The report shifts from fleshing out a story behind Joyce's acts to foreclosing it. This shift transforms Joyce into a scarred mimic who in turn scars the report's coherence.

Whenever "The Revolutionary" probes the origins of Joyce's treason, it modulates from specificity to abstraction and transposes from what Roman Jakobson calls the associative, metonymic pole of language—a move, however minor, toward narrative expansion—to the redundancy of the metaphoric pole of substitution. Metaphor and metonymy designate expressive modes here; tendency toward positional similarity and replacement or tautology defines the first, and semantic contiguity, expansion, and combination, the second.[76] West continually replaces referents, concepts, and events that plot treason within a historical trajectory with metaphors that substitute the tautology of mystery for narrative causality. She claims, for instance, that the trial centers on the "fantastic and ironical story of a family who, for obscure reasons springing from one convulsion of history, engaged in disingenuous conduct which, long after, brought their dearest member a peculiarly nonsensical doom in another convulsion of history" (8). "Convulsions of history" obscures the reenactment of colonial trauma in Ireland in England during World War II. Citing "obscure reasons" for the Joyces' behavior masks what West narrativized as a typical effect of colonial subject formation. A "peculiarly non-sensical doom" pretends the British state did not shape Joyce's life and death, first through colonization and then through the death penalty. And a "fantastic and ironical story" disguises that many other Irish concealed their nationality and fought on the English side, some for monetary reward, but "many were people who honestly loved law and order and preferred the smart uniforms and the soldierly bearing of the English garrisons and the Royal Irish Constabulary" (16). This tautology of mystery manifests again when West asks why this American by birth masqueraded as British and regrets that "in the third trial, as in the first and the second, that question was never answered" (43), insisting "this mysterious imposture, and this alone, brought Joyce to the gallows" (43). Legal narratives fail to explain anything: "The arguments of his counsel could not disguise the ineluctable process" (43).

"The Revolutionary" asserts that treason is the effect of inexplicable physical abnormalities and idiosyncrasies—that Joyce's body *is* metaphor, resistance to narrative. West transfers onto Joyce the traumatic effects of limited vision that Joyce inflicts on England and English law, when fragmented prose "explains" treason through tautology and redundant metaphors: "there was at some point a partial blackness, as if a perforated ear drum or a detached retina, and the consequence was barbarity. This was apparent even when the unscarred side of his face revealed his humor and acuteness, to a degree that was remarkable" (41). The first sentence not only refuses to narrativize treason as effect with historical cause but, by expelling the grammatical subject as passive recipient of the wounds, it even refuses to complete the narrative of treason as physical trauma. The passage confuses the physical and historicopolitical, and Joyce's body becomes at once unreadable and immediately readable. Rather than a metonym that points elsewhere, to a colonial past, Joyce's "wound" refers back to itself as absolute resistance, legible as illegibility. The abstract phrase "partial blackness" denotes a psychic condition that invites narrative expansion, which a simile appears to provide through concrete referents. Instead of explaining the abstract, however, these concrete, physical afflictions entirely supplant it. Mystery substitutes for explanation, redundancy for contiguity. Consequently, the scar on Joyce's face does not operate as a sign of the political effect, "barbarity," but is conflated with it. Physical ruptures, a "perforated ear drum, a detached retina," transform from figural analogies into literal causes of treason. Making treason the effect of chance bodily rupture tightens the tautological circle that articulates revolutionary violence as blackout, blindness, the fall from culture into nature. In attacking England, Joyce attacks "the complex social organization of Western civilization" (115).

By treating his body as that of a scarred mimic, the report forestalls Joyce's insertion into the *Bildung* narrative and thereby recodes England from a territorial state vulnerable to boomerang effects of imperialism incarnated in the intimate enemy it hosts into a cultural formation secured from the colonial outsider within. Although Joyce was an American citizen, he testifies that "we were generally treated as British subjects . . . we were always treated as British during the period of my stay in England whether we were or not" (11). The state issued him a passport, enabling him to travel to Germany and broadcast propaganda, but also, by providing him an extensive education, first in the sciences and then the humanities, it allowed him to become, in theory, a member of the English nation, a "brother." By insisting that he was incapable of being remade by this English education, West consolidates a legacy of philosophical nationalism summarized in the Fichtean concept of the separation and subordination of the machine state to the living, organic nation, whose development relies on education as acculturation.[77] By casting Joyce as a desiring but aberrant subject of the *Bildung* narrative of development, whose end is the civilized, or civicized, individual,[78] West corrects for the laws that enable Joyce to pass as English and turns England into a national culture secured from a revolutionary death drive. As Pheng Cheah writes when glossing Fichte's nationalism, "when the nation's physical borders have been penetrated, it must preserve its invisible spiritual borders to avoid total destruction. The alien power may have overcome political borders, but as long as the cultural borders remain, the seeds of resistance are preserved."[79] To preserve resistance, West devises a discursive strategy in which the colonized becomes "the effect of a flawed colonial mimesis, in which to be Anglicized is *emphatically* not to be English."[80]

Here, as throughout literary and cultural histories of colonial representation, the civilizing education of a colonial subject does not create an English person but a farcical double, a buffoon. "Passionately he longed to enjoy certain things which are the fruits of a highly developed civilization" (41), but Joyce's extensive education fails to surmount his shortcomings. "It had not mattered . . . how he cancelled the disadvantages of pygmyhood by courage and learning. . . . There was something there which would have been a bar between him and advancement, whatever he made of himself" (41). This mysterious "bar," the "illiterate quality never dispelled by his University education" (181), emerges throughout the text. Joyce shifts from *almost* part of the English family, "*as if* he had been a husband or a brother" (3, my emphasis), to radically other. This radical alterity is figured, for example, through West's invocation of the shibboleth, evidence of a physical resistance to acculturation, as well as buffoonery. The shibboleth leads to his arrest in Germany, for "he among men spoke with the blended voices of Tamerlane and Punchinello, and . . . whatever he said he also said 'I am William Joyce'" (178). Soldiers jeer him, "crying out, 'This is Jairmany calling.' This must have been the first intimation to him that he was considered by the British public as a comic character" (178), hence his farcical title Lord Haw Haw. By mocking his voice, however, West contradicts her claims that it allows him to pass as English and that it was dangerous and tempting rather than comical.[81]

Staging Joyce as mimic disrupts the report by generating not only contradictions, tautologies, and redundancies but also a residual "scientific" system whose premises conflict with ideals espoused and practiced in West's other writings. The act of subjecting the colonized to a civilizing mission that refuses them Englishness is often menaced, Homi Bhabha writes, by the colonized's "displacing gaze" on the level of form. This displacing gaze inspires "pseudo-scientific theories . . . spurious authorities, and classifications" that constitute a "desperate effort to 'normalize' *formally* the disturbance of a discourse of splitting that violates the rational, enlightened claims of its enunciatory modality."[82] If the mission of the *Bildung* narrative is to repair the divide between citizen and subject, West revives a pseudoscience to prove that this divide cannot be repaired in Joyce's case, that he could never be (English) citizen, only (colonial) subject. His stunted development, "infancy"(115) and "adolescence" (82), is realized through a rehashed Victorian criminal anthropology and its taxonomy of social types, which charts Joyce's transition from mimicry, "a difference that is almost nothing but not quite—to *menace*—a difference that is almost total but not quite."[83]

High modernists employ ethnology to produce more ethical cross-cultural encounters, and late modernists employ it to imagine Englishness on shared cultural values rather than race.[84] Yet West does neither. In an effort to restore national integrity by denying colonials culture, her deployment of ethnology in fact menaces her own modernist theories and practices. West departs from the principles of character and subject formation that appear in her most extended work of literary criticism, *The Strange Necessity*, published in 1928. Like Woolf in "Modern Fiction," West criticizes the Edwardians Galsworthy, Bennett, and Wells for focusing, in Woolf's words, on the "body" more than the "spirit." West contends that Wells reduces the variegations of characters' thoughtworlds by "flat statement" of innate traits. In *Lord Raingo*, he "gives no explanation of the girl's cruel desertion of her old lover for death except an innate melancholic taint, acted upon by the appearance in the casualty list of a former lover."[85] Suggesting that these traits are not legible on the body, she also implies that a character cannot be reduced to a social type based on physical appearance. "Never once," West chides, "does he invent the phrase, the speech, the incident that would be the right hieroglyphic to stamp on our minds forever the conviction that this creature, though young and beautiful and passionate enough to make an aging man feel that his age was an adjustable defect like something a little wrong with the eyesight, had nevertheless looked on the waters of life and seen them dark."[86] Attention to the outwardly visible, the physical, elides the complexities of Lord Raingo's mental theater, too. Although "the physical circumstances of his death are magnificently described," physical appearance cannot on its own tell us what occurs within; "the obvious poignancy of his mental situation, the despair which must have crept over the old man . . . is simply not stated."[87] Compare these articulations of (literary) character that emphasize the discrepancy between exterior features and interior world to what serves as her theory of (historical) character in the trial report.

> Men who are perfect specimens of a type feel pleasure in their representative perfection, even though the type itself is not happy. . . . A work of art gives satisfaction to the artist and the spectator because it analyzes an experience

> and synthesizes its findings into a new form that makes people eager for fresh experience. It is natural enough that something of the same sort of satisfaction should be enjoyed by a human being whose character lies limned before the eye with the particularity of an anatomical drawing, so that it can be comprehended as never before, and judged.
>
> (187–188)

The model of character representation, "an anatomical drawing," describes the representational system that makes Irish subjects objects of comprehension and judgment in this work. "The Revolutionary" details Joyce's stalled development not merely "with the particularity of anatomical drawings" but actually *through* a form of anatomical drawing: physiognomy.

West draws from the imaginary of physiognomy—an ethnology that, more than others, obtains energy from visual analysis—to racialize Irish subjects and make English culture and civility unavailable to them. Physiognomy taxonomizes social types based on the premise that physical features mirror innate traits, make visible the invisible. Deployed during the nineteenth century to identify criminal types, it also classified Irish and English into separate and unequal races.[88] Among these Victorian ethnologists who helped transform popular understandings of race was John Beddoe, a founding member of the Ethnological Society and president of the Anthropological Institute. Through his "Index of Nigrescence," Beddoe used "science" to contrast the lighter-skinned upper classes and darker lower and working classes of the British Isles, positing an "Africanoid" Celt, a "Celtic Caliban." Physiognomy was later discredited, and this image recedes by the 1920s, but it reemerged in English popular media such as *Punch* at moments of Irish anticolonial revolt. The Celtic Caliban does not appear in its exactitude, but its lineaments are visible in descriptions of Joyce and other Irish "revolutionaries," or British fascists.

> Men of violent and unhappy appearance, with a look of animal shyness and ferocity, and, in some cases, a measure of animal beauty, they were for the most part darker in complexion than one would expect in subscribers to the Aryan theory. One especially, looked like a true gipsy. Most of them had an Irish cast of feature, and some bore Irish names. It must be remembered that these men were not followers of Sir Oswald Mosely, who picked a more varied and more cheerfully brutal type. Joyce had seceded from Mosely's movement some years

> before the war and started his own. This was his private army, part of his individual hell.
>
> (8)

Shifting between desire for ("animal beauty") and fear of ("animal shyness and ferocity") the other, this passage expresses the ethnological vision of the Irish as closer to ape than human and more negroid than Caucasian. More important than whether it presents the Irish precisely as Beddoe describes, however, is that it enacts a residual epistemic that ossifies the Irish into an immediately legible "type" based on "cast of feature" and denies what West articulates in *The Strange Necessity*: the gap between outward appearance and inner worlds. To be guided by this epistemic is to refuse the possibility of development on the grounds of perceived physicality. Indeed, "the net effect of Victorian ethnology . . . was to undermine the environmentalist view that Englishman and Irishmen were fundamentally alike and equally educable."

That this physiognomic discourse is a response to blackout and constitutes an effort to the defend the English nation from colonial masquerade during war and imperial decline seems clear when one compares "The Revolutionary" with West's other reports on trials where issues of race are at the center, but not Englishness or Irishness. Consider, for example, the report on the 1947 trial in which white taxi drivers stood accused of lynching the African American Willie Earl in Greenville, South Carolina. Although West refers to the defendants as a "type," it is a professional type (a more specific marker than class). West does not racialize or nationalize their character and asserts that environmental factors played a part in their crime.[89] She condemns the racist attitudes of white attorneys.[90] Significantly, however, when she attacks the argument that racial struggles do not exist outside the United States by citing European and British cases, she refers to Germany and South Africa. She only mentions England in order to analogize intra-U.S. relations, and she does so, ironically, by emphasizing England's difference from Ireland. By proposing that the gap between the northern and southern United States "was a breach as divides England and Ireland,"[91] West insinuates a racial character to this latter by analogizing it to the U.S. North and South. In the Nuremberg trial reports, West does not racialize German fascists by treating them as animals, as she does the Irish fascists in "The Revolutionary."

She depicts them as humans, a status they of course denied their victims based on their alleged racial compositions.

In both the Nuremburg reports and "The Revolutionary," criticism of anti-Semitism might occasionally function as a foil for colonial racism informing depictions of the Irish. In the former, West recalls an encounter with a German woman—critical of the Nazis—who mistakes the British chief prosecutor for a Jew because she "has seen him" and because his name is "David."[92] West and her companions correct her, noting that Scots can physically resemble Jews and that David is a common name in Britain. "Oh, you English are so simple; it is because you are aristocrats. A man who called his son David might tell you that he was English, or Scottish, or Welsh, because he would know that you would believe him," the woman replies. "But we Germans understand a little better about such things, and he would not dare to pretend to us that he was not a Jew."[93] West's choice to present this reply without comment proves the woman's point. The English would not make judgments about race based on sight and name; only the Germans would. Highlighting Joyce's anti-Jewishness in "The Revolutionary" serves a similar self-exonerating purpose. West recalls a broadcast "of the familiar and ill-advised type" she implies is authored by Joyce: "'Next time you travel by train or bus and one of your companions is obviously a Jew, I want you to observe his actions. You can hardly mistake their dominant characteristics—their coarse, greasy hair, their greasy foreheads, their negroid lips—but their actions betray their race more than their appearance'" (131). Joyce's deployment of the physiognomic in his Nazi propaganda distracts from West's deployment of it throughout the report.

The discourse meant to establish Joyce's mimicry repeatedly menaces the report's coherence, however. These textual disturbances challenge the validity of the epistemological system on which the denial of Joyce's access to acculturation rests. Commenting again on his "resistance" to the narrative of development, West muses,

> it also appeared that Joyce's body had the same resistance to culture as his mind. He was a graduate with honours of London University, but there was a quality about all his sayings and doings which suggested illiteracy; he was good rider, he swam and dived to Polytechnic Standard, he had tried hard as a featherweight boxer, he fenced, but his body looked as if he had been a poor child without exercise.
>
> (48)

This passage struggles, and fails, to create a seamless parallel between the body and soul of the desiring subject flung back from English acculturation. The semicolon after illiteracy suggests that West will prove how his mind and body, "saying and doings," resist cultivation, but she proves the opposite by cataloguing how he cultivates himself as an effective athlete. The fastening of these examples of athleticism to the final clause, therefore, is also a breach in logic as well as a departure from expectations. Because she inadvertently illustrates his successful acculturation, physical literacy in English sport, she undermines her aim while simultaneously attacking physiognomy's premises: Outward appearance does not reflect inner world. The look of Joyce's body does not testify to his resistance to culture but, on the contrary, testifies to the discrepancy between physical appearance and reality. Such logical ruptures undermine the representational system on which the report's protection of English national integrity relies.

Yet faced again with the specter of violence inhabiting English law—and this time legal violence in its most naked form, the death penalty—West finally does allow Joyce to succeed in the narrative of development, if only for a moment. Crafting a narrative of rehabilitation, West has the trials tame Joyce's Irish "animal ferocity" and make him into a man. The cost of orchestrating this rehabilitation narrative is that Joyce becomes an English citizen rather than a colonial mimic. The gain is that the apotheosis of English state violence can be converted into the climactic victory of legal reform, or *Bildung*.

The Rehabilitation of William Joyce

West's presentation of the trials creates a narrative arc, a story with a plot, protagonist, conflict, and resolution, elucidating further affinities among artistic and legal practices. West does not simply impose literary conventions onto law, though, for law relies on narrative. As Kieran Dolin remarks, discussing Robert Cover's contributions to the study of law and literature, trials are "contests over narrative, not just at a surface level of evidence presented and contradicted, but at a deeper level of established versus alternative social visions."[94] The Joyce trials rehearse the contest between a social vision of English law as the triumph of a civilizing mission and an alternative vision of English law as a form of retributive violence. Extracting from the piecemeal and interrupted trials a connected story, the report, like law, marshals "formulas . . . to impose form and rule on stories,"[95] finessing the violence of both Joyce and the English state.[96]

The narrative of law's rehabilitation of a "demonic" Irish soul is a story of the trials' illumination of darkness and its restoration of physical and spiritual fulsomeness. The legal process makes Joyce's trauma visible as physical affliction rather than historical phenomenon, for "whoever followed William Joyce from the Old Bailey to the Law Courts found themselves thinking of him no longer as base and shabby, but as damaged and deformed" (41), and then ministers to the wound. "Time had acted on him during the trials . . . strongly. . . . At the Old Bailey he had seemed meanly and repulsively ugly. At the Law Courts, where he appeared before the Court of Appeal he was not so . . . the alteration in effect was in part due to a considerable improvement in his health" (40). The law cares for and transforms not only biological life but mental and spiritual life. It acculturates the revolutionary: "Here at the house of Lords he had endured a further change. . . . He still followed the legal argument with a bright eye. But the long contemplation of death had given him a dignity and refinement that he had lacked before" (42). Though Joyce's crime originates—mysteriously—in a moment of "disaster, when a demon entered" into him and he said "yes" instead of "no" (185), after the first trials, "he changed to the man we saw at his later trials, who seemed no longer to trouble himself about his demon's unfortunate reply, but to ponder on an answer he must shortly make to another question" (185). Stimulating in Joyce a "process of enlightenment" (43), the trials theatricalize English law's rationalism and continuity, embodied, for example, in the Lord Chancellor, "the symbol of the continuing rule of law" (51).

The rehabilitation narrative also relieves anxieties about the growing legitimacy of anti-imperial movements around the world. Fearing that the courtroom might erupt in violence by imperial subjects, West turns it into a forum in which British civil and civic structures are honored and desired. Among the trials' spectators were many "Negroes and Hindus," and "nothing seemed more unhappily clear than that these must be discontented members of the British empire's subject races, sympathetically attending the trial of a fellow-rebel" (33). By "eavesdropping" (33), however, West gathers with relief that no sympathy for Joyce exists among them. The trial's draw is not that it offers an occasion for alliance against the imperial power but that it offers instead an appreciation for its institutions. These Africans and Indians "belonged to that large class of person, to be found in all races, which delights in the technicalities of Western Law for their own sake, and would exchange a native dance or the Taj Mahal any day for a good tort" (34). And rather than serving as a rallying point for a worldwide anticolonial insurgency, Joyce fragments and divides it. The trials are a theater for colonial masochism and sadism, for "subjected races" to dramatize the enjoyment of their own and others' oppression: "they were interested in Joyce only as a golfer might be in a ball that has taken up an unusual position in the rough" (34). Shattering any "fellowship" among the "rebels," this remark pits colonial subjects against each other as one becomes the plaything the other strikes for sport while the colonizing power referees.

By rehabilitating Joyce's body and soul, however, the courts destroy the "bar" that prevents the civilizing and civicizing narrative from accomplishing its work, turning Joyce into an English person. To resolve this intolerable situation, West ensures that Joyce's transcending of that bar coincides with his death, which allows her to recode the death penalty as nonviolent, just, and legitimate simultaneously. West disputes the popular and professional sentiment that prevailed at the time, now widely accepted, that the Joyce trials were a miscarriage of justice and the death sentence an excessive use of force. Among laity and legal professionals alike, the trials were accused of marshalling state power as a form of vengeance. In his report for the Notable British Trials Series, the law reporter J. W. Hall criticized the prosecution's methods and argued that death was not a punishment commensurate with Joyce's crime. Alan Dershowitz also writes that the trial "succumbed to the passions of the day" and asserts that it "shows the British legal system in far from its best light."[97] West rejects such positions, censuring the "vehemence" of Hall's preface to the trial and contesting his insinuation that the law was operating in "haste and venom." She also disputes the position voiced not only by Hall but many legal professionals that the sentence was unjust and motivated by passion and emotion. Recall Menke's observation about discourses of the legitimation of law: "violence—in the relevant sense of the term—is not the same as restriction or even violation. Violence is a restraint or violation imposed by somebody on somebody against their will. But if the legal verdict is justified, it is valid also for the person sentenced, and insofar as it is not against her will, it is not violence."[98] West transforms state killing into nonviolence while articulating the execution as the climax of the *Bildung* narrative, the transformation of subject into citizen.

The sentence marks the victory of reform over revolution because it reflects Joyce's own desires and is proof of English law's natural justice, which is accessible to the "finite mind" through the moral sense. "In the infinite mind there is reconciled justice and injustice. The moral sense of a man is clairvoyant: if he chooses to love rather than to hate he shall be right both in time and eternity" (184), West maintains. By defining treason as a strike against "his own flesh," the report asserts that the trials have transformed Joyce—soul *and body*—into an English citizen, made him part of the body politic. The trials create a moral sense in him, which enables him to see that an Englishman turned against himself is unjust: "William Joyce, knowing that he had struck against his own flesh, had written it down that every time he had broadcast he had committed treason. He took a short cut to the same conclusion reached by the lawyers who knew so much about him that he did not" (184). At the moment the report converts Joyce and reveals a death drive at work in what is rhetorically constituted as an English citizen, it simultaneously articulates English law's death dealing as nonviolent. Capital punishment is not violent or unjust if Joyce's moral sense makes him agree with the court, makes it "valid" for him. Moreover, it cannot be violent if he accepts it without coercion, even if not for the right reasons. Dying would mean "an end to mediocrity" and resolve the "war between the forces in himself which desired to live and those which desired to die" (196). Execution "was the beginning of such distinction as would ideally be conferred on him in a society which believed that a man's soul was immortal and precious to the higher powers. Thus made serene (for all who saw him would concede his serenity), he waited his time" (196–197).

The need to assure readers of his serenity by parenthetically invoking other witnesses signals West's struggle to prove that the death sentence is both nonviolent and just, however. The social vision of the trial as rehabilitation rather than retribution is punctured when blackout again reveals the sentence as a form of legal violence discontinuous with reason and natural justice. Efforts to distinguish the English distribution of justice from violence and limited sight strain under the language of abyss, repression, and mystery. West criticizes the logic of calculation or measurement of guilt and punishment in Hall's claim that Joyce should not have been hanged because the sentence was not commensurate with the crime. In doing so, however, she admits that one can never verify if the (death) penalty is just: "The mind seeking justice envies such measurement, but must content itself with erecting on the edge of an abyss signboards crudely warning of disaster" (61). "Abyss" refers both to the beyond of legal knowledge as well as Joyce's crime, which exceeds law's ability to justly measure and which execution can only "crudely signpost." West also defends the punishment by maintaining that a double repression shapes criticism of the death penalty, but at the same time, she admits without admitting that law is violent and that law's relation to justice remains inaccessible to vision and reason.

> Like the journalists, like the public, [the lawyers] felt distaste for any attempt of the law to lay hands on Joyce which proceeded from the emotions and did not consult the intellect until it was asked to furnish an explanation for its own vehemence. They felt it more sharply and personally, because it was their *mystery* which being *profaned*: and as they, as all of us, are forced sometimes to doubt whether *the mystery of the law* is not itself a *profanity*, since we live in the New Testament world, and justice has been blown upon by mercy. This reluctance has forgotten its cause, since we are no longer Christian. Hence, it remains as an arbitrary awkwardness about inflicting punishment, which is the more passionate by reason of its puzzled ignorance of its origin, and which reverts to the fiery prejudices of the Old Testament without regaining the caution which is characteristically patriarchal. One cannot live to be a patriarch without being careful as well as violent.
>
> (58, my emphasis)

This passage relates, without ever directly stating, that law was originally violent and that Joyce's sentence is a repetition of violence. Diversionary tactics displace legal violence onto critics of legal violence. The report manages the abyss it generates between law and justice and violence and mercy through chiasma in order to achieve rhetorically a symmetry between logically asymmetrical terms. Lawyers criticize the passion of Old Testament violence in the name of mercy; mercy is justified by recourse to the passion of Old Testament violence. Law profanes the mystery of justice; the mystery of justice profanes law. These neat reversals distract from the discrepancies dividing each term in the set: the difference between the instrumental violence of "passionate" and "fiery" criticism of the death sentence and the performative violence of a death sentence—words that actually kill—and the difference between the profanation of law's mystery and the profanation of justice's mystery *by* law. The second chiasmus obscures that the term "profane" bears two separate meanings in usages here. The lawyers fear that the law ("their mystery") will be *desecrated* by violence, but "the mystery of the law" is a profanity because it is a *curse*. West implies it is a curse because its relation to justice is inaccessible to knowledge and cannot be grounded in reason. The justice of legal punishments, repetitions of divine violence, cannot be verified, remain a "cautious" mystery. Justice is incalculable.

The trials' civilizing and civicizing of Joyce enables West to have it both ways. The legal institutions accomplish the reform that colonial trauma prevented (and caused), but at the moment this is accomplished, Joyce has to die. He is only a good English citizen insofar as he is a dead one. Through narrative and ethnography, the report tries to establish a legally and culturally stable English community and identity in the wake of communism and fascism's rise on the one hand and the imminent end of empire on the other. Attesting to individual and collective historicopolitical crises with colonialism at their root, *The Meaning of Treason* marks a continuity and a break with *The Return of the Soldier*. The novel contends that the narrative of an insular, idyllic English nation and Pax Britannica relies upon the interment of structural violence, the uneven social and economic formations within England and abroad generated by colonialism and capitalism. The trial report attempts to establish an insular, organic nation by suppressing colonial and state violence through a vindication of English law. In the next chapter, we shift focus to Jamaican authors who confront colonial trauma from within the colony rather than metropole. In their own ways, they, too, endeavor to vindicate English law.

THREE

Vindicating the Law

H. G. de Lisser, V. S. Reid, and the Morant Bay Rebellion

The previous chapters examined how efforts to bear witness to historical traumas, events in which the nation and empire are threatened by revolt and state violence, shaped the formal strategies of British modernist writing. To glean a fuller sense of how twentieth-century Anglophone literature responds to crises in collective memory when the status of a nation and empire, and the laws that secure them, are particularly unstable, I shift focus now from works written from the metropole to writings produced from within the colonies during colonial and postcolonial periods. In the second half of this book, we will see how the staging of testimony to such crises by authors who were *not* part of the great waves of postwar and postcolonial migration manifests the difficulties of managing the often conflicting demands of national and transnational forces. These works also invite us to reassess divisions between categories that govern contemporary literary study. In this chapter, those categories are national literature and world literature, in the next chapter, modernism and postcolonial literature.

This chapter functions as a transition between the preceding chapters, centered on works written before and immediately after the Second World War, and the final chapter, which will address a text composed in the recent aftermath of postcolonial independence in Kenya. Here, I consider three writings that span the period of anticolonial nationalism in Jamaica: H. G. de Lisser's 1919 historical romance *Revenge: A Tale of Old Jamaica*; V. S. Reid's 1949 epic novel *New Day*; and, finally, Reid's 1960 young-adult novella *Sixty-Five*, published two years before Jamaican independence. Each one presents a version of the Morant Bay rebellion, an event in imperial modernity still largely overlooked in literary criticism.[1]

By analyzing these particular works by these particular authors, I respond to Paul Gilroy's request to investigate this key historical moment in black Atlantic history, but I do so with aims and a method distinct from the approaches initiated by Gilroy. In his groundbreaking and field-generating book, Gilroy argued that "the specificity of the modern political and cultural formation I want to call the black Atlantic can be defined, on one level, through this desire to transcend both the structures of the nation-state and the constraints of ethnicity and national particularity. These desires are relevant to understanding political organizing and cultural criticism."[2] Twenty years later, these desires drive contemporary literary and cultural criticism. Explorations of how fiction imaginatively transcends the structures of the nation-state and the constraints of national and ethnic particularities organize postcolonial and world literature studies. This work continues to be important, but because migration and diaspora narratives have taken center stage in critical scholarship, and because mobility and rootlessness have become master tropes for contemporary ontology, literature that does not thematize these conditions increasingly eludes our attention. Alison Donnell makes this point in her study of twentieth-century Caribbean literature.[3] I consider two Caribbean writers who were important in their own times but whose works have fallen out of print, not having triumphed in what Pascale Casanova calls the "world republic of letters."[4] These novels are set within the space of the colony. I focus on them because, like Donnell, I want to "draw attention back to the local and the dweller as figures worthy of intellectual attention."[5] I also want to question critical models that oppose world literature to national literature.

I acknowledge that "the kinds of transcultural and intercultural work that Gilroy locates as somehow exceeding and even deconstructing the nation can actually be located within the Caribbean nation, city, or even village."[6] My goal, however, is not only, or even mainly, to show how de Lisser's text and Reid's responses to it enact a transcendence of national particularities through intercultural and transcultural work. It is, instead, to demonstrate how the Morant Bay rebellion and the legal controversy that followed it determined for both the antinationalist de Lisser *and* the cultural nationalist Reid that the intercultural and transcultural history of Jamaica could not form the basis of an independent nation-state nor provide sufficient conditions by which to work through colonial trauma. For de Lisser to argue against national independence and for Reid to argue for it, each must vindicate English law.

The details of the rebellion are by now well established.[7] On October 16, 1865, several hundred Jamaican men and women, mostly black, entered the town of Morant Bay. They were led by Paul Bogle, a native Baptist minister. Bogle made clear that he was not rebelling against the Queen, to whom he even appealed to help Jamaicans resist the inequities and injustices produced by the colonial government. The rebels targeted the Morant Bay courthouse and the vestry. They were protesting unfair wages, decisions regarding land distribution, and among their grievances also listed the expulsion from the vestry of another of their leaders, the minister and politician George William Gordon. At Morant Bay, eighteen officials and members of the militia were killed and thirty-one were wounded, and seven members of the crowd were killed. The rebellion then spread throughout the parish of St. Thomas in the East. Thomas Holt explains that "at its peak, the rebellion involved an estimated fifteen hundred to two thousand people, men and women, African and creole, estate workers and settlers" and that "the rebels' grievances included proletarian issues such as higher wages and better working conditions on the estates along with peasant issues such as lower taxes and more land."[8] In response to the uprising, Governor Edward Eyre declared martial law, and Jamaica was placed under Crown colony rule until 1944. The counterinsurgency was of a length and violence such that it gave rise to an enormous controversy in England, which set conservative Victorians such as Thomas Carlyle and Charles Dickens against liberals organized as the Jamaica Committee, led by Charles Buxton and John Stuart Mill.

On July 7, 1866, the Jamaica Committee made a case for trying Governor Eyre before a court of law in England. The committee framed its argument in terms of vindication. The word "vindicate" appears numerous times in this brief appeal. To be vindicated, however, are not those Jamaicans who suffered multiple and varied acts of torture and killing under Eyre's authority, or even the colored leader Gordon, who was hanged following a court-martial that the English government's extensive inquiry into events in Jamaica through the Jamaica Royal Commission (JRC) had determined broke with procedures under martial law.[9] To be vindicated is law itself. "When there is reason to believe that a British subject has been illegally put to death, or otherwise illegally punished by a person in authority," the Jamaica Committee claims, "it is the duty of the Government to inquire into the case; and if it appears that the offence has been committed, to vindicate the law by bringing the offender to public justice."[10] Although "the Government declined to take any steps for the vindication of the law," the committee persists, but not because it is motivated "by vindictive feelings." Rather, its goal, "besides upholding the obligation of justice and humanity towards all races beneath the Queen's sway, is to vindicate, by an appeal to judicial authority, the great legal and constitutional principles which have been violated in the late proceedings, and deserted by the Government."[11] Upholding justice and the humanity of colonial peoples is presented not quite as an afterthought, but certainly not as the central motivation of the committee. What has been deserted and abandoned by law are not those who suffer its violence but law itself. Law is outside of itself, because English law is discontinuous with violence, which has been inflicted in its name, according to Mill and the Jamaica Committee. Eyre was charged with murder but was never found guilty.[12]

Neither de Lisser nor Reid would comfortably identify with the philosophies of Mill or the Jamaica Committee, and they certainly would not identify with each other's positions on colonial rule. Yet both, I will argue, try to vindicate English law in their representations of the rebellion. They do so in ways distinct from Mill and from each other. *Revenge* attacks Mill's liberal principles and supports the ideals espoused by an acolyte of Carlyle, Mill's antagonist during the Governor Eyre controversy. *New Day*, which Reid composes as rebuttal to the racist portrayal of Jamaican history he ascribes to de Lisser's historical romance,[13] vindicates law through the performance of a dialectical history of liberation whose rhythm and pacing in fact reflects that of historical romance.[14] Despite their antithetical positions on colonial rule, both authors' works attempt to vindicate English law by separating it from violence. In both works, too, the formal production of witnessing generates unintended effects that create a friction with the strategies of vindication. This friction alerts us that structures of feeling underwriting the nation as an autonomous political formation either to be strived toward (in Reid's case) or prevented (in de Lisser's case) conflict with the demands of transcultural as well as global economic forces that would crosshatch and even constitute the nation.[15] In de Lisser and Reid's novels, the effort to vindicate law is the symptom of this conflict, which stymies the effort.

Catching the Myal Spirit: Revenge *and the Temporality of Necessity*

Herbert George de Lisser, a brown Jamaican of Portuguese Jewish and African ancestry, began his career as a writer for the *Jamaica Times* in 1898, became editor of the *Daily Gleaner* in 1904, a position he held until his death in 1944, and was also an editor of *Planter's Punch*. Mervyn Morris named him "the first competent Caribbean novelist in English."[16] Many of the twenty-five novels and novellas he composed beginning in 1913 were made available to Jamaicans in the pages of *Planter's Punch* and were also published in England. de Lisser's career and racial and class identifications shifted drastically between the 1890s and 1920s and thereafter. Transforming from a brown-indentified supporter of the middle classes to a strong supporter of the white business elite, de Lisser opposed struggles for economic and social justice by the working class, serving as secretary of the Jamaica Imperial Association. Leah Reade Rosenberg argues that these personal shifts reflected the changing place of Jamaica in the world system.[17] In her recent study of nationalism and the formation of Caribbean literature, Rosenberg asks, "Why, having achieved such influence in Jamaican literary production, has de Lisser been eclipsed from literary scholarship?"[18] Her answer is persuasive: his historical romances, which cover events spanning the Spanish Conquest of Jamaica in 1492 to the labor riots of 1938, do not meet the aesthetic or ideological standards of later twentieth- and twenty-first-century scholarship. "Insidiously and unremittingly antilabor and antiblack," these works, of which *Revenge* is one, are "derivative of European popular romances and opposed to the political empowerment of Jamaica's black majority . . . the antithesis of a liberated poetics."[19] Add to this that de Lisser's literary output precedes that of the great wave of migrant writers from the Caribbean in the 1950s—the reputedly authentic origin of Caribbean literature, as it has become canonized through postcolonial studies[20]—and it is no surprise de Lisser's fiction has been forgotten.

Revenge is worth revisiting, however, not only because it engages a legal dilemma that returns in different ways throughout the twentieth and twenty-first centuries, but because it is one of very few representations of the Morant Bay rebellion in fictional prose form. Moreover, it is written by a prolific author known as one of the "'pioneers' of 'authentic Jamaican literature'"[21] whose works were enormously popular in the first part of the twentieth century. *Revenge* thus helped shape how both English and Jamaicans understood an event that was the site of transnational legal and cultural contestations in imperial modernity. Reid underscores this point by delivering not one but two literary counterattacks to challenge de Lisser's portrayal of this historical event. The rebellion was a turning point in Jamaican history because it initiated a culture war, an "open war for civilization,"[22] a bid to control what constitutes culture, which involved white and educated brown elite policing (literally and figuratively) of Afro-Creole religions, rituals, and languages. The rebellion also caused a dilemma in British law: how to define the concept of necessity so as to judge whether the violence that occurred under emergency and martial law was legitimate. The rebellion and the controversy that followed elucidated that legal definitions of necessity rest upon specific cognitions of time. Through its staging of temporality, *Revenge* attempts to solve the legal problem of defining necessity; however, it also relies upon principles of witnessing shared by cultural systems that law is enlisted, both historically and in the text, to control.

Set in the weeks leading up to the rebellion, *Revenge* emphasizes from its first to its final pages that thwarting the insurgency, and thus avoiding the brutal counterinsurgency, demands a correct cognition of time. The novel's main characters include the mixed-race Rachael Bogle, the fictional daughter of Paul Bogle; Dick Carlton, a member of the white plantocracy whose sympathy with black estate workers and refusal to engage in cross-racial sexual dalliances sets him apart from that plantocracy; and Joyce Graham, Carlton's English cousin and fiancée recently arrived in Jamaica. The plot centers on the relationships among these three in the context of growing unrest in the colony. The novel is obsessed with marking time, and it chastises Carlton, its liberal protagonist, for failing to recognize threat in order to deter the rebellion—that is, for failing to see how various events in the present are urgent signs of future catastrophe. de Lisser contrasts the near-sightedness of Carlton with the far-aiming scopic drive of a time-obsessed Eyre: "Fifty miles away the Governor of the colony was pacing to and fro like a caged lion. . . . Now and again he would look out of the window of his house in the direction of St. Thomas, as if he would pierce through the darkness and see what was happening there," for "one question obsessed his mind. Would the relief he had sent arrive in time? Could it arrive in time?"[23] The novel concludes that liberalist perspectives, or ways of looking, did not try hard enough to penetrate darkness of the present to read the future, and consequently they are responsible for the violence of both the insurgency and counterinsurgency. The passage describing the launching of the counterinsurgency summarizes this point neatly in its formal conduct. By filling sentence after sentence with minute temporal indices, de Lisser performatively scolds his protagonist while instructing readers about the importance of attending to the infinitesimal intervals that compose time:

> Over the sea came the deep roar of a cannon. Starting up Dick saw a steamer in the distance heading toward the shore . . . *in an instant* the beach was alive with people all gazing intently at the ship *which momently* grew nearer. . . . Then the vessel was seen to come to a stop in the open roadstead *and one, two, three* boats dropped from her side into the water. . . . The crowd around Dick was thinning *rapidly*; Bogle's garrison were *fleeing as fast* as their limbs would go. Straight towards the beach *flew* the boats, each crowded with black soldiers and with marines. . . . The first boat grounded, the men leaped ashore, and a young lieutenant came *hurrying up* to where the wounded men were grouped. . . . "*Not quite too late*, I hope?" were his first words; then, glancing at the haggard, blood-stained men before him he added sadly, "it looks so."
>
> (85, my emphasis)

The desire to control events through a minute-by-minute narrative of them can be read as a response to the crisis of the temporality of necessity that was at the center of the arguments of the defenders and accusers of Governor Eyre in their respective efforts to vindicate law.

At stake in defining necessity on the basis of a particular cognition of time was nothing less than protecting English law from charges of illegitimate violence. The conduct of colonial administration, coupled with the proliferation of instances of anticolonial resistance throughout the nineteenth and into the twentieth centuries, make this protection increasingly difficult to achieve. As we saw in our exploration of West's reports on the treason trials, violence is often viewed as external rather than internal to law, or as an exceptional aspect of it. In the aftermath of the Morant Bay rebellion, Victorian jurists and intellectuals debated whether violence was internal or external to law, whether it was justified under martial law and emergency. The legal scholar Nasser Hussain explains that "emergency is an elastic category, stretching over political disturbances such as riots, the situation of sovereign war, and even constitutional crises within the sphere of the state," and he argues that much political theory and constitutional jurisprudence mistakenly treat it as an external "third term" between sovereignty and law. History shows, however, that emergency is not external or exceptional, but forms "a constitutive relation between modern law and sovereignty."[24] Moreover, it is colonialism that challenges the claims of English jurists that emergency was an exceptional rather than constitutive facet of English law. "The nineteenth-century empire, covering India, and later Africa and the Middle East, consisted of people who were not slaves but, because they seemed utterly incapable of participating in their rule, were not quite free subjects either," Hussain writes. "This empire required a new conception of sovereignty, one that was neither despotic nor democratic. And for such a historically specific reason, it was in this empire that law in general, and the problematic of a rule of law and emergency in particular, assumed a greater ideological weight."[25] During the Governor Eyre controversy, the question of how to defend the violence that occurred under the emergency while portraying martial law as an exception or "third term" was answered inadequately. This is because justifications for Eyre's actions were based on a category impossible to define rigorously: "necessity," which, in legal terms, is a temporal condition. The rebellion and its suppression raised the question: what is the temporality of necessity?

It was the transference of martial law from the metropole to the colonies that made clear that the concept of necessity was an irresolvable epistemological and juridical problem or, rather, a problem that could be solved not with logic and constitutional principles of English common law but only through colonialist ideologies of uneven racial formation. This, Hussain asserts, was the lesson of the Governor Eyre controversy. The rebellion demonstrated that in the colonies "the legal definition of necessity would prove more varied and vexing" than in England.[26] To justify the use of martial law, there must be evidence of a pressing danger, an imminent threat to the security of the state. Based on the testimonies gathered by the JRC, Eyre had extended martial law well after that danger had expired. "What keeps the line between very similar acts of violence intact here is a correct cognition of necessity," but "the rhetorical structure of martial law begins to crumble the moment one asks for some exactness to the description of 'pressing danger,'" Hussain explains. This is because "the category 'necessity' is itself a temporal condition . . . it must be represented as an interruption in the otherwise smooth functioning of lawful politics. Only its minute by minute narrative, its always so closely anticipated ending, can make legitimate the exercise of violence."[27]

The arguments of Chief Justice Sir Alexander Cockburn and the jurist William Francis Finlason clashed when they confronted the question of necessity. Cockburn maintained that imminent threat collapsed immediately after the troops arrived in Jamaica. Under English common law, imminent violence was the only justification for martial law. Acts committed during the month-long emergency were illegal violence, therefore. Finlason disputes Cockburn's arguments by citing racial difference as the grounds for another definition of necessity that he asserts must be applied in the colonies. This concept of necessity pivoted on an alternative cognition of time: it replaced imminent threat with deterrence as its guiding principle. As justification for this, Finlason claimed, first, that English common law in the colonies pertained only to white descendents, not those of Africa, so the definition of necessity must be adjusted to suit the situation. Second, the situation during the Morant Bay rebellion was that Jamaica was poised to become another Haiti during the revolution—a genocidal scene. Necessity did not collapse with the arrival of the troops, Finlason maintained, because the blacks greatly outnumbered the whites, because blacks were of a different species from whites, and because, he alleged, they had been planning to kill the entire white population. This definition of necessity based in deterrence demands a dilated temporal view that travels backward to events in the past (in this case, to the Haitian revolution) and then forward to project what will happen in the future. To assess accurately what the correct course of action is one must look into the temporal and spatial distance, like de Lisser's Eyre, rather than with the nearsighted presentism of Cockburn and Dick Carlton. Violence committed by the counterinsurgents during the entire length of the emergency in Jamaica was legal, and English common law protected from charges of illegitimate violence under this definition of necessity.

Finlason's definition does not rest on stable ground or constitutional principles. It is propped on sociological categories of race and historical precedents. Hussain points out that Finlason's argument proceeds tautologically.

> Finlason's criticism of the chief justice's charge ends then with an explanation of dizzying circularity:
>
> "He utterly failed to realize the danger of the rebellion, and therefore he of course failed to recognize the necessity for deterrent measures, of which the necessity could only be recognized by realizing the danger, and without realizing which severities would easily appear to have been cruelties."
>
> Martial law appears here as a deeply cognitive problem. We can now recognize the anxiety over the slippage between the same act of violence as it can appear within the authority of the law and opposed to it, so that an excessive cruelty can easily be mistaken for a warranted severity.[28]

The tautological formulation fails to express the reality of the situation in Morant Bay. While the argument for deterrence dictated that Eyre had to look to past events in Haiti as evidence of what would occur in the future in Jamaica, doing so did not provide an accurate assessment of the situation Eyre faced. The Morant Bay rebellion was not an attempt at secession from the empire, nor was there any plan to eradicate the white population that needed to be deterred. The contested definition of necessity was also central to the debates between two intellectuals involved in the Governor Eyre controversy, Thomas Carlyle and John Stuart Mill.

Given de Lisser's extensive historical research, he was no doubt aware of the jurists' debates about imminent threat versus deterrence, but likely, too, is that these debates were also filtered for him through Mill, Carlyle, and Carlyle's disciple, James Anthony Froude, who was a strong influence on de Lisser's political thought and whom he references directly and indirectly in his works. Examining the Jamaica Committee and the Eyre Defense Committee's testimonies, along with Froude's discussion of the rebellion in his travel writing, enables us to see how *Revenge* reworks Mill's and Carlyle's arguments under the more recent influence of Froude and in response to contemporaneous cultural and legal practices in Jamaica.

To vindicate English law, Mill argues for imminent threat as the definition of necessity and claims that violence committed during the emergency was illegitimate.[29] In a speech delivered in the House of Commons on July 31, 1866, Mill asserts that "martial law is another word for the law of necessity, and that the justification of acts done under that law consist in their necessity. Well, then, we have the right to dispute the necessity."[30] He attempts to vindicate English law not only by charging Eyre for extending martial law past the point that imminent violence had ended but also by arguing that the treatment of Jamaicans was inhumane and that "feelings of humanity" cannot legitimately be suspended when ordinary law is suspended. Counterinsurgents

> are not justified in the use of excessive or cruel means, but are liable civilly or criminally for such excess. They are not justified in inflicting punishment after resistance is suppressed, and after the ordinary courts of justice can be reopened. The principle by which their responsibility is measured is well expressed in the case of Wright v. Fitzgerald. Mr. Wright was a French master, of Clonmel, who, after the suppression of the Irish rebellion in 1798, brought an action against Mr. Fitzgerald, the sheriff of Tipperary, for having cruelly flogged him without due inquiry. Martial law was in full force at that time, and an act of indemnity had been passed to excuse all breaches of the law committed in the suppression of the rebellion. In summing up, Justice Chamberlain, with whom Lord Yalverton agreed, said:—"The jury were not to imagine that the legislature, by enabling magistrates to justify under the indemnity bill, had released them from feelings of humanity, or permitted them wantonly to exercise power, even though it were to put down rebellion."[31]

If for Mill the colonial administration's suppression of the rebellion was inhumane, for Carlyle and Eyre that suppression served to protect a higher form of civilization from a lower form: the "white race" from the "black."

Carlyle argued for the definition of necessity as deterrence by claiming that black subjects act under the influence of superstition rather than according to reason. A crucial part of his defense of Eyre was that the governor safeguarded the boundaries between races by protecting white women from rape by black men, thereby preventing miscegenation. Catherine Hall analyzes Carlyle's defense and demonstrates that statements in Eyre's testimony before the JRC recall those of Carlyle's 1849 notorious essay "Occasional Discourse on the Nigger Question," published anonymously in *Fraser's* magazine. (J. A. Froude assumed editorship of *Fraser*'s for fourteen years, relinquishing it in 1874 at Carlyle's request.) Eyre testified "that the negroes form a lower state of civilization and being under the influence of superstitious feelings could not properly be dealt with in the same manner as might the peasantry of a European country." Their attachment "as a race" to superstition proves that deterrence rather than imminent threat must operate as the guiding principle of necessity outside of Europe: "As a race the negroes are most excitable and impulsive, and any seditious or rebellious action was sure to be taken up by and extend amongst the large majority with whom it came in contact."[32] Carlyle commended Eyre for his deployment of a correct variety of English masculinity in suppressing the rebels, whose sexuality posed as much of a threat as their superstitious natures. Hall explains that Carlyle's defense drew together antiliberal concepts of racialization and gendering while displaying fears of black masculinities and femininities. For Carlyle, "Eyre was not only the hero who had saved Englishmen from a gruesome death; he had also protected Englishwomen, and protecting 'the weaker sex' was, of course, a crucial aspect of independence and manliness."[33] Moreover, she writes, "Englishmen's fears of black male sexuality and the threat it posed to 'their' women were linked with fears about unleashing the powers of black women."[34] Fears about the mixing of races through sex are expressed throughout *Revenge*.

Before returning to the novel, let us consider a final reflection on the rebellion, one whose date is closest to *Revenge*'s publication: Froude's 1888 travelogue *The English in the West Indies; or, the Bow of Ulysses*. Although well received in England, this ethnography was pilloried by colonial writers for its polemical meditations on race, colonial rule, and chattel slavery.[35] Froude, who wrote biographies of Carlyle (which eventually gave rise to a Froude-Carlyle controversy), constructs a similar defense of Eyre and argues for deterrence as the basis of necessity, citing black colonial subjects' superstitious natures as justification. Declaring that black Jamaicans belong to "an inferior race," he claims that "they have shown no capacity to rise above the conditions of their ancestors except under European laws, European education, and European authority, to keep them from making war on one another," and also "their notions of right and wrong are scarcely even elementary; their education, such as it may be, is but skin deep, and the old African superstitions lie undisturbed at the bottom of their souls."[36]

Revenge suggests that de Lisser envisions Froude's work as a mediator between the immediate postrebellion controversy and his own historical situation of anticolonial activity. It indicates this most clearly by generating narrative energy through multiple employments of an image that occurs in the travelogue's pages. This image concretizes the juridical arguments for the redefinition of the concept of necessity in an astonishingly literal way—as the eradication of whiteness by blackness. Through this image, Froude makes a connection between the Morant Bay rebellion and his own time, a period of growing anticolonial consciousness, increasing desertion of whatever white land owners remain in the colony, and battles over the place of Afro-Creole culture in Jamaicans' resistance to Crown colony rule. These three conditions have only intensified by the time de Lisser writes *Revenge*. The temporal perspective of the image Froude draws underwrites the arguments for making deterrence rather than imminent threat the basis of necessity. Froude looks to the future by gazing into the distance of the past, envisioning the Morant Bay rebellion as a reiteration of the Haitian revolution, which is imprinted in his, Finlason's, and Eyre's minds as the attempted eradication of whites by black subjects. The removal of whites by blacks from colonial spaces is on the verge of materializing once again, he warns. This time it portends the loss of British economic power in the world. "The only good that came of [the Morant Bay rebellion] was the surrender of the constitution and the return to Crown government, and this our wonderful statesmen are beginning to undo,"[37] he laments, and he continues in an ominous tone that

> Lands once under high cultivation are lapsing into jungle. . . . Every year the census renews its warning . . . The white is relatively disappearing, the black is growing; that is the fact with which we have to deal. . . . The West India Islands, once the pride of our empire . . . are passing away out of our hands; the remnants of our own countrymen, weary of an unavailing struggle, are more and more eager to withdraw from the scene, because they find no sympathy and no encouragement from home, and are forbidden to accept help from America when help is offered them, while under our eyes their quondam slaves are mul-

> tiplying, thriving, occupying, growing strong, and every day more conscious of the changed order of things.[38]

The image of an encroaching blackness that eclipses whiteness structures de Lisser's entire novel. *Revenge* deploys it to make a case for deterrence as the basis of necessity during the rebellion.

The novel reacts to the unsettling of racial divisions and political hierarchies within Jamaica and to Jamaica's changing place in the global economy during the time of the rebellion as well as during the time of *Revenge*'s composition. By mounting a defense of Carlyle and Eyre through the use of Froude's imagery, *Revenge* responds to exigencies produced in the immediate aftermath of the rebellion. By framing this imagery within a scenography and iconography associated with Myal, an Afro-Caribbean religion it (mis)identifies as Obeah, the text responds to exigencies contemporaneous with its composition. In the first decades of the twentieth century, Jamaica instituted laws to control various creolized indigenous and diasporic cultural practices, especially Obeah. These laws operated in an effort to keep pace with an intensified anticolonial movement that drew upon such practices and beliefs. Though he invokes Afro-Creole practices and beliefs, de Lisser does not depict those that were actually used in Jamaica during the rebellion. Moreover, he confuses the rituals he depicts with practices in use in Haiti during the revolutionary period. Combining the imagery found in Froude's travelogue with such rituals to tell the story of the rebellion, the novel makes claims for understanding necessity on the basis of deterrence by warning readers about the dangers of mixing of races during both Eyre's time and de Lisser's time.

The novel rehearses the ideologies of racial separatism that it projects onto the insurgents in order to mark their difference from the English and the white plantocracy. Prohibition against miscegenation is the law of the rebel father, not the law of liberal Dick Carlton and Joyce Graham, who treat Rachael Bogle as a token friend of color. "Colour for colour" is both Bogle's war cry and the basis of his domestic rage. After Rachel disobeys Bogle's orders forbidding her to visit Carlton (who confronts her romantic overtures with polite but firm civility, advising her to obey her father), she and her dead mother become victims of that rage. "'You forget your colour? Don't you always hear me say 'colour for colour'?" an incredulous Bogle asks, then accuses, "you are common . . . an' you get your commonness from you' brown mother, for you don't get it from me. You sambo slut! it is a white man you want, eh?" (53). Rachel responds that she wants a white man because a white man is human while the maroon to whom her father wants to marry her in a bid to secure the rebellion's victory is not. But while *Revenge* attaches the prohibition of racial mixing to a genocidal insurgency led by a savage and superstitious misogynist, it just as stridently ratifies that prohibition in order to make an argument for deterrence as the basis of necessity. The mixing of races is articulated as contamination. Contamination occurs through acts of witnessing.

The episode freighted with the most evidence for implementing Finlason's theory of necessity in the colonies relates how Carlton's English fiancée witnesses the conception of the rebellion, presented as a Myal ritual the novel calls "obeah" (41). The text warns that Afro-Creole religious practices create the conditions for moral, political, and economic catastrophe: a nation where whiteness disappears. It issues this warning by showing how easily English womanhood can become compromised by atavistic forces once one leaves the metropole for the colony. In this episode's attack on liberals' charges against Eyre and the concept of necessity based in imminent threat, *Revenge* addresses English as well as Caribbean readers. The colonial settlers, most of whom sided with Eyre and against the Jamaica Committee, insisted that those safely ensconced in England could not know the terror of being outnumbered in the colony.

By tightly focalizing on the English woman and charting her descent into a heart of darkness where she watches a ritual with Bogle as its "high priest" (27), the text turns the Morant Bay rebellion into an iteration of the Haitian revolution. It does so while elaborating the sexual conquest of English white femininity by superstitious black masculinity, a trauma Eyre, according to Carlyle, was able to prevent. Joyce leaves the security of the big house and rides into the woods with a black servant guide. The second she leaves the grounds, she becomes vulnerable to the infectious Jamaican landscape: "A wave of excitement flowed through her; the weird, wild beauty of the night had thrown its spell upon her; she was in the throes of its fascination. . . . Then she came to a path which plunged into a wood on her left hand and seemed to lead into its innermost recesses" (38–39). She descends further into "semi-obscurity" until she hears a "cry that came stabbing through the gloom," which she recognizes as part of "a revival meeting. Her heart began to beat faster, her pulses quickened" (39). She is driven to descend still farther inward, proceeding onto a trail that only natives, perhaps settlers, but certainly not an English woman, should be able to manage, for "no horse could go that way, but a human being used to such places, could scramble up and down it with no great difficulty" (39). Comingling desire and fear are written onto Joyce's body as she approaches a place from which to witness the meeting. This comingling produces a characterological break. Joyce transforms from an embodiment of English civility to a voyeur attracted to what is presented as a perverse primal scene. She travels through a narrowing canal that opens onto a wider, hidden enclave from which she watches the conception of a monstrous birth. From her place high above the scene at Stony Gut, where, as her guide relates, "'you can see from . . . an them can't see you'" (39–40), she witnesses the insemination of the spirit of rebellion into the people that occurs through the movement of the black man's wand. Bogle, "standing erect within the circle," bears "a slender wand, and this he sometimes moved from side to side with a quick nervous jerk" (40), to which the members who circle him respond. They "followed the motion of the rod, rocking their bodies to and fro" and "thundered denunciations at times, shrieked agony, sobbed contrition, and surged upwards in frenzied supplications" (40). Joyce is not immune to the wand's power.

Afro-Jamaican masculinity's conquest of English femininity is represented as a trauma that portends a miscegenated future, a nation in which the white disappears under an encroaching black mass. Such is the image that justified for Finlason, Carlyle, and Froude a definition of necessity based in deterrence. According to the young guide who accompanies her, Joyce is protected from the "arousal" Bogle's rod inspires in him and others.

> Charles was trembling with excitement. His superstitious fears and beliefs were fully aroused; he dreaded lest the woman and the man below should smell him out and hurl some deadly curse at him. His mistress, he thought, was safe; she was buckra, white, and above the black man's evil. . . . From her presence, too, he drew a certain courage. . . . his young mistress could look calmly down upon a scene which even the principal actors regarded with secret awe.
>
> (41)

Charles's assumptions are false, however. Despite his confidence that her race acts as a shield against contamination, the English woman, too, is inseminated by the act of witnessing, and her body becomes part of the rebel body. Joyce's body's reactions to Bogle's moving wand evince her "arousal." The "fascination" and "shudders" that accompany her approach of the primal scene are followed by breathlessness after witnessing it: "gasped Joyce, 'I have stayed here long enough'" (41). She exits the narrow trail and emerges onto "the open road" (42), but the damage is done: she now resembles the rebels. The act of penetration leaves her cold blooded like the insurgents, with a " pallor" that would have "startled" her if she could see her reflection, "shivering" while "nervous tremors ran through her" (42). Joyce cannot bear witness to this contamination through insemination that will result in a monstrous birth—a mixed-race nation, where the white will continue to disappear as black "superstition" spreads. She tries and fails to tell Dick what has occurred: "'I went on to Stony Gut, and I saw—O, it is too dreadful!' She broke off sharply, fighting desperately the hysterical wave that surged through her" (42). Emphasizing that this event should not be passed on, the text orchestrates a thunderclap that prevents its transmission: "He knew that she was saying something, but heard no words" (42). de Lisser locates the rebels' racial and sexual conquest of white femininity at the root of the rebellion and diagnoses these as traumas that only Eyre's counterinsurgency and cognition of time can cure.

Revenge's author, like its farsighted Eyre, looks with a dilated perspective into the future and past to grasp the rebellion. de Lisser shapes it anachronistically by invoking the legal management of Obeah that occurs decades after the insurgency and attributes to Afro-Creole religion a role it did not play in Jamaica in 1865 but rather later, earlier, and elsewhere. Between 1907 and 1920, as part of the civilizing mission and culture wars in Jamaica, a series of new laws were passed that regulated Obeah and denied it the legal status of a religion. Defined as superstition, it was now also codified as fraud, which marked a shift from its legal designation as witchcraft during the pre-emancipation era.[39] Obeah had its own literature in the 1900s, and this had to be outlawed because it was accessible to the middle classes of all colors, could be read by them, and thus culturally, and potentially juridically, legitimized.[40] Diana Patton has shown that in Jamaica and throughout the Anglophone Caribbean "Obeah" was produced as a discursive formation through the interactions of transnational, colonial, and regional forces and had "locally differentiated meanings . . . that engage with, but are not determined by, the meanings produced by ruling groups both within and outside the region."[41] In historical and critical analyses, Myal and Obeah have been treated as alternately interchangeable and oppositional;[42] as noted, de Lisser refers to a Myal ritual as "obeah" (41). de Lisser's portrayal of Myal as Obeah is anachronistic because during the period of legal reforms in which de Lisser writes, Afro-Caribbean religions operated in a way that they did *not* during the Morant Bay rebellion, that is, as sites of social and legal contest over cultural and political autonomy.[43] Also, not until after the 1860s does Myal become connected with the rituals *Revenge* describes, possession trances, circles, and dances.[44] Calling Myal an "Africanization of Protestantism," Dale Bisnauth locates the aims of possession in individual spiritual growth,[45] but other scholars claim that these serve the aims of a community, and one often struggling against an oppressive enemy, white or black.[46] By naming Myal Obeah, de Lisser anachronistically identifies the former with a practice that was being legally regulated in the twentieth century on the basis of its imputed destruction of community, the fraudulent use of "superstition" for individual gains at the cost of others' losses.

Yet, paradoxically, it is precisely the communitarian character of an Afro-Caribbean religion that de Lisser wants to highlight in order to support his argument for deterrence as the basis of necessity. The articulation of the rebellion's conception through the ritual is anachronistic because it imposes a discourse of religion's connection to anticolonial revolt that postdates the insurgency as well as to one that predates it and that occurs outside of Jamaica. The Myal ritual serves in the narrative to connect Morant Bay to Haiti, where Voudou, another religion used to galvanize a community, played an important role in the mounting of the revolution. While it is true that the creolization of the Moravian Baptist religion in Jamaica involved the revivalism that Bisnauth claims is another name for Myalism[47] and that Native Baptist communities were key to the formation of black publics that resisted oppression, which culminated in the rebellion,[48] the insurgency was not a revolution and attempted secession from the empire, as was the case in Saint Domingue. Moreover, although Myal "was a significant spiritual resource for Afro-Jamaicans under stress," historically, it "did not stage a successful revolution like the Haitian revolt, and its political role in the struggle against slavery and colonialism in Jamaica is not comparable to that of Vodou."[49]

de Lisser conflates them, but in actuality Myal was often a countermeasure to Obeah, a way of getting to the truth and resetting the moral balance by reading the natural world. This required that one become infected. Nathaniel Murrell points out the feature with which Myal becomes most associated after the 1860s—"its spirit possession catalepsy," which "is still referred to as 'catching the Myal spirit.'"[50] Catching the Myal spirit enables one to read signs and mediate between known and unknown worlds. Through possession, "Afro-Jamaicans believed Myal brought them revelations of the invisible world: a state of mind that allowed the initiates to see Obeah works and to transmit messages from that other world to their community."[51] Murrell relates that "during the dance ritual, worshipers formed the famous circle to communicate with the divinity, who bestowed on the new shaman the powers to heal and to see unusual things in the sacred and profane worlds."[52]

By invoking Afro-Creole religion while looking through the lenses of Morant Bay's past and future, *Revenge* presents the rebellion as a genocidal secessionist movement. The chapter relating the Myal ritual, entitled "The Sign from Heaven," enacts the disappearance of whiteness under blackness, but it also illustrates that in order to be able to read this disappearance as sign one must become infected. The multiple situations of infection that occur in the chapter's central scene disclose that black femininity is as threatening as black masculinity, if not more so.[53] Here, again, Joyce becomes infected when she witnesses another act of witnessing: a black woman, a "crone" who is the "chief hierophant" (27), reads the night sky during the ritual over which Bogle presides. The Myal woman's testimony to what she witnesses seems illegible at first, for "Joyce heard the sounds that came from the woman; gibberish, it seemed, an incoherent meaningless sputtering from foaming lips" (41). Yet the "gibberish" becomes coherent speech. Through it, the novel relates that nature is a sign system that provides knowledge about future events once one is possessed by the spirit:

> still the stream of meaningless sounds poured out of the woman's foaming mouth, and still she whirled round the circle. Then the *peninsular-like cloud* which had been threatening the moon *detached itself from the parent mass* and drifted towards the now, dimmed, half-enshrouded orb. The woman stood stock-still and darted one arm toward it: "A sign!" she screamed, "de answer of de Spirit!". . . .
>
> . . . "the answer is coming!" thundered Paul Bogle. "We will know tonight whether black or white will win!"
>
> Steadily the cloud moved forward, and after it came creeping the dense black mass that now covered half the sky. At this moment the moon struggled

> out from beneath the veils of vapour that had dimmed it. Serenely it shone, as though conscious of its own triumph. A groan burst from Paul Bogle and was echoed by hundreds of the expectant crowd.
>
> But still they stared, and inch by inch the darkness drew towards the light. *Joyce, too, infected by the spirit of the people*, watched the scene with intensest interest. At last the cloud touched the edge of the moon, a moment after it had swept over most of it. Darker and darker grew the night, swiftly the light departed. Soon it was all gone. . . .
>
> Now there arose a wild cry of triumph, and high above it rang the voice of Paul Bogle—"A sign, the Spirit give us a sign!"
>
> (41, my emphasis)

In this mise-en-abyme of infection, the hierophant and Bogle catch the Myal spirit, which allows them to read the sky's prophecy that the Morant Bay rebellion will formally repeat the structure of insurgency in Haiti, a colony that attempted to "detach itself" from a "parent mass," or empire. Joyce, "infected by the spirit of the people," can read the sky as Bogle and the hierophant do and then warn Carlton of the necessity of deterring future events. And finally, the novel itself reveals how it is infected by a practice of witnessing it invokes in order to police while simultaneously obscuring this by generating a contradiction.

This scene expresses that nature is and is not readable as sign. This contradiction is the consequence of spatial and temporal telescoping and can be explained by approaching the scene from multiple perspectives. The problem de Lisser confronts in his effort to vindicate law is this: nature must be a sign system, as the insurgents' and Joyce's reading of the sky imply, because then, according to narrative logic, a counterinsurgency based on the necessity of deterrence can be justified. But nature cannot be a sign system because if it is, Myal's interpretive methods do not reflect atavistic superstition but rather constitute a powerful epistemology that allows us to understand politicoeconomic forces of modernity. From the perspective of Jamaica in late October 1865, Bogle's interpretation of movements of darkness and light in the sky is based on superstition because what he names a sign is not in fact a sign—it does not correctly designate who will be victor and who vanquished at Morant Bay. The novel indicates, however, that we must also look from the perspective of those who witnessed the Haitian revolution, and from this angle, it is a sign. It is the sign of *intent* of secession and genocide. In this way, the scene justifies Eyre's cognition of the temporality of necessity and asserts that those who define necessity as imminent threat do not know how to read nature as signs. After Carlton's fiancée manages to relate "all that she had heard and seen the night before" (42), Carlton's response illustrates that what is legible to Joyce, and to readers, is illegible through the framework that uses imminent threat as the basis for action. "We can only watch them" (42), Carlton says, because there is no evidence of pressing danger. Only by reading signs of intent by referencing the historical memory of Haiti was de Lisser's (and Carlyle's) Eyre able to prevent what Bogle interprets, that "black . . . will win." But there is another angle of vision in play here that contradicts these first two statements on the status of the sign. From Froude's perspective in 1888 and de Lisser's perspective in 1919, the sky does display a sign, and not merely of intent but of events that will actually occur in the future, decades after the rebellion takes place. This passage restates Froude's argument and even uses the rhetoric Froude uses to makes it. In Froude's formulation, changes in the natural world are anagogical to and reflect population shifts, which are also moral, political, and economic shifts: "lands once under high cultivation are lapsing into jungle. . . . The white is relatively disappearing, the black is growing."[54] The sign Joyce and the insurgents gaze upon is also a warning addressed to readers outside and inside Jamaica. Anticolonial nationalism in the twentieth century is confirming that "black" is triumphing over "white." Because the novel endorses the methods of witnessing and assumptions about the semiotic potential of nature it attributes to a superstitious insurgency to make this point, it reveals that it cannot vindicate law without breaking from its own value system.

The novel articulates that diasporic and indigenous cultural formations mobilize agitation for national economic and political independence in ways that threaten reason, order, and civilization. As a result, the text insists, law must be vindicated from charges of illegitimate violence when it suppresses agitation. The literary and formal strategies *Revenge* uses to make these claims, however, paradoxically endorse the epistemology and interpretive methods of the systems that it claims law must suppress. Like de Lisser's Bogle, de Lisser himself treats nature and landscape as the means by which to assess future events throughout *Revenge*. In doing so he obstructs the novel's attempts to reestablish a boundary that the process of witnessing the rebellion's conception dismantled: that between European civilization, which Joyce figures, and atavistic superstition, which the insurgents engaged in Afro-Creole ritual embody.

The novel's treatment of nature and landscape illustrate that techniques European literary forms use to interpret social and political conflict share with Afro-Creole religions premises about nature's semiotic potential. Although *Revenge* takes place entirely within Jamaica and therefore seems an example of national literature, the line between national and world literature blurs when we consider that efforts to manage crises of insurgency and counterinsurgency whose effects extend beyond a single nation and historical moment structure the novel. Through these efforts British literary aesthetics are creolized: The text's literary techniques become doubles of and legitimize the hermeneutics of Myal, an Afro-Jamaican cultural system that was employed, the text shows, to produce effects in Jamaica that transform the places of England and the United States in the world system. On the one hand, de Lisser must insist that Myal has no epistemological purchase, which is why he calls it Obeah. To argue otherwise would be to repeal its codification as fraud and treat it as a religion, a system with a truth value that inheres in its ability to mediate between transcendent and finite temporalities and worlds. On the other hand, de Lisser is composing a literary work, and the methods Myal uses to make meaning are not so different from those of the literary genres de Lisser's fiction references. The author represents Jamaican history, as one critic notes, through the "literary models available to him in colonial Jamaica at the end of the last century. These models were British—eighteenth-century Gothic, and the Victorian 'sensation' writing."[55] These models treat nature and landscape as semiotic systems. They often do so in order to tell stories in which femininity is made vulnerable by brutal masculinity and racial otherness. Because *Revenge* employs their aesthetic techniques to argue for the necessity of deterrence while simultaneously revealing that their interpretive principles overlap with those of Myal, he demonstrates how a supposedly atavistic process and a "modern" British literary tradition share techniques for making sense of social, economic, and political phenomena.

Among the many figurations of landscape and nature as signs of blackness encroaching on whiteness, two tropes are particularly important in the novel: hurricanes and fires. Hurricanes and fires are analogous to the night sky whose cloud formations Bogle and the Myal women interpret as signs.

Hurricanes and fires are signs of the future catastrophic storm and holocaust that is the Morant Bay rebellion; however, they are not legible as signs when viewed through the lens of necessity as imminent threat. The novel's formal conduct suggests that de Lisser assumes that readers are conversant with the conventions of Gothic fiction and Victorian sensation writing and therefore know to read landscape and natural events as signs of conflict, strife, or disaster. *Revenge* shows that Dick Carlton does not know how to read this way. The text's handling of fires and hurricanes serve as reading lessons for him and the novel's other liberal characters.

The text relies upon an understanding of nature and landscape as sign systems from the first page in order to make its argument for deterrence and to criticize, through the use of dramatic irony, those who do not know how to read their signs. Chapter 1 opens with a question of how to interpret what is disclosed as a sign: fires on the horizon outside the big house. Three possibilities are offered from three perspectives. The first interpretation is scientific; they are nature's evidence of the drought, a sign of "how severe it has been" (1). The second is that they are signs that the profane world is continuous with, and signs of, the sacred world. Dick Carlton claims the Jamaicans read the fires and the drought as a "sign of God's displeasure, and that they are called upon to purge the wickedness out of the land. Some of those fires are lighted as a warning to the unrepentant" (2). The third possibility is that the fires are not only "warnings" but "signals" sent between black Jamaicans to commit genocide, that "we [the white plantocracy] are the 'wickedness' to be purged out of the land" (2). Carlton's mother offers this last reading. By rejecting it while assuring his fiancée that "the danger is purely imaginary" (2), Carlton strengthens de Lisser's argument for a conceptualization of necessity based on deterrence. Carlton's nearsightedness makes him incapable of protecting white femininity. His mother and fiancée are captured by the rebels, and the only reason they are not raped and killed is that a planter who supports the argument for deterrence prevents this.[56] Linking Carlton's failure to read the signs in the novel's opening episode to his failure to protect white women in distress, *Revenge* uses gothic literary conventions while affirming Myal's premise that nature operates as signs of the supernatural world that also reflect human desires.

Like fire, the hurricane functions as a sign and signal that liberal colonial officials cannot recognize as such. At a dinner party on the eve of Joyce's return to England, the Custos describes hurricanes to the English woman, who has never seen one. He tells her that by October, hurricanes are generally "all over. There have been hurricanes in October though" (66), he admits. Joyce asks, "Hurricanes are almost as dangerous on land as at sea, aren't they?" (66). The Custos responds, "Rather! They are terrible. Hundreds of lives are sometimes lost in them; they are what we have most to fear in Jamaica. Take away our hurricanes and our droughts and we should go on our way rejoicing" (66). His response associates hurricanes with fires by mentioning the droughts, which the opening episode's scientific interpretation mistakenly identifies as the cause of the fires. The novel therefore asks us to read the Custos's words in the way he does not intend them to be read—through the hermeneutics of the Gothic tradition and Myal. Underscoring the novel's prescription to replace a realistic or scientific reading of nature with one that follows the protocols established by Gothic literature and Myal, a passage in another chapter relates that "When the West Indian hurricane is approaching the atmosphere gives warning. . . . So too, before the bursting of the storm of human rage and passion, the wild expression of hate and anger and madness, there are signs and warnings which the clear-sighted may plainly read," and finishes with a rebuke: "in the month of October, 1865, such signs were not lacking" (43). Neither Carlton nor the Custos are clear sighted enough to read these signs. Both also fail to understand that signals operate as signs of the rebellion. When a planter warns that the conch shell's signaling of a revival meeting "may herald a hurricane worse than any we have ever known in Jamaica," the Custos replies, "it may and it may not . . . I prefer to think that it means nothing more than some fellow summoning his friends" (67).

The final vindications of law occur at the novel's conclusion, where de Lisser reduces the month-long emergency to two weeks, thus falsifying the detail that was at the center of accusations against Eyre, and exonerates law from its most naked instrumentalization of violence: the hanging of a witness following a hasty drumhead court. Like West, who detaches capital punishment from violence in her trial report by making the colonial subject a willing participant in his own death at the hands of the state, de Lisser protects English law from violence by enabling the death penalty to do its work without the colonial subject's conscious resistance—indeed without her consciousness that it is even taking place. The character hanged is Rachael

Bogle, whom the spurned and vengeful maroon suitor has falsely accused of killing Dick Carlton. She is without an alibi and is starved to the point of madness because she has been hiding from the counterinsurgents searching for her. Consequently, though her testimony to the court accurately describes events that should prove her innocence, it is dismissed as "hysterical raving" (95). de Lisser uses the statements and actions of the British soldiers charged with hanging her to vindicate law. The soldiers' comments suggest that violence committed by the state during the counterinsurgency is exceptional—not typical in England—but also that colonial situations demand that law be applied in the colonies in ways that it is not in England: "It might be harsh to hang a woman, but women were hanged every year in the colony for murder" (95). de Lisser has Rachael faint from mental and physical exhaustion on the eve of her hanging so that he can both commend the soldiers for their empathy and protect law from charges of violence, punitive actions inflicted against the will of a subject. "She was alive, but unless they restored her to consciousness, she would know nothing more, feel nothing more, on this earth," the text assures readers, and the officer "was emphatic in his order that the woman should suffer no unnecessary torture" (96) by being brought to consciousness.

Critics have argued that by using the British literary models available to him, de Lisser's prose suffers; his "style recaptures and amplifies some of the sentimentality, repetition, indulgent explanations, and florid descriptions of British writers who are nowadays considered of less than first rank."[57] The overwrought descriptions of landscape and nature are evidence of this. But through this "bad" style, *Revenge* illuminates connections between secular European discourses and Afro-Caribbean religious discourses and asserts the epistemological force of both. This style conveys that practices that are legally deemed fraudulent actually produce truth. The novel formally makes an argument its author rejects. It does so because it is contoured by the imperatives of Jamaica's shifting place in the world system as much as by a historical trauma of its national past. *Revenge* enacts a return of the repressed. It addresses a rebellion that destabilized social, political, and economic structures so as to argue for legal procedures that would prevent such disturbances from happening again. Its formal conduct relates, however, that such disturbances have not only continued to occur but that their effects have been amplified and intensified by the time the novel is composed.

Revenge is a world text, but not because it has conquered the global literary market (which it hasn't) or because it critiques models of community based on exclusionary categories such as race and nation (which it doesn't), or, finally, because it is "locally inflected, and translocally mobile"[58] (the fact that, according to WorldCat, the only copy currently available in the world is located in the British library and not available for checkout, suggests in a very literal way that it's not). *Revenge* is a world text because its use of diasporic and creolized cultural and aesthetic practices to bear witness to a historical trauma of imperial modernity demonstrates that contemporaneous pressures of a global economic system structure and destructure it as a literary work. These pressures, that is, both enable the work to come into being and mark the limits of its coherence. de Lisser's text raises a question that Simon Gikandi puts to us in light of Catherine Hall's influential analysis of the postemancipation period in Jamaica, in which apparently oppositional missionary and planter discourses in fact collude in disavowing the agency of black freedmen and women.[59] Gikandi asks, "Where were the free villagers in themselves in this economy of debate? Could they as subalterns speak or were they simultaneously silenced in the discourse of the planters and the missionaries alike? Were the new black subjects masters of their own technologies of self in the postemancipation order or inherently overdetermined?"[60] *Revenge* suggests that planter and missionary alike failed to hear the freed villagers' voices—or rather, read their signs—to catastrophic effect. de Lisser, however, represents insurgents not as rational agents of change but as victims of what he would like to insist is an irrational system that confirms the Afro-Jamaicans' "unconsciousness": The novel dramatizes the origin of the insurgency as the loss of consciousness that occurs when its leader catches the Myal spirit. *Revenge* endeavors to silence subaltern discourse, but it returns as a displaced force that disrupts the coherence of the novel's argument for a particular legal codification of necessity.

de Lisser addresses the rebellion to bulwark dominant forces under attack at least since 1865; Vic Reid addresses the rebellion to support the working classes in struggles toward Jamaican independence. Like *Revenge*, *New Day* and *Sixty-Five* have also fallen out of print, entering neither the canons of World Literature nor the canons of postcolonial literary studies, where focus on works of migrancy and exile still dominate. This seems to confirm that Reid's are decidedly national works. Both take as their subject key moments of national history and take place within the nation, and *New Day*'s linguistic mode has even been referred to as "nation language": It is the first Anglophone Caribbean novel written entirely in a Creole vernacular.[61] But as in *Revenge*, the techniques *New Day* and *Sixty-Five* use to bear witness to the rebellion challenge critical models that distinguish national from world literature. Reid's works elaborate tensions between national and global forces and show how these tensions spark eruptions of anticolonial revolt throughout Jamaican history. His writings attempt to imagine a way to work through these traumatic eruptions, and they do so by vindicating English law from charges of violence. Thus, neither text entirely breaks with the responses to the rebellion and the counterinsurgency offered by de Lisser or the Victorians before him. *New Day* presents historical events through the perspectives of a middle-class brown family, and the young-adult novella *Sixty-Five* presents them through the perspectives of a poor black family. Whether Jamaicans were "masters of their own technologies of self or inherently overdetermined," as Gikandi put it, is the question each work raises through its vindications of law. Both writings suggest, in different ways, that while brown and black subjects harnessed some of these technologies of self, they are not masters of them but rather "conscripts of modernity." Examining Reid's portrayals of this condition enables us to see how the historical trauma of the Morant Bay rebellion generates literary testimonies that erode distinctions between national and world literatures.

Taking Time and Leaping Ahead: New Day *as Modern Epic*

Vic Reid described *New Day* as a corrective to the racism of de Lisser's portrayals of Jamaican history, but by arguing for a specific cognition of temporality, it, too, vindicates English law and depicts the insurgency as the violent expression of politically unconscious subjects. Where de Lisser redefines the temporality of necessity to stall anticolonial nationalism, Reid advocates for the necessity of a certain temporality as the condition for achieving an authentic national independence. The refrain that organizes *New Day* is "take time," that is, wait for conditions to be favorable to make claims for political independence. The novel maintains that English legal education teaches how to develop a cognition of time that will enable Jamaica to flourish and compete in a global economy with England, under whose protection the novel asserts it should remain, though not as a Crown colony but as an entity with "full representative government within the British empire."[62]

That *New Day* expresses this tutelary cognition of time seems oddly anachronistic, considering that the novel is composed when anticolonial agendas were articulated through a rhetoric of urgency in the Caribbean and abroad. This ideology of temporality is all the more striking because it occurs in what otherwise appears an exemplary work of its moment. Published in 1949, five years after the lifting of Crown colony rule, *New Day* emerges out of 1930s and 1940s cultural nationalism. Literature of this period used the conventions and vernaculars of realism and portrayed local landscape, labor, and social practices of the peasantry and working classes to interrupt colonial imaginaries and forge a national consciousness. *New Day* features all of these elements. It depicts eighty years of postemancipation struggle beginning with the Morant Bay rebellion and concluding with the end of Crown colony rule. On the eve of the new constitution in 1944, the elderly narrator John Campbell spends the night looking backward in time, starting with early October 1865, and takes readers through major events in Jamaican history, which are given narrative shape as a family saga. This form's genealogical thrust makes it particularly compelling for a writer confronting a newly reconfigured nation because it enables him to imagine that nation as the result of a continuous development. The family saga smoothes over the discontinuities of the Morant Bay rebellion and other violent eruptions, such as the 1938 labor riots. Campbell's older brother Davie is a conflicted insurgent at Morant Bay who, after the rebellion, fathers a son, James. James becomes a successful capitalist who cares only for business and has no interest in anticolonial politics. He marries a white English woman, and both die soon after from influenza, leaving a young son, Garth, behind. *New Day* replaces *Revenge*'s anxiety over miscegenation with delight: Garth displays the best aspects of his parents' respective racial and national backgrounds and embodies a synthesis of his father's business acumen and his grandfather's anticolonial spirit.

Where the novel breaks from other works of its era is in its usage of a European model, that of *Bildung*, to confront what it criticizes as premature attempts at national independence. The third and final part of the novel relates the effects of Garth Campbell's education in England on the movement of Jamaica toward independence. Garth's personal development, or

Bildung, models an ideal national *Bildung*, which, as uninterrupted, rational, and nonviolent, does not reflect the actual history of Jamaica. Because English law makes possible Garth's development, it will make possible Jamaica's development toward self-rule, the novel claims. This means that English law will redeem the Morant Bay rebellion.

The novel intimates that the rebellion was a necessary but false start in the movement toward national independence for two related reasons: first, the rebels did not recognize that a nation that sees itself divided from a world system could not succeed, and second, the rebellion was an attempt at achieving national independence that used violence instead of law to try to accomplish its goal. Like *Revenge*, *New Day* misrepresents the rebellion as secession from England led by a figure who appears in Reid's novel not unlike he does in de Lisser's. A bloodthirsty Bogle demands, "Secession! Secession! Total freedom!" (16). When the spirit of rebellion enters Davie Campbell it transforms him into this predator: "Firecoals make his eyes, teeth are wild boar's tearing down Warieka Mount. All of a sudden I see Davie is Deacon Bogle, and frighten comes on me" (32–33). The narrator figures Bogle as a persecutor of Christians, a "herring-Jew merchant" who extracts "the price of blood" (33). Condemning the minister's disregard for all life ("*who it runs over, it runs over!*" [33]), the novel claims that Jamaicans died for his sins, sacrificing themselves to secession: "black was the cloud o' singing that day piling up on Morant courthouse. Did they hope say rain would fall from it? All the same, rain did fall. Rain, like the rain from the side o' Mas'r Gods Son, the Golgotha rain . . . and it drowned some o' me brethren" (112–113). Bogle both demands and preys on sacrifice, for "Deacon is a hunter-dog quartering the hole o' the German boar. Deacon is a cult shepherd in Yallahs Valley waiting for the sacrificial lamb. He will be a quartering *John Crow*, working up his appetite before he swoops for carrion meat" (139). By portraying the rebellion as sacrifice, the novel establishes that it is the task of history to redeem it.

English legal education redeems this sacrifice and provides the lesson the novel imparts: to "take time." Belaboring this point, *New Day* issues the warning in multiple, seemingly unconnected contexts. Not until the final section does it relate the refrain to the prescription of colonial tutelage:

> "The scene is changing, Uncle. We are growing up. We are getting out of the chrysalis."

"We? We who?"

"The Colonial Empire. Once it was the British Empire, now it is the British Commonwealth and the Colonial Empire. Soon it will only be the British Commonwealth—each of us with our own pair of wings, but flying together."

"And how will we get our wings?"

"We will ask for them, but first we must learn how to use them . . .

"We had them once, you know, Uncle."

I nod me head, "Yes, true that."

"We lost them. We flapped too heavily, so mother bird clipped them. For our own good, she said. She was probably right. They would have flapped us into trouble."

(338–339)

The loss of self-representation through Crown colony rule, the result of the rebellion, is deemed necessary because Jamaicans did not know not to leap ahead. The demand for immediate sovereignty (which of course in historical terms was not made during the rebellion or leading up to it) only proved that Jamaicans required more tutoring. A hasty secession from the empire would only have resulted in the incapacity to manage the world system. A nation that cannot suture itself into that system, Garth and the novel assure us, is a nation that is not truly independent, "mature," and free.

Garth Campbell's legal education in England enables him to help Jamaica cope with pressure of multinationals like United Fruit and WISCO, effectively deal with the rise of trade unionism, and forecast and exploit the changing role of the sugar industry in the global economy during World War II. Garth understands Jamaica as part of a world that is necessarily one and stitched together into a system of economic dependency: "Mr. Hitler is determined that Germany should expand, and in this close-fitting world, expansion by any one nation means somewhere there will be a tear. Wherever this tear occurs there will be resentment, and there you will have your war and a terrific demand for our sugar" (333). He is able to acquit himself and hundreds of workers in a trial following a trade union meeting that turns violent. He can do this because, our narrator regularly reminds us, he learned to "talk strong but with reason before the King's bench" (273). "This boy . . . whom many learned men ha' taught how to speak before the King's bench" (329) also resolves disputes between capital and labor and secures a thriving economy on the Campbell estate and in the parish, which becomes a utopic, parallel colony in miniature, a foreign body enveloped in a colony plagued with poverty and violent labor disputes. As Thomas Holt writes, 1938 "was a year as violent and consequential as 1831–32 and 1865," and in the decade following the strike, "new forces emerged—some beneficial, some sinister—that would reshape the political, economic, and social futures not only of Jamaica but of the entire colonial empire."[63] By establishing conditions of rational discussion and consensus among the plantocracy, Garth prevents a violent uprising by estate workers, which the novel identifies as potentially another Morant Bay rebellion. Persuading parish planters to join with the Campbells in raising wages and in teaching their workers how to lobby for rights and privileges, he warns, "in some countries unionism was born in blood; in others, wise heads who saw the inevitableness of the birth took steps to prevent violence" (334). The novel draws a connection between political independence and business acumen by stating that both require a correct cognition of time. Garth preaches, "In doing business you know there is one cardinal rule, never act in haste" (329). When Crown colony rule is finally lifted as a consequence of Garth's mediation between the colony and his legal connections in England, to whom he petitions, John Campbell declares that the sacrifices of the Morant Bay rebellion have been redeemed. His comments assert that Garth's *Bildung* parallels that of Jamaica. Redemption happens as the result of an organic process of personal and national development, the ripening of a seed: "*Aie*, what a fruit our seed has borne . . . Glad, I am glad that Naomi and me had sent Davie's offspring to learn of the law in England" (365). Jamaica has finally "reached our age of reason" (271) because now "men can march with the banner o' the law waving over them 'stead o' shells talking of blood and fire" (366). The novel equates this age of reason or enlightenment in which law enables Jamaica to manage effectively the demands of the world system with modernity: "Get rid of those horse-and-buggy concepts, Mother England, before the rest of the world speeds out of sight leaving you wallowing in the mire of prejudiced tradition" (367).

In its staging of history as an uninterrupted dialectical progression that redeems an initial sacrifice and that is guided by a future horizon of hope in recent gains toward national independence, *New Day* seems at first glance to typify what David Scott calls "the mythos of Romance" he claims organizes anticolonial revolutionary discourse as well as postcolonial criticism.

Through his reading of *The Black Jacobins*, C. L. R. James's classic study of the revolution in Haiti, Scott argues that this future horizon determines a shaping of the past through epic romance, a genre of the quest that is, in Northrop Frye's words, "nearest of all literary forms to the wish fulfillment dream." Scott explains:

> the protagonists (invariably associated with the new, with Light, with order) undertake a perilous journey; there are encounters with antagonists or enemies (invariably associated with the old, with Darkness, with disorder); the inevitable conflict ensues between these irreconcilable principles; there are heightened moments when Darkness seems poised to vanquish Light; and finally the victorious deliverance or overcoming from bondage, from evil, comes: what Frye calls "the point of epiphany."[64]

Published just eleven years after James's text, *New Day* reflects the rhythm and pacing of epic romance as Scott describes it, but its vindication of English law also distinguishes it from *The Black Jacobins*. The novel eschews and even criticizes two defining features of the anticolonial mythos of romance—the employment of a form of vindicationalism and the longing for total revolution. Vindicationalism here is a narrative mode, often a tone of "moral indignation" or outrage devoted to redeeming wrongs under slavery and colonialism, which it characterizes as processes of total dehumanization and victimization.[65] Vindicationalism accompanies the demand for "total revolution," a complete and immediate break from an empire to be orchestrated by an autonomous subject, an epic romantic hero.[66] Later anticolonial movements and criticism take up this "unequivocal demand for immediate sovereignty."[67] Instead of rehearsing vindicationalism, an outrage over the besmirching of the dignity and humanity of black subjects under colonialism, *New Day* vindicates English law. Instead of presenting as heroic a figure who redeems wrongs suffered under colonialism by initiating total revolution, as James presents Toussaint, *New Day* portrays as a predator the historical figure it misrepresents as an initiator of total revolution whose sacrifices must be redeemed by law. Instead of demanding immediate sovereignty, *New Day* demands that colonial subjects "take time."

Reid's work depicts colonialism not as a totalizing process of victimization but as an epistemic violence that also enabled the emergence of agents who could help bring it to crisis. These "conscripts of modernity" were not autonomous masters of their destiny. They were subjects who harnessed technologies imposed by colonialism to resist it. Garth Campbell is the conscript the text privileges. Although the novel interrupts the mythos of romance by rejecting the notion of colonialism as totalizing victimization that demands total revolution, it also enacts this mythos by plotting a progress narrative that molds a brown middle-class subject into the novel's, and Jamaican history's, hero. By making Garth the singular hero, Reid ignores how black subjects of lower economic status, including Paul Bogle, were conscripts of modernity whose resistance tactics challenged colonial power and did so *without* calling for total revolution. These men and women redeployed Moravian Baptist missionary discourse to create new counterpublics and bypass the colonial government to appeal to the Queen for economic and political justice. They also formed their own justice systems to confront the widespread injustices produced by the plantocracy.[68] Moreover, *New Day* renders Enlightenment thought—English legal thought—the pathway to organic, national *Bildung* but does not show, as James does in his appended comments on tragedy in *The Black Jacobins*, what Scott calls "the inevitable costs that accompany relentless and unheeding enlightenment thinking."[69] A brutal counterinsurgency was the result of Enlightenment codifications of race, gender, and sexuality, of the human and the inhuman. Enlightenment thought shaped the arguments of jurists such as Finlason, who asserted the need for the redefinition of English constitutional principles on the basis of colonial exception, proposing that emergency law could not be transferred from domestic to colonial space without the concept of necessity being transformed to reflect racial difference. Carlyle's defense of the counterinsurgency on the grounds that Eyre had safeguarded white femininity was the product of Enlightenment thought. Even among the Jamaica Committee, Enlightenment thought determined the initial response to the insurgency. Mill and Buxton argued the rebellion was a spontaneous riot because they could not imagine that Jamaicans were capable of organizing and planning anything like a widespread, coherent act of anticolonial resistance.[70] By advocating the tutelary cognition of time without showing what Scott calls the "paradoxes and reversals" that interrupt the progress narrative of history, *New Day* seems more like a colonial than an anticolonial or a postcolonial work, if the "post-" refers to a critical mode and not only a historical period.[71]

But although the novel challenges the rhetoric of nationalism shared by so many anticolonial works of its time and after, it also illustrates that it has difficulty rejecting the unequivocal demand for immediate sovereignty without equivocation. In tension with the plotting of the epic as romantic discourse is its formal staging as something like what Franco Moretti calls the modern epic. This form configures a relation between past, present, and future in ways that are sharply distinct from the linear trajectory of romance. As this epic form, the text incessantly presses against the ideology of tutelage; the novel refuses, structurally, to "take time." In refusing to take time, *New Day* also challenges oppositions between world text and national saga.

Moretti distinguishes the modern epic from what he calls the "premodern" epic as well as from the national saga in a number of ways. First and foremost, the modern epic, unlike the other two, formally testifies to the fact that the world system has taken hold. "The construction of national identity—henceforth required of the novel—is thus replaced, for the epic, by a far larger geographical ambition: a global ambition."[72] According to the classification Moretti devises, *New Day* is a national work or a "premodern" epic. In the latter, we find "the weight of the past . . . the epic is not just inherited from the past, but also dominated by it . . . imposing on author and readers alike 'the reverent point of view of a descendant.'"[73] The modern epic finds the present invaded by the past, too, but does not approach that past with reverence or position itself as a descendant. This form is defined by geographical expansion and temporal contraction. By contrast, the national saga is defined by spatial contraction and temporal expansion, a tightening of space and lengthening of history. And in a reversal of the Bakhtinian thesis that the epic is monologic while the novel is polyphonic, Moretti claims that polyphony reigns in the modern epic. In place of an intelligent ordering of many voices, however, is cacophony because "in the expanding universe of modernity, many things are as yet unclear; and it is necessary to learn to live with noise."[74] The expansion of time rather than space, the monologic narration, the focus on the Campbells' parish, the retelling of the historical past as family saga, which places hope for the future in the descendents—all of this puts Reid's text on the other side of the modern epic, suggesting it is a thoroughly national work, not a world text. Critics assert that this is the case, some arguing that the novel supports Fredric Jameson's controversial claim that third-world texts are national allegories.[75] Yet when Moretti turns his attention away from the works of Western Europe to analyze a postcolonial novel of the Americas, he offers a reading of epic form that suggests the division between world and national text is not so rigid.

Deploying Moretti's close readings to examine *New Day* means redirecting the work of the advocate of a world literature studies constituted by distanced reading.[76] Those close readings, which explore *One Hundred Years of Solitude*'s depiction of colonial space, its staging of time, and its plotting of history, expand the category of modern epic and bring us closer to seeing *New Day* as something other than "premodern" and "national." In Moretti's reading, these three narrative elements of Márquez's text disclose that what seems a national work, a family saga focused on the House of Buendia, is in fact a world text. In family sagas such as Thomas Mann's *Buddenbrooks*, focalization "is like a zoom shot: from the world to the nation-state to the city to the house. Spaces ever more tightly defined, ever more smaller and more homogenous."[77] Márquez's novel, too, is focused on a tighter space than the world and never migrates out of Macondo, "yet Macondo is, as it were, larger than Lübeck: because more open to the world . . . [Márquez's novel is] the story of *Buddenbrooks*—in the context of the world-system."[78] Within Macondo appear people and objects from the farthest-flung parts of the globe, and the narrative tracks the varied effects of the world system in its plotting and in its staging of time. This staging of time, an interplay of prolepses and analepses that has the narrative traveling repeatedly, in each episode, from the future, to the past, and then back to the future is what gives the work its "epic grandeur," Moretti explains, citing Vargas Lhosa, who describes the "basic narrative cell" of the novel:

> At the start of an episode, the main fact in the narrative unit is mentioned: it is usually the last, in chronological terms. In other words, the episode begins with a leap towards the future. . . . The narrative then jumps to the remotest past of the fact mentioned, whence it follows a linear chronological account of events, until it reaches the future fact that has been displaced and reported at the start of the episode: in this way the circle is closed, and *the episode ends where it began, just as it had begun where it would end*.[79]

This description of narrative time as a leap toward the future, a jump back to the remotest past, and return to the future fact that has been displaced and reported at the episode's beginning describes almost exactly the structure of *New Day*. Two important aspects distinguish Reid's text's staging of time from Márquez's text's. In the latter, the circular temporal motion of the novel is often sparked as a consequence of processes that begin outside of the nation and that produce decisive and lasting effects on its plot, transforming it into a "*Buddenbrooks* in the context of the world-system." The world system also produces decisive and lasting effects in *New Day*'s plot, but what sparks the temporal motion of each episode is not portrayed by the plot as economic processes that begin outside of the nation. What organizes the proleptic and analeptic epic structure and creates its temporal motion is something else: the syntactical structure of its vernacular. The novel's temporality rehearses the rhythm of its linguistic code. This code is the crystallization of national as well as transnational forces and histories and also irreducible to them.

While *New Day* advises to "take time" in order to manage best the processes it plots that begin outside the nation, from the beginning, the narrative continuously leaps ahead and disobeys the order that vindicates law's cognition of time as well as the concept of time underwriting the novel form as a nation form. The novel's other refrain is "Is remember I remember," which occurs in each episode. This refrain rehearses in miniature the almost circular temporal motion of the narrative that occurs in each of the novel's episodes. "Is remember" is a comment delivered in each episode by the narrator from a point in the future; its utterance signifies that the narrative has leapt forward, jumped over a time that the text will then proceed to recount in the episode that follows so as to try to catch up with the point from which this account begins. Rather than progress immediately into its account of the past that has been leapt over, however, the text first turns backward as the narrator repeats the phrase, yet with a difference: "I remember." Just as the phrase begins with two words and travels backward, repeating the words with a difference ("Is remember I remember"), so too does the novel as a whole follow this structure. Every episode moves from a future to a past that has been leapt over, and then, instead of bringing us back to that exact moment from which the episode's narration began, it leaps ahead, past events leading up to that moment and lands on a future moment from which the utterance "Is remember, I remember" will be issued. The leap forward at the end of each episode spurs the cycle to begin again in the next episode. The narrative "circle" is never closed, therefore;

there is always a disjuncture, a leap forward, a refusal to "take time" that leaves each episode open.

The novel's proleptic and recursive structure marks a departure from the novelistic structures that create the effect of an imagined national community. Novels "take time," we might say, and in doing so, they interpellate their readers and depict their characters in ways that Benedict Anderson argues distinguish it from the epic. The novel does not leap forward and backward through a limited perspective as the epic does, a form that historically precedes the development of nations and nationalisms. Simultaneity, a "meanwhile" that suggests temporal coincidence and an omniscient, "bird's eye" view are the defining features of the novel form as nation form, Anderson maintains. The novel shows characters that might never interact or even meet progressing though an empty, homogenous time, and thus it simulates the nation as imagination of serialized, anonymous subjects both within the text and "in the minds of the omniscient readers."[80] By contrast, Reid's novel does not take time and therefore does not generate this notion of the nation as serialized, anonymous subjects in either characters' or readers' minds. Rather than enact an omniscient perspective or the linear progression of homogenous empty time that facilitates national identification and address—a concept of time on which the vindication of law is propped—*New Day* rehearses time as prefiguration and fulfillment whose rhythm is forward, backward, and forward again. Because of its epic form, then, it would seem this text is not even "modern" enough to be considered a "national" work, much less a world text. The novel's epic form, however, enacts its connection to the nation and to the world beyond it because its temporality obeys the structure and rhythm of its "nation language"—a national language which, it turns out, is not one.

New Day's narrative structure is modeled on the structure of its vernacular, a reworked mesolect of Jamaican Creole and British and American English. Reid provides a glossary of Creole terms and a note on Jamaican vernacular in which he underlines a particular feature of the grammar, the repetitions of words for emphasis and rhythm, and says this is what "give[s] the dialect its uniquely poetic character" (374). This repetition is evident in the refrain that triggers the "circle" that gives the work its "epic grandeur," "Is remember I remember." This spacing rhythm of a step forward and backward and then forward again structures the phrasing of memory as well as that of textual temporality, as the text returns to 1865, then returns to 1944, then returns to 1882, then returns to 1944, and so forth, while never coinciding with its previous moment. Less of a circle, time is more of a spiral, which is itself, as Nico Israel argues, an aesthetic and politico-philosophical feature of global modernity that questions the closures of national discourse.[81] *New Day*'s temporal spiral does not imagine the nation in terms of serialized subjects in empty time but does manifest the desire to reappropriate what had been devalued under antinationalist cultural programs—Jamaican Creole. By deploying Jamaican Creole's rhythm as the basis for its temporal structure of leaping ahead and turning backward, Reid's novel undercuts the ideology of tutelage expressed in the economic-political phrasing of "take time" and rejects the colonial models of acculturation that insisted that British English must replace Jamaican English and Creole.[82] This epic temporality also stalls the progress narrative that vindicates law, as it continually transgresses the law of that law.

If it seems that *New Day*'s deployment of the linguistic mode simply replaces its romantic hero's global outlook by reasserting a concept of the nation as a *Volk* naturally connected to a language untouched by imperial modernity, this is not the case for a number of reasons. First, as discussed, the narrative time provided by the linguistic mode refuses the logic of seriality and temporal homogeneity associated with a literary imagination of nation form. Second, this "nation language" in fact belongs to no particular nation. Finally, Reid operates as a bricoleur, reappropriating linguistic material of the past in order to *denaturalize* nation, language, and the connection between them and to address audiences both within and outside of the nation. The apparent monologism of *New Day* is internally constituted by a multilingual bricolage. The glossary does seem to suggest that what we are reading is a language at once premodern and confined to Jamaica, though certainly also the result of extranational forces: "the dialectic spoken in Jamaica derives in part from the English of an earlier day and in part from Welsh. It is characterized by repetitions of words and by the use of forms that have gone out of fashion in England and the United States" (374). But the language of *New Day* is neither "premodern" nor a national language. This is not only for the more obvious reasons that, first, there is no Jamaican monolinguilism because many dialects, mesolects, acrolects, and basolects are spoken, and, second, as a combination of Creole and Anglo-English, the novel's form of expression is also the result of a history of migrations and movements of peoples and languages shaped by the forces of imperialism and capitalism as well as resistance to these. Less obviously, this is because Reid employs a "vernacular" that is not spoken by anyone, anywhere. In an interview, Reid asserts that the novel's language was an attempt to counter colonialist depictions of Jamaican history that served antinationalist agendas. His example is de Lisser, "one of the old fashioned brown imperialists who thought people should be kept in their places," whose novels put Jamaicans "in the worst light possible. . . . And so I thought the thing to do would be to write a book in the dialect, in the Jamaican vernacular."[83] Although this statement seems to indicate that the novel, and specifically its language, serves a cultural nationalist program, Reid goes on to explain that the novel's counter to colonialist representations of culture is not guided by an attempt to restore a true national language of the *Volk* nor to address a national audience alone, but a transnational one. Reid does not pretend that an anticolonial transnational address is divorced from economics, the pressures of a transnational literary market, and he represents fiction writing as a form of labor that deserves a livable wage:

> The trouble was of course that being slightly commercial in my outlook, and also I think quite sensible, I saw no reason why the writer should really not make a living from his work. And so I decided that if I'm going to use the dialect, it must be used so that it can be read by people all over the world, who can read English. And I went to work to style the language, the English language and the Jamaican vernacular . . . into the sort of language that people could read and understand, always bearing in mind very deliberately, that the rhythms, the beautiful rhythm of all the West Indian English-speaking people would be in the book as far as Jamaican rhythm and nuances were concerned.[84]

Moreover, rather than address English speakers within and outside of Jamaica in a familiar language, he sought to defamiliarize the language for them: "I devised this way of using some of the old Elizabethan styles but bringing in the atmosphere of the Jamaican language all set in a rhythm . . . and they'd understand the language although it was rather exotic to most of them, also to my own people."[85] Reid's description of language as defamiliarizing, invented, and aimed beyond a single nation challenges George Lamming's reading of Reid's (and Sam Selvon's) works' language as pure, unmediated "peasant tongue . . . no artifice of techniques, no sophisticated gimmicks."[86] It also troubles Lamming's position that Reid's ability to render this "organic music of the earth"[87] is the result of his being more closely tied to the nation because he did not emigrate like so many other Caribbean writers. As Sylvia Wynter points out, Reid's novel practices a psychic emigration and return, if not a physical one.[88]

Rejecting a natural connection between nation and language through what Reid calls this "devised language," *New Day* delivers a rejoinder to "take time" by practicing the temporality that underwrites demands for immediate sovereignty while detaching this temporality from ethnicist concepts of the nation as a demos rooted in language and shared tradition. Internally heterogeneous, this mode was a practical strategy that allowed Reid to address both Jamaican people and people who could read English all over the world, but without addressing them in the idioms of the dominant and through the antinationalist cultural systems of de Lisser's work. *New Day* therefore questions the ideology that vindicates English law and the progressive movement toward Enlightenment and modernity through a temporality modeled on the subnational discourse that is also transnational. This language forces readers to learn to engage with a language unfamiliar or defamiliarized that is *not* of the dominant. As the North American reviewer in the *Sewanee Review* noted in 1950, the novel forced readers "to readjust . . . linguistic expectations."[89]

Another way that *New Day* troubles the relationship between monologism and polyphony, thereby challenging the vindication of British law and disturbing the conception of time as a progressive unfolding, occurs in a crucial scene. This scene elaborates the staging of testimony before the JRC. Rather than defining modernity as what gives rise to many voices, "cacophony," or noise, as Moretti claims, *New Day* defines modernity as what silences many voices through colonial conquest and consolidation. The novel choreographs a scene of endeavoring to convoke those many voices in order to bear witness to a history of violence that challenges England's legal response to the rebellion. This depiction refuses the idea that underwrote the concept of necessity—that the rebellion was a traumatic rupture that provoked an exceptional manifestation of British violence. The rebellion is a trauma that silences witnesses, the novel maintains, but also insists that the rebellion is not a rupture and that the violence practiced by the colonial state during the counterinsurgency is not exceptional.

When Davie Campbell bears witness before the commissioners, his testimony is orchestrated not simply as his own voice but as prosopopeia: as spectral witnessing. Davie asks the commissioners, "Do you know how we came these last three years? Or how we come before that?" (207). In other words, he asks them do they know how and when the rebellion originated. Their reaction is "Just what do you mean, Campbell?" (207). His response is presented not as his testimony but as an effort to speak for those who cannot, without guarantee that he can speak for them. "*That now I would speak for the dead ones!*" (207), he responds. The conditional tense is crucial because it expresses the act of speaking for others as a necessary betrayal. It acknowledges that this witness cannot stand in for all those others who were deprived of the capacity to bear witness as a consequence of historical traumas of imperial modernity that precede the rebellion. Through this testimonial act—a speech act presented here as neither verifiable or even rigorously possible—the novel acknowledges the limits of using a single heroic figure as the conscript of modernity and recognizes that a brown middle-class witness cannot speak for all those who have lived and died under slavery and colonialism. This testimony passes through that impasse by translating collective damages into wrongs before the JRC, breaking the protocols of this inquiry, which was based on individual eyewitness accounts of events that transpired during October 1865. "I *would speak* for such as do no' speak any more! I *would* tell you that for two hundred years before October gone, men were a-march on Morant Bay courthouse. Say it was not from Stony Gut they marched, nor Bath Town, nor Port Morant, nor Cuna Cuna Mountain. Say that they marched from all over the island and ha' been marching for two hundred years!" (208, my emphasis).

This insurgent testimony presents history as a steady destruction under British power and situates the Morant Bay rebellion not as the exceptional event that shamed English law and required its vindication but rather as the rule of British law's "shaming" of labor. "For these two hundred years they saw the shaming of man's highest calling—the calling o' labor with the hands" (208), Davie testifies. The rebellion is another effect of the culmination of events that began in Jamaica with chattel slavery and, most recently, with the postemancipation government's withholding of lands for Jamaicans to work. After emancipation, black and brown Jamaicans obtain their own lands and can leave the white landowner's estates, but by "that time, then, there is no labor, and there is new laws in the House o' Assembly which will prevent people getting good lands to buy, so they will return to buckra estates. There is even talk among the plantermen of bringing indentured labor from India and China" (211). By attempting to bear witness for those who do not share the witness's privileged economic and racial status, Davie presents the representatives of English law with a portrayal of the Morant Bay rebellion not as an exception, "an interruption in the otherwise smooth functioning of lawful politics,"[90] which forms the basis of the legal concept of necessity, but as business as usual in the longue durée of imperial political economy whose networks are ever expanding and globalizing.

As such, the rebellion exceeds resolution by English law even as it demands a response in the form of an official inquiry. Testimony in the novel therefore exposes the failures of England's response to the crisis. As the legal scholar Rande W. Kostal notes, "to the modern observer, to many contemporaries, the Government's obsession with things legal was more than passing strange. After all, in the 1860s Jamaica faced profound economic and social crises. The sugar economy had collapsed, and nothing viable had taken its place. The colony was densely populated but desperately poor. Race relations were hopelessly poisoned," yet "the leaders of the imperial state in London either did not want—or did not know how—to respond to the Jamaican crisis at the level of political economy. What it thought to do . . . was consult lawyers and mount a series of legal initiatives."[91] The government attempts to remedy what it mistakes as a rupture through law.

Ultimately, however, *New Day*, too, puts its faith in English law to redeem the rebellion. Although the prosopopeia before the JRC and the temporality and address of the linguistic code intercept the relentless unfolding of the dialectic that vindicates law, the progress narrative triumphs in the end. Davie is reborn and improved in the lawyer Garth, and by the third section of the novel, the British English spoken by this romantic hero is far more dominant than the devised language that organizes the entire first section but that slowly retreats as the novel continues.[92] Reid attributes this disappearance to the fact that the "foreign editors" liked the idea because it would give those outside of Jamaica a chance to "catch their breath."[93] It is difficult, however, not to read the shift from one linguistic code to another also as another indication of the tension the novel conveys between taking time and leaping ahead. This tension manifests an ambivalence toward its vindications of English law. For these reasons, *New Day* is not a total rupture from the literary history to which it reacts, and it remains attached to the models from which Reid attempts to break, specifically de Lisser's. Not until a decade after *New Day* is published will Reid move closer to acknowledging in literary form the violence of English law, which again occurs through the interruption of testimony.

Story of the Eye: Sixty-Five*'s Pedagogy of Perception*

It is not surprising that Reid would revisit the Morant Bay rebellion in 1960, two years before Jamaica achieves full national independence. During this era, the rebellion became the site of renewed interest in culture and politics, and it was reinvented as the origin of the new nation.[94] Also not surprising is that Reid would revisit the rebellion in the form of a young-adult novella. Reid's commitment to intervening in colonial constructions of Jamaican history extended beyond his novel writing; he also wrote books for schoolchildren, including *The Young Warriors*, which tells the story of the Maroons, and *Peter of Mount Ephraim*, which examines the Sam Sharpe rebellion. Like *New Day*, *Sixty-Five* presents history as a family saga, though here narrative time is linear and spans only a short period before, during, and after the rebellion. Paralleling the middle-class brown family the Campbells are the Murrays, a black family of lesser means whose father and son also clash over the insurgency. Like *New Day*, this novel places hope for the future in the grandson, who, like Garth Campbell, represents a synthesis of the father and grandfather's conflicting perspectives. Twelve-year-old Japheth is not only the narrator but also the novel's main focalizer, and the narrative consistently highlights his and others' acts of looking to carry out its pedagogic mission. That mission is to train its readers to find the correct angle of vision through which to view the past in order to judge the best way to proceed toward the future.

Whereas the conflict that centers *New Day* pivots on a cognition of time—whether to leap forward immediately or wait to confront colonial power—the central conflict of *Sixty-Five* is figured in terms of a cognition of space: whether to advance and attack or "fall back" from colonial power. By advocating the latter and deploying it as a refrain, *Sixty-Five*, like *New Day*, endeavors to vindicate English law. But as is also the case in the earlier novel, in the later one this vindication is interrupted. Here, the interruption occurs through the novel's elaboration of double vision, a critical strategy about which the work says little but regularly puts on display through its handling of focalization.

This critical strategy discloses an orchestration of British legal violence in imperial history that the novel will not express through the voices of its characters—indeed, that its most privileged character will deny. The disclosure articulates history as structured by paradoxes and reversals and demonstrates that it conscripts subjects into complicity with colonial subjectifications, both their own and those of others. This is history as tragedy rather than epic romance. In tragedy, as Scott asserts, "the relation between past, present, and future is never a Romantic one in which history rides a triumphant and seamlessly progressive rhythm, but a broken series of paradoxes and reversals in which human action is ever open to unaccountable contingencies."[95]

Sixty-Five provides two different testimonies to the Morant Bay rebellion, one through voice and another through vision, reminding us of the distinction between focalization, the narrative act of looking, and the broader term narrative perspective, which can include voice.[96] The story told through voice is complicated through the story told through acts of looking. This story of the eye does not contradict the novel's order to fall back vocalized by the grandfather, "an old servant of the Crown"[97] who served in the West Indian regiment. It does, however, reconfigure the meaning of those words to reject his claim that the counterinsurgency is an act of exceptional violence. "Never have I beheld the Crown dragged through the mud the way Governor Eyre has done. The Queen will be ashamed" (99), Joe Murray complains. The novel's drama of focalization challenges both of Murray's statements.

Sixty-Five calls attention to characters' eyes on almost every page, usually multiple times, detailing how characters see, the angles from which they direct their gazes, and assessing whether they possess suitable distance from the objects of their regard. At times the book's illustrations' constructions of focalization depart from the narrative's verbal focalization of the scene represented; at other times they overlap. Readers are sutured to different perspectives by each illustration so they "see" events from different angles, through the eyes of different characters. The novel first introduces a drama of looking through text and image in an episode that also underlines a distinction between voice and vision. Here, both text and illustration make readers aware of the importance of looking. The narrator relates that "when I entered the hall and blinked the glare from my eyes, what I saw sent me quietly to my stool near the window. . . . I turned my rounded eyes toward [Queenie]," and he asks his sister about the meaning of the conference occurring between their father and grandfather. "Be quiet," Queenie responds, "you should be seen and not heard" (7). An illustration following this text places Grandpa Joe in the foreground. His most striking feature, his one good eye, squints critically at his rebel son and at the novel's readers, who are sutured to the latter's point of view and positioned at a 180-degree angle from the narrator, who watches the drama unfold from the background. Grandpa Murray was "always telling his friends about my 'sharp black eyes,'" the narrator boasts; "he always said there was nothing I missed" (8).

The novel implies that gaining control over the rebellion requires that one *see* clearly. Before Japheth schools Queenie on recent events leading up to the rebellion, the Queen's advice and the Underhill meetings, the novel relates twice that he "cleared the shreds of cerosee bush from [his] eyes" (31). Seeing clearly is a problem for the rebels. One insurgent is twice noted to be "near-sighted" (15, 17), and Bogle himself is blindsided by the counterinsurgency. *Sixty-Five*'s Bogle is not a secessionist but a loyal subject of the Queen. Neither a persecutor nor vulture, as in *New Day*, Bogle comes under assault here for his ways of looking, which prevent him from heeding the old soldier Murray's advice to fall back. When we first encounter the Minister, his eyes are "flashing like swords around him, thrusting into the crowd" (18). When he speaks of preparing to march on the Morant Bay courthouse his eyes are not wide open but "half-closed like Queenie's, when she daydreamed that she was a great lady in silks and satins" (72). Surprised by the immediate launching of a counterinsurgency, Bogle's "eyes closed to mere slits" (75) when he hears the news.

What of the single eye of the grandfather who has fought for the empire "all his youthful days" (10)? Using "the one good eye an Indian spearman left him with when he campaigned in Central America" (10), Murray teaches Japheth the best angle from which to view the current conflict, that is, from a distance instead of in its midst. On the day of the rebellion, the two leave the square in front of the Morant Bay courthouse for a place "a bit up the side of the gorge. We had the gorge below us and we could see everything as if they were on the stage and we were in the gallery" (46). This comment instructs readers that remaining outside the fray, *falling back*, allows a better vantage point from which to perceive the entire situation. Murray scrutinizes the colonial government's militiamen, "his one eye tearing into [them], seeing all their faults" (48). This scene figuratively criticizes anticolonial violence as *lexis talionis*, an eye for an eye. Of the crowd, Japheth relates, "There were scores of others perched on the scaffolding, looking down like huge birds. Maybe, I thought, they will take wings and fly down to peck out the small eyes of the lieutenant peering out below the peak of his cap" (50). After the lieutenant prohibits the rebels from crossing into the vestry, Murray remarks, "A good man, that" (51). The power of Murray's "one sharp eye," which can access the future by looking toward the past, contrasts with the nearsighted and cloudy vision of the rebels. Because they are unprepared for the force of the counterinsurgency, their response proves disorganized, foolhardy, and futile.

By making a servant of the crown and the critic of the rebellion the voice of reason with the best view of events, and having him condemn the counterinsurgency as exceptional violence that will shame the Queen, *Sixty-Five*, like *New Day* and *Revenge* before it, also appears to vindicate British law. But appearances are deceiving, and things not always clear in this novel. The deployment of two trompe l'oeil challenges the distinction between law and violence that subtends the grandfather's bafflement at the brutality of the counterinsurgency. Only by learning to recognize a trompe l'oeil for what it is—only by seeing double—can readers view what the novel refuses to state: As long as it has operated in the service of quashing anticolonial resistance, British law has been violent.

Two overdetermined emblems teach that having one's eyes deceive one can lead to unexpected and violent consequences. The first emblem is the Murrays' donkey. The opening chapter describes how "one morning the soft brown eyes had fooled us" (4–5) and assures readers "none of us would ever forget that morning" (4–5). The unforgettable event is a show of force and violent disruption that is the result of thinking that things are as they appear. It is a result of being fooled by the eyes—both by one's own and by those of others who appear nonviolent. The donkey's "soft brown eyes" indicate that she is securely tied down, intends no resistance, and poses no threat. "We had put on the harness and hampers and stepped away from her. And before you could yell 'Look out!'—forward had gone her forefeet, inward had shot her hindlegs, and she had slipped to the ground, trying to kick in the air, while carrots and cassavas and sweet potatoes and tomatoes were smashed and tumbled all over the yard" (4–5). This cautionary tale seems to cast the animal as Morant Bay rebel, an interpretation strengthened when in subsequent chapters she is twice identified with the narrator's insurgent father. But she is also figured as the ostensible opposite of a rebel: "She was big and strong, with a head on her shoulders that she must have stolen from a Morant Bay lawyer" (3), and in fact, "Grandpa said [she] was smarter than a lawyer" (4). This figure not only fools the narrator but also fools readers if their perspectives separate law from the disruption of law. Law and its violent suspension must be seen as inhabiting a single image. This trompe l'oeil intimates the violence structuring law in Jamaica and suggests it is "illegitimate" or at least ungrounded, by connecting it to insurgency and rebellion that challenge official law. The other trompe l'oeil, the weapon used in the West Indian regiment, expands this disclosure of violence and ungroundedness to include British law.

Like that of the donkey, the meaning of the grandfather's gun is overdetermined, but recognizing this figure as a trompe l'oeil proves far more difficult. This difficulty suggests that not only the grandfather but also Reid does and does not want to disclose the truth this fetish conceals and reveals: that whenever British law operates in territories of colonial contestation it is caught up in a history that resembles the tragedy, not epic romance, of Enlightenment reason. The gun, like the donkey, serves pedagogical purposes. Murray uses it to educate and discipline the narrator and his sister by calling them to attention and chronicling the past. The musket that accompanied the grandfather on military campaigns is a precious object in the narrative. He keeps it "glistening with care. He called it Beelzebub because, he said, it had done the Devil's work in its time" (10). Readers might wonder why a critic of anticolonial revolt and a "strong Church of England man" (30) would expend so much energy on such a profane object. It is, however, precisely the paradoxical character of this situation that makes the gun an important teaching tool, one whose effects extend beyond the purposes to which the character, and even perhaps the author, put it. At one point, Murray uses the musket to educate and discipline Bogle and the rebels. Here the novel resists what it simultaneously avows about the relation between British law, violence, and history.

An episode that rehearses the musket's concealment and revelation shows how it fools the rebels' eyes. "Nobody could know that beneath that blue coat was the musket that had won for England the war in Haiti . . . and had quelled the mutiny at Fort Augusta" (25), the narrator relates. Murray waits for Bogle to approach and then confronts him and his men. The novel makes much of the revelation: "'A great Israelite,' Grandpa said, his voice wrathful. 'A man of peace, a singer of psalms who believes in *this!*' Down he swooped to brush aside the coat and sweep Beelzebub into his hand. There was a long-drawn *aaah* from the men as the afternoon light spoke of beauty in the oiled stock and shining iron of the gun" (27). But exactly what has been revealed? Despite this elaborate spectacle of unveiling, is it at all clear that once the concealed weapon has been made visible, its meaning has also been made known? The use of the pronoun "this!" is a symptom of the novel's difficulty in naming a referent.

The rebels' enthrallment with the shiny surface indicates that the gun is a fetish whose surface masks another meaning. The gun indexes a history that is itself overdetermined. The four military theaters in which the musket has seen action condense complicity and reversals between colonial and anticolonial forces, muddying clear lines between colonial and anticolonial projects. By referencing "the war in Haiti," the War of 1812, the battles over the Mosquito Coast, and the slave mutiny at Fort Augusta as events in which the colonial subject has been conscripted, *Sixty-Five*'s articulation of history departs from the model of progressive history articulated in *New Day*. This novel edges closer toward acknowledging the paradoxes and inversions that attend conscription. In each of the first three examples named, the British have aided anticolonial resistance but have done so in support of colonial interests. The British aligned with Toussaint not from a moral commitment to a free Haiti but because of economic interests and battles with the French. The War of 1812 pits former colonizers against former colonized, but the once-colonized are also colonizers. Britain's alliances with Native Americans obstruct U.S. settler colonialism, but again, these alliances were motivated by British interests. In Central America, the British aided the Miskite Indians in resisting other regional forces but did so to safeguard their economic interests in the mahogany trade. The complicity of the subjects of empire with British imperial violence is crystallized in the events at Fort Augusta, where the slaves who were taken to Jamaica to become part of the West Indian regiment revolted, and the mutiny was put down brutally not only by the British but by other soldiers in the regiment.

Each event named, therefore, bears witness to the doubling of anticolonial and colonial force, reminding us how one slides into the other, how one uses the techniques of the other. To be a conscript of modernity is not only, as *New Day* relates, to use the techniques of colonial education to generate a successful anticolonial resistance. It is also to use these techniques to support the systems of slavery and colonial subjection that constitute imperial modernity. *Sixty-Five* portrays the history of conscription less as romance and more as tragedy, or even trauma. It suggests "the past is a wound, it is one that may not heal; it cannot be evaded or cleanly overcome. It doesn't go away by an act of heroic agency. . . . History, in short, is not a series of neat resolutions; the future does not grow triumphantly out of the wicked turmoil of the past."[98]

The novel cannot state this, however; it can only perform it. The historical condition of conscription is a trauma the text (dis)avows through a fetish that disrupts the coherence of the pedagogical scene in which it is called upon to offer up its truth. The trauma of conscription is avowed and disavowed in the pronoun "this!" whose exclamatory force registers at once the desire and failure to say what the text never does utter aloud—that anticolonial and British law are both violent, neither "legitimate" in themselves. Reid's text thus performs both an acknowledgment, and the difficulty of acknowledging the character of law, which West's trial report also performed. "This!" is a testimony, a call to investigate what its referent might be. The pronoun is a sign that the novel cannot decide whether to vindicate British law or to accuse it, and this failure to decide destroys the coherence of Murray's accusation. When Murray insists Bogle believes in "this," what the gun signifies, the implication is that he believes in using violence toward anticolonial ends. But as the examples above relate, the gun condenses the long history of British violence as well and collusions and slippages between colonizer and colonized. Because it choreographs this scene as the revelation of a trompe l'oeil, the novel implies that Murray brandishes the gun to show Bogle that his eyes deceive him and thus to convince Bogle to fall back. The pedagogical aim of the gun, therefore, is similar to that of the donkey, that is, to warn of a disruptive violence to come that one cannot see if one fails to recognize the coexistence of violence and law. Therefore, the gun represents not (only) what Bogle believes in but what he *does not believe in*, what he cannot see: that imminent anticolonial violence is inextricable from imminent British state violence. The incoherence of the accusation discloses that Eyre's counterinsurgency is not an example of exceptional violence, as the grandfather claims. The advice to "fall back" is issued not, as is "take time" in *New Day*, as a call to use law rather than rebellion against law to ground resistance. It is issued as a warning that imperial responses to revolt are brutal, and this violence operates in the name of reestablishing British law, which is thus precarious, always on shaky ground.

New Day insisted that rebellion could not found an independent Jamaica because only by "marching under the banner of the law" can a nation become free, but *Sixty-Five* is far less clear on this point. The novel's own double vision, its connecting of British law to violence in these two trompe l'oeil, leaves undecided whether law should dominate and control rebellion or rebellion should challenge law. The novel's conclusion has Murray teach his grandson "Discipline—knowing how to obey orders—that is the rule for victory, Japheth . . . you cannot win battles if you have no discipline" (108). What follows is another instance of the paradoxes and reversals that compose the history embedded within and figured by the gun. Murray uses the weapon that served British power to stall it: "Grandpa's hands were busy as he loaded like lightning and the musket spoke again and again" (109). In *New Day*, the conscript harnesses British legal tutelage to redeem the violence of rebellion. In *Sixty-Five*, the conscript marshals British military tutelage to repel what the novel implies is inextricable from British law—violence. The novel's final words are doubled and overdetermined and can be read as a compromise formation that both connects and disconnects this novel from Reid's earlier work. Murray and Japheth head into the mountains to wait out the counterinsurgency; "I jerked the rope which was her bridle and turned her head up the mountain. . . . Theresa went willingly, with the butt of Grandpa's musket persuading her in the rear" (110). Because both emblems are doubled, rebel and law, anticolonial and British force, they are doubles of each other. The novel leaves undecided whether rebellion should master law or law master rebellion. This undecidability indicates that even on the brink of full Jamaican independence, *Sixty-Five* does not, or cannot, entirely break from the desire to vindicate British law. Unlike *New Day*, however, it acknowledges this inability to do so as part of the trauma of the history of conscription in imperial modernity.

Emergency increasingly became the rule rather than the exception as the empire grew and as it declined. Hussain writes, "In the colonies martial law was frequently resorted to throughout the nineteenth-century: Barbados in 1805 and 1816; Demerera in 1823; Jamaica in 1831–32 and 1865; Canada in 1837–38; Ceylon in 1817 and 1848; Cephalonia in 1848; Cape of Good Hope in 1834 and 1849–51; and the Island of St. Vincent in 1863. All of these instances . . . produced debate, controversy, and an effort at justification."[99] In the twentieth century, in response to imperialism's decline, Emergency is declared in colonies such as India and Kenya. We discussed the situation of the emergency in India in the introduction's analysis of *A Passage to India*. I turn in the next and final chapter to a work that approaches the Emergency in Kenya. It is written soon after Kenyan independence, when the history of conscription, its paradoxes and reversals, have emerged in the form of a system of global capitalism and a neocolonial government that has betrayed the hopes of the nation by repressing traumas that occurred under the emergency. Ngũgi wa Thiong'o's *A Grain of Wheat* makes no attempt to vindicate law. Instead it elaborates a struggle to find a language with which to speak to and of the past that does not repeat the silencing that occurs under first British, and then Kenyan, law. Through this elaboration, the work questions the boundaries between modernist and postcolonial literatures.

FOUR

Testimony and the Crisis of the Juridical Order in Ngũgi wa Thiong'o's *A Grain of Wheat*

> African literature, even that in European languages, starts with that rejection of the master's narrative of history.
>
> —NGŨGI WA THIONG'O, *Globalectics*

The previous chapter sought to enrich a postcolonial studies dominated by the cultural problematic of migrancy and deterritorialization by analyzing writings of colonial and postcolonial authors that were not migration narratives but that instead bore witness from within the nation to law's disruption of it. This final chapter also focuses on a work that eschews a narrative of movement out of the nation for one of detention inside it. Like the Jamaicans Reid and de Lisser, the Kenyan Ngũgi wa Thiong'o elaborates how traumas of a colonial past under Emergency threaten the transition from colony to postcolony. Ngũgi's postindependence 1967 novel *A Grain of Wheat* rewrites *Under Western Eyes*, Joseph Conrad's novel from 1911, which Chapter 1 explored. Scholars once censured Ngũgi for using the work of *the* novelist of European imperialism as a template for representing African history under colonialism, but more recent studies argue that Ngũgi is critical of Conrad's modernist depiction of revolution even as he uses it to warn against the dangers of an emerging neocolonial state in Kenya.[1]

Like Conrad's novel, Ngũgi's is directed toward its protagonist's confession of betrayal. Featuring flashbacks and diversions into 150 years of Kenyan history, but focusing most prominently on the Mau Mau uprising and counterinsurgency, *A Grain of Wheat* takes place four days before Independence in 1963 and leads toward a commemorative event, the honoring of fallen freedom fighters at the Uhuru celebrations. "Let it never be said Thabai dragged to shame the names of the sons she lost in war. No. We must raise them—even from the dead—to share it with us,"[2] Warui, a village elder insists. Mugo has been called upon to make the dead speak, not least of all the heroic insurgent Kihika, whom the community does not know Mugo betrayed to the colonial authorities. Mugo's testimony on independence day is not the prosopopeia of insurgents, however, but a confession to his betrayal of the movement's leader.

Mugo's confession is always read as the textual act that most clearly expresses Ngũgi's wish to halt the compulsive repetition of betrayals the novel claims defines colonial, and newly postcolonial, Kenya. The text tells us, repeatedly, that "life was only a constant repetition of what happened yesterday and the day before" (269), from its most mundane to spectacular aspects: Mugo "liked porridge in the morning. But whenever he took it, he remembered the half-cooked porridge he ate in detention . . . everything repeats itself . . . the day ahead would be just like yesterday and the day before" (4). Betrayals reconsolidate colonial structures after eruptions of anticolonial resistance seem about to destroy them once and for all. The most recent at the time of writing occurs under Jomo Kenyatta's rule. The novel refers to it by having characters imagine what does in fact come to pass after Kenyatta is tried for insurgency in *The Queen against Kenyatta and others*. "They avoided talking about Jomo or speculating about the outcome of the case in Kapenguria," the novel relates. "Long ago, young Harry [Thuku] had also been detained, and sentenced to live alone. . . . He had come back a broken man, who promised eternal co-operation with his oppressors, denouncing the Party he had helped to build. What happened yesterday could happen today. The same thing, over and over again, through history" (122). Kenyatta betrayed the independence movement by ordering a compulsory forgetting of the Emergency and establishing the conditions for a comprador state. He described Mau Mau as "a disease that needed to be eradicated, and must never be remembered again"; as one historian notes, "Kenyatta's use of criminal analogies and disease metaphors directly recalled the British discourse on Mau Mau."[3] Critics contend that Mugo's confession speaks directly to Kenyatta's betrayals of the community, exposing and condemning the ethos of individualism underwriting economic and political policies that organize the neocolonial state.[4] As Byron Caminero-Santangelo argues, this confession dispels irony, which in the novel perpetuates deception and trust in individuals as false heroes. Mugo shares "his true history, with the community," and his confession is "also an act of self-sacrifice for the good of that community."[5] The narrative seems to support this reading of confession as sacrificial when it relates immediately after the confession occurs that "a few other elders remained behind to complete the sacrifice before the storm" (253).

Throughout the text, however, practices of witnessing push against the dominant assessment of Mugo's confession; they also constitute a significant, unexpected, and unexplored departure from those of Conrad's novel. Whether readers criticize or commend Ngũgi's adaptation of *Under Western Eyes*, they have neglected a major formal contrast between the works: the treatment of confession. While Conrad's novel multiplies confessions endlessly, *A Grain of Wheat* withholds them. It is surprising that formal tactics would differentiate two works that share a plot of revolution and its betrayal because form is what connects these writers while perspectives toward revolution set them apart. Ngũgi explains the attraction Conrad held for him in his early career as a novelist. He admired Conrad in part because here was a colonial subject who wrote in, and thus had to negotiate with, a language that was not his first (or even second): English.[6] Also, although Ngũgi remained critical of what he calls Conrad's liberal humanist support of imperialism, he found the formal procedures of Conrad's work "tantalising" and employed them to compose what he names the Afro-European novel.[7] This "hybrid form" arises in the midst of the worldwide postwar anti-imperialist upheavals, continues after the postindependence betrayal of national liberations, and attempts to represent, address, and touch the peasantry and working classes. But this genre is still confined within European languages and can only reach the petty bourgeoisie, Ngũgi acknowledges. Because *A Grain of Wheat* is such a novel, it must therefore make all the more effort to work against its limiting condition in order to loosen itself from the colonial legacy it bears and risks perpetuating through its linguistic expression.[8] As Ngũgi famously argued in *Decolonizing the Mind*, "the domination of a people's language by the languages of the colonizing nations was crucial to the domination of the mental universe of the colonized."[9] The tactics Ngũgi employs in *A Grain of Wheat*, however, are frequently associated with an aesthetic discourse thought to convey colonialist mindsets—European modernism. Ngũgi explained why these tactics, rather than conventions of realism and naturalism that shape so much colonial and postcolonial African literature, were useful for composing the story of Kenyan history and people. "The story-within-a-story was part and parcel of the conversational norms of the peasantry," he relates. "The linear/biographical unfolding of a story was more removed from actual social practice than the narrative of Conrad."[10] Given his admiration for Conrad's use of form, it is notable that Ngũgi modifies, even jettisons, the organizing formal strategy of the particular Conrad novel he selects to tell the story of Kenya on the brink of independence.

We should consider, then, what it is about the specific historical and literary-historical situation that encourages or even demands this formal change. Not only does *A Grain of Wheat* take as its focus a turning point in Kenyan history, the transition from colony to postcolony; it is also written in a moment of limbo. It is composed after what Ngũgi identifies as the first period of African literature, which manifests "self-assuredness, a confidence . . . optimism" in the emergent nation,[11] and before the third period, those works that were to "reveal what really had been happening in the sixties: the transition from the colonial to the neocolonial stage."[12] During the intermediary period of independence, the structural shifts in national and global forces have not yet become clear:

> The writer in this period was still limited by his inadequate grasp of the full dimension of what was really happening in the sixties: the international and national realignment of class forces and class alliances. What the writer often reacted to was the visible lack of moral fibre of the new leadership and not necessarily the structural basis of that lack of a national moral fibre . . . although the literature produced was incisive in its description, it was nevertheless characterized by a sense of despair. The writer in this period often retreated into individualism, cynicism or into empty moral appeals for a change of heart.[13]

Ngũgi is not discussing his own work here (at least not directly), but his remarks might pertain to *A Grain of Wheat*. In contrast to his later fiction's foregrounding of the structural basis of the nation's turmoil, the effects of global capitalism and internal class struggle, this work foregrounds the psychology of betrayal—of Mugo's and of many other characters. The novel's examination of a pivotal moment in Kenya through characterological dramas of betrayal suggests that it believes that historical conflicts can be explained by individual moral shortcomings and psychological motivations. It would seem, therefore, that this work is "characterized by a sense of despair." Readers have indeed argued that this is the case.[14] Yet the text's management of silence and speech around the novel's betrayals indicates, on the contrary, that problems emerging in the new nation cannot be understood this way—that they possess a structural basis. That structure is the deployment of state power during colonial modernity, which reaches a crisis point during the Emergency: it creates an impasse of witnessing, making confessions to the past at once necessary and difficult, if not impossible.

In both demonstrating and negotiating this impasse while confronting its underlying conditions—a suspension of law under a state of exception, whose brutalities the English state only began to address legally in 2011—the novel replaces cynicism or despair, the responses of a literature unaware of structural conditions shaping the nation-state, with a modernist response that questions traditional and revised definitions of modernism. This response challenges the perceived rupture between modernism and African postcolonial literature as well as the notion that *A Grain of Wheat* is a copy of a modernist source text. Because formal elements distinct from, as well as those that overlap with, Conrad's novel are harnessed to different ends in the Kenyan work, the latter cannot be understood as a "belated" modernism. This harnessing also pressures Eurocentric tendencies in global modernist studies to approach modernism as an enlightened aesthetic discourse that exposes nationalism as a retrograde ideology of a residual political form while articulating alternative—diasporic and cosmopolitan—identities and commitments. Postcolonial scholars have highlighted the differences between Anglo-European modernism and that of African writers and have sought to reconfigure the category modernism from the perspective of the latter. Neil Lazarus maintains that African literature requires an expansion of the term modernism that also replaces the fetishization of particular aesthetic techniques with attention to the political work such techniques perform.[15] Simon Gikandi describes that work as giving symbolic form to the nation. "While their Western counterparts sought to use the ideology of modernism to undo nationalism, African artists adopted the same ideology to imagine and to will into being new nations," Gikandi writes, and he remarks that "nationalism has become a dirty word in some circles, but for the colonized it was a redemptive project that needed an aesthetic dimension in order to fulfill its mandate."[16] Ngũgi writes *A Grain of Wheat* when confidence in the nation-state is eroding under the weight of global capitalism, with which national elites collude, yet when the nation-state also remains a form many still hope can be marshaled to resist the depredations of an expanding neoimperial world system. The novel strives to address the past in ways that would bolster the nation against a future shaped by historical amnesia imposed by a neocolonial regime complicit with contemporaneous globalization but also strives to detach a national imagination from a history of colonial thought and language that authorizes practices of exceptional violence. The orchestration of testimonial speech, and testimonial silence, is the vehicle of this striving.

Ellipses

As many have noted, *A Grain of Wheat* is replete with silences, a fact that seems strange when we consider that the novel is written to give voice to the Emergency. British colonial and postindependence Kenyan governments both attempted to foreclose the possibility of bearing witness to this period of insurgency and counterinsurgency that lasted from 1952 to 1960. The novel relates the effects of foreclosed attestation when it describes insurgents

> abandoned in a desert where not even a straying voice from the world of men could reach them. This frightened Gikonyo, for who, then, would come to rescue them? The sun would scorch them dead and they would be buried in the hot sand where the traces of their graves would be lost forever . . . that his identity even in death would be wiped from the surface of the earth was a recurring thought that often brought him into a cold sweat on cold nights.
>
> (123)

This fear of silencing in turn silences, for "at such times, words formed in prayer would not leave his throat" (123). If it is crucial that being buried without a grave, trace, or remainder, left unmourned and forgotten, not occur, then the novel's central rhetorical strategy poses a conundrum. That strategy is ellipses, the repeated imposition of silence where speech is anticipated.

Although the work's "excessive silences"[17] have been noticed, unacknowledged is that these silences are systematic: they emerge wherever confessions are anticipated, and they are created by ellipses. This device thus insists on the importance of confessions, paradoxically by preventing them. "Ellipsis" derives from the Greek *ellipsis*, "a falling short, defect, ellipse," from *elleipein*, "to fall short, leave out," from *en- in* + *leipein*, "to leave." Embedded in its etymology are two senses of leaving: leaving out and moving away from. The novel exploits both tendencies in its uses of this figure. Ellipsis calls attention to itself *as* device, not only enacting incompletion and substitution but emphasizing that it does so. Whatever the content around which, or through which, it appears, ellipsis simultaneously signifies "I point elsewhere," whether to a passage of time between thoughts, omitted words, or any number of affects it creates—anxiety, confusion, the desire to narrate, the desire not to narrate, the failure to narrate. Ellipses convey that whatever is stated is haunted by what is not stated. By frustrating confessions of virtually all the characters at some point, this strategy formally challenges oppositions between colonizers and colonized, insurgents and counterinsurgents, and public and private spheres.

The novel's elliptical style might represent Ngũgi's nod to Conrad's work in general, though not *Under Western Eyes* specifically. Conrad was famous for creating meaning through "sudden holes in space time," but while he does so in his "Russian novel" by keeping confessions behind closed doors, he nevertheless portrays characters engaged in confessional acts, however interrupted. Ngũgi, on the other hand, regularly withholds such satisfaction from readers as well as characters. Ellipses stress the connotative rather than denotative meaning of a passage and often also play upon the interactive quality of a text, its interpellation of readers. The first ellipsis in the novel is directed at readers, from whom it withholds a confession of Mugo:

> There was, for him, then, solace in the very act of breaking the soil: to bury seeds and watch the green leaves heave and thrust themselves out of the ground, to tend the plants to ripeness and then harvest, these were all part of the world

> he had created for himself and which formed the background against which his dreams soared to the sky. But then Kihika had come into his life.
>
> (11)

Although the passage ends with a single period rather than three, the former functions in the same way as the latter. The final sentence raises an expectation (the significance of Kihika's interruption of Mugo's "dreams"), but what follows it typographically is a literal gap, a blank line space and section break that does not proceed to a completion of the thought in the section that follows and that turns the final sentence into a dangling phrase that trails off into silence. This doubled utterance emphasizes that the passage's primary meaning is not what is said but rather that there is more to say and that it is being withheld. Creating the effect of a subject driven to confess but unable to do so, ellipses multiply after Mugo receives a visit from Gikonyo:

> Suppose I had told him . . . suppose I had suddenly told him . . . Everything would have been all over . . . all over . . . the knowledge . . . the burden . . . fears . . . and hopes. . . . I could have told him . . . and maybe . . . maybe . . . Or is that why he told me his own story? At this thought he abruptly stopped pacing and leaned against the bed. A man does not go to a stranger and tear his heart open . . . I see everything . . . everything . . . he pretended not to look at me . . . yet kept on stealing eyes at me . . . see if I was frightened . . . see . . . if . . .
>
> (142)

When Mugo finally approaches Kihika's sister Mumbi to confess his betrayal of her brother, an ellipsis suspends the confession. After Mumbi asks, "What is it Mugo? What is wrong?" (211), the novel jumps into the future instead of proceeding to Mugo's confession. Leapt over, it occurs in a hole in narrative space and time and is narrated belatedly: "Suddenly at her question, he had removed his hands from her body. He knelt before her, a broken, submissive penitent" (236), and confesses. The use of past tense underlines that readers cannot witness the confession when it actually occurs. Thus, in various ways, the novel censors an act to which critics impute so much critical weight.

While the prevalence of ellipses might seem unremarkable, even cliché, Ngũgi handles the device in unconventional ways that indicate its function is more than aesthetic, that its primary role is to express the need for confession so as to refuse it. Common in detective fiction, a genre Ngũgi references in this novel and others, ellipses are typically used to generate narrative tension; although in the first appearance of ellipses, which is cited above, they are used this way, in the vast majority of instances, they are not. This is because the "secrets" ellipses hide or interrupt are always in fact disclosed, but elsewhere and outside of the confessional frame the novel erects only to have the device leave empty. The most striking proof that the ellipses are not employed to generate narrative tension is that the novel discloses its organizing secret, Mugo's betrayal of Kihika, less than a third of the way in, thus making elliptical evasions excessive to plot fomentation or suspense. But just as important is *how* that secret is disclosed—in an offhanded aside in the middle of a chapter that nearly begs readers to overlook its revelatory status: "Unless they had suspected him could General R. have asked those pointed questions? Meeting somebody after a week? Karanja? Yes, could they really have asked him to carve his place in society by singing tributes to the man he had so treacherously betrayed?" (77–78). The ways ellipses structure multiple situations involving many other characters confirms that it serves an alternative function to the production of suspense.

Through the elliptical strategy, confession is constantly proposed as a way to reveal betrayals, only for their disclosure to readers and other characters to occur otherwise, if at all. This pattern of anticipation and frustration repeats three times within one chapter that details betrayals in the domestic sphere. While engaged in an extramarital affair, the colonial administrator John Thompson's wife, Margery, felt "the impulsive desire to confess, to clean her breast, was very strong" (60), but the novel replaces confession with ellipsis. The weak rationale for such silence is a contrived missed opportunity: the sudden death of the lover allegedly makes the confession to the husband unnecessary. This is no explanation, however. Guilt rather than fear of being caught was shown to have motivated the desire to confess. This scene proposing and then thwarting the wife's confession of infidelity also includes her determination to "compel" (61) her husband to confess his feeling about the couple's imminent return to England on the eve of independence, for "Uhuru had brought their lives into a crisis and he behaved as if nothing was happening" (52):

> Yes, she would compel him to talk, tonight, she resolved, and stopped wiping the dishes, walking back to the sitting-room with determination. John was peering

> into the mass of notebooks and papers before him, occasionally scribbling something with a hand that appeared to be shaking. She bent behind him, put her arm around his neck, and lightly touched the lobe of his left ear with her lips. She was surprised at herself, since she had not done this for years. Suddenly her grim determination to force their relationship into the open crisis subsided.
>
> (61)

The desire to make Thompson confess "suddenly" subsides without explanation, and the final sentence reads as a dangling thought, ellipsis again "leaving" or moving away from confession. Margery's plan to confess is coupled with Thompson's plan to confess to Margery why they must return to England. The reason, that Kenya has betrayed him by unseating him from power, is provided to readers through free indirect discourse: "why should people wait and go through the indignity of being ejected from their beds and seats by their houseboys?" (65):

> He braced himself for the effort. His heart livened with hope and fear as he went into the bathroom to prepare himself for the great confession.
>
> He opened the door to the bedroom cautiously and stepped in. He did not put on the lights, feeling that darkness would create the right atmosphere. A man was born to die continually and start afresh. His hands were shaking, slightly, and he felt darkness creep towards him, as he reached for the bed. But Margery was already asleep. Thompson saw this and felt enormous relief and gratitude. He got into bed but for a long time he could not sleep.
>
> (65–66)

The passage elliptically leaves off again, the final sentence highlighting not only the failure but the persisting need for confession.

The struggle to confess extends beyond the home and civilian life to the military sphere, the borders between which the Emergency collapses. The specter of the Emergency chases both British and Kikuyu characters toward confessions. An episode involving Thompson, who is the former district officer at Rira camp, implies that confession alone can cure the compulsive returns of the "Rira disaster," which is based on actual events that occurred at Hola camp. Years later, on the verge of Uhuru, the specter of this disaster reemerges in civilian space. Thompson watches from his office window at Githima library as the dog belonging to his colleague Dr. Lynd prepares to attack the black Kenyan workers, who arm themselves with stones in self-defense. Lynd appears and restrains the animal, but, Thompson muses, "what would have happened if the bull-mastif had jumped on Karanja and torn his flesh? The hostility he saw in the men's eyes as he approached them. The silence. Sudden. Like Rira" (53). We learn that "at Rira, the tragedy of his life occurred. A hunger strike, a little beating and eleven detainees died" (54). Consequently, "he was whisked off to Githima . . . But the wound had never healed. Touch it, and it brought back all the humiliation he had felt at the time" (54). Thompson attempts to confess to Lynd to heal the wound. "Everything seemed a visitation from the past: Rira and the dog" (50) and even the setting seems to evoke elements of the camp, "a big tree-nursery surrounded by a wire fence" (51). Confession is continually called upon to stop the past from reemerging: "He wanted to tell her about the dog but somehow found it difficult" (50); he "wanted to tell her the truth—but he would have to tell her about his own paralysis—how he had stood fascinated by an anticipation of blood" (51). The episode builds to a confession—"he tried to tell Dr Lynd what had happened—the difficulty lay in separating what had occurred outside his office on the grass—only tell her that—from what had gone on inside him" (51–52), but it concludes with abrupt silence: "He fidgeted on the grass, felt his ridiculous position in relation to this woman from whom he wanted to get away now that the urge to tell her about the dog had faded" (52). The novel declines to explain why the desire to confess vanishes, why the text elliptically moves away from the testimonial act the return of a spectral past seems to require. In another episode, that spectral past literally chases the character Gikonyo toward a confession:

> He seemed to hear, in the distance, steps on a pavement. The steps approached him. He walked faster and faster, away from the steps. But the faster he walked, the louder the steps became. . . . The steps on the pavement, so near now, rhymed with his pounding heart. He had to talk to someone. He must hear another human voice. Mugo. But what were mere human voices? Had he not lived with them for six years? In various detention camps? Perhaps he wanted the voice of a man who would understand. Mugo. Abruptly he stopped running. The steps on the pavement receded into a distance. They would come again, he knew they would come to plague him. I must talk to Mugo. The words Mugo had spoken at a meeting two years before had touched Gikonyo. Lord, Mugo would know.
>
> (33–34)

The next sentence frustrates expectations: "But by the time he reached Mugo's hut, the heat of his resolution had cooled" (34). This inconclusive concluding remark, yet another ellipsis, denies resolution.

How, then, to explain the consistent, inexplicable fall into silence when confession is demanded? The abrupt fading of Thompson's desire to confess, the sudden loss of Margery's desire to compel Thompson to confess, the "cooling" of Gikonyo's need to confess, the censorship of Mugo's confession to Mumbi—not one is accounted for through either character psychology or plotting. While it is tempting to read the climactic delivery of Mugo's public confession as the novel's telos, the organizing elliptical strategy pressures this reading. What also pressures the privileging of this confession are its effects in the narrative. Rather than an act of self-sacrifice that unifies the community, Mugo's confession disperses those gathered at the Uhuru celebrations: "Then they rose and started talking, moving away in different directions, as if the meeting ended with Mugo's confession" (253). Moreover, after he confesses, Mugo disappears from the novel. This might of course be a sign that the narrative no longer needs the protagonist once he has fulfilled his catalytic function by confessing; however, given the resistance to confessions peppered across the entire work, the confessant's disappearance might also be a sign of ambivalence toward his testimonial act. After all, Mugo's confession does not halt the cycle of violence that characterizes colonial and postcolonial Kenya but rather inspires yet another instance of it, if, as the novel implies, he is executed without witnesses or the consent of the village judge who tries him for his crime.

The novel guides us most clearly toward a reason for its elliptical strategy when it connects confession to a history that has only recently come to light in official British archives and is still suppressed in Kenya—that of indefinite detention under the Emergency. Detained for years at Yala camp, Gikonyo desperately confesses to having taken the Mau Mau oath. The novel elliptically censors the act that precipitates his release from the concentration camp:

> Gikonyo fixed his mind on Mumbi, fearing that strength would leave his knees under the silent stare of all the other detainees. He walked on and the sound of his feet on the pavement leading to the office where screening, interrogations, and confessions were made, seemed, in the absence of other noise, unnecessar-

> ily loud. The door closed behind him. The other detainees walked back to their rooms to wait for another journey to the quarry . . .
>
> * * *
>
> As Gikonyo left the road and took a path into the fields, he could still hear the echo of his steps on the pavement four years back. The steps had followed him all through the pipe-line, for in spite of the confession, Gikonyo was not released immediately.
>
> (130)

Examining the novel's portrayal of state power and detention under the Emergency and imperial nationalist principles guiding colonial consolidation suggests why *A Grain of Wheat* refuses to deploy confessions, even though this refusal seems only to perpetuate the silencing and amnesia Kenyatta's rule enforced.

States of Exception

A Grain of Wheat details an insurgency and counterinsurgency whose role in distinguishing its ethics and politics of witnessing from that of *Under Western Eyes* has been overlooked in criticism on the novel; this history has also been overlooked in theories of trauma, sovereignty, and biopolitics. Confronting scholarship long focused on European histories, theorists have begun to consider how colonial situations might shift analyses of trauma and even occasion what Michael Rothberg calls "multidirectional memory." A comparative approach that "draws attention to the dynamic transfers that take place between diverse places and times during the act of remembrance,"[18] such a practice would, in this case, challenge Giorgio Agamben's claim that the only situation to which indefinite detention in Guantanamo Bay after September 11, 2001, "could possibly be compared is the legal situation of the Jews in the Nazi Lager [camps], who, along with their citizenship had lost every legal identity, but at least retained their identity as Jews."[19] By confronting another world of the concentration camp, which Ngũgi reminds us were "named detention camps for the world outside Kenya,"[20] *A Grain of Wheat* invites us to "posit collective memory as *partially* disengaged from exclusive versions of cultural identity and acknowledge how remembrance both cuts across and binds together diverse spatial, temporal, and cultural sites."[21] Multidirectional memory is "partial" in the sense that it struggles to maintain singularities while searching for points of connection; its goal is not synthesis. Placing Ngũgi's novel in conversation with studies of sovereignty and biopolitics that take other historical events as their focus elucidates how the novel relates that the Emergency was a crisis of the juridical order in which states of exception create the impasse of witnessing that the elliptical strategy manifests.

The novel's representation of the anticolonial movement's aims and the rhetoric of nationhood it deploys, however, obscures the nature and extent of this crisis and the mechanisms of imperial power it battles. Critics, historians, and Ngũgi himself at times describe the insurgency as a reaction to two specific losses at the hands of colonialism: land and freedom. Indeed, the name the resistance movement gave itself was the Kenya Land and Freedom Army (*not* Mau Mau). The many references to intimacy with the land convey that it defines Kenyan character and operates as the rhetorical base of claims for political independence.[22] "Is he a man who lets another take away his land and freedom?" (112), Kihika asks. "Whether the land was stolen from Gikuyu, Ukabi or Nandi, it does not belong to the whiteman. And even if it did, shouldn't everyone have a share in the common shamba, our Kenya?" (113). Kenya is regularly defined as fertile land from which its people are biologically descended, from Kihika's statement that "with us, Kenya is our Mother" (103), to the depiction of Mumbi as substitute for one of the founders of the Kikuyu, a mother who, according to the novel's conclusion, metaphorically gives birth to a new nation,[23] to the myth of the warrior Waiyaki, who took arms against the first European settlers because "the white man had imperceptibly acquired more land to meet the growing needs of his position" (15). Waiyaki is challenged by the white man, whose "menacing laughter remained echoing in the hearts of the people, long after Waiyaki had been arrested and taken to the coast, bound hands and feet" (15). The story of Waiyaki's resistance is elevated to myth through rumor. "Later, so it is said, Waiyaki was buried alive at Kibwezi with his head facing into the centre of the earth, a living warning to those who, in after years, might challenge the hand of the christian woman whose protecting shadow now bestrode both land and sea" (15). The next sentence transforms this rumor into an epic event that enables transgenerational memory, mediated through Kenyans' natural connection to the land: "Then nobody noticed it;

but looking back we can see that Waiyaki's blood contained within it a seed, a grain, which gave birth to a political party whose main strength thereafter sprang from a bond with the soil" (15). The foundation on which anticolonial nationalism is erected posits the autochthon as the legitimate inheritor of Kenyan earth and identifies two concrete losses that must be recovered.

The novel's portrayal of the Emergency, however, and of the image of imperialism the Emergency threatens indicates that more than land and control of the polity have been lost. This portrayal also illustrates that the terms the anticolonial movement uses to justify its aims—seeds, birth, "natural" life—are what drive colonial power in its various forms. According to the novel, a supposedly universally shared biological life becomes the contested site of, and justification for, earliest imperial rule and then, later, exceptional state violence in Kenya. *A Grain of Wheat* relates that what Giorgio Agamben calls the metaphysical "fracture" between an imputed "bare" or natural life and political life that shapes modernity leads to a situation in Kenya in which witnesses are silenced but also forced to speak in ways that will make attestation to this period a complicated affair.

The novel casts open the abyss of law[24] generated through what Agamben theorizes as the paradox of sovereignty in modernity. In *Homo Sacer: Sovereign Power and Bare Life*, which is launched from Michel Foucault's and Hannah Arendt's studies of biopolitics, Agamben analyzes how "natural life begins to be included in the mechanisms and calculations of State power, and politics turns into biopolitics."[25] This process is an "inclusive exclusion" in the polis of biological or bare life, what the ancients called *zoe*, as distinct from *bios*, or good life. "The peculiar phrase 'born with regard to life, but existing essentially with regard to the good life' can be read . . . as an inclusive exclusion (an *exceptio*) of *zoe* in the *polis*, almost as if politics were the place in which life had to transform itself into good life and in which what had to be politicized were always already bare life,"[26] Agamben writes. Bare life is not only excluded but also maintained as exclusion for the production of (politicized) existence. Once located at the margins of the domain of the political, in modernity, bare life comes to coincide with the political realm in totalitarian and parliamentary democratic regimes alike—indeed, "the only real question to be decided was which form of organization would be best suited to the task of assuring the care, control, and use of bare life."[27] In modern managements of bare life, distinctions between inclusion and exclusion and right and fact dissolve through a paradox enacted in the state of exception.

To account for what Agamben describes as the twentieth century's unprecedented orchestrations of state violence, which he claims are typified in the Nazi concentration camp, he focuses on what Foucault's studies of biopower allegedly neglected, the "hidden intersection between the juridico-institutional and the biopolitical modes of power." Arguing that "the production of a biopolitical body is the original activity of sovereign power,"[28] Agamben contends that that power's paradox is enacted in a state of exception that creates *homo sacer*, a subject suspended between life and death who is both inside and outside of law. The sovereign who decides on the state of exception is also inside and outside of law, but this is because he or she suspends the juridical order of which he or she is also a part. This situation institutes a threshold of indistinction

> between [right and fact]. It is not a fact, since it is only created through the suspension of the rule. But for the same reason it is not even a juridical case in point, even if it opens the possibility of the force of law. . . . What is at issue in the sovereign exception is not so much the control or neutralization of an excess as the creation and definition of the very space in which the juridico-political order can have validity. . . . The "ordering of space" that is, according to [the jurist Carl] Schmitt, constitutive of the sovereign nomos *is therefore not only a "taking of land"—the determination of a juridical and territorial ordering—but above all a "taking of the outside," an exception.*[29]

Once exceptional, the state of exception becomes normalized throughout the twentieth century and into the twenty-first. (Although, as our discussion in the previous chapter indicates, we could counter that emergency law was increasingly invoked by the British empire throughout the nineteenth century and was also legally coded as "exceptional.") Agamben argues that the Nazi camp is the pure topological expression of the breakdown between inside and outside and right and fact under sovereign exception. There, the detainee is transformed into *homo sacer*, both outside and inside the law, deprived of law's protection yet subject to it. The camp therefore makes visible "the hidden paradigm of the political space of modernity."[30]

A Grain of Wheat suggests that the paradox of sovereignty that produces and maintains bare life finds a different manifestation in Kenya under British rule. The novel articulates that the sovereign ordering of space under colonialism was more than a "taking of land," in the words of both Carl Schmitt and the anticolonial movement; it was also a "taking of the outside." The inclusive exclusion of bare life is presented as central to imperial aims across history in Kenya. It shapes the discourse of rehabilitation that initiates conquest and colonial consolidation under the mantle of imperial nationalism as well as the discourse of contamination and elimination that defined the totalitarian Emergency state.

The text relates that as a civilizing mission, British imperialism creates a fracture between bare life and good life that it unsuccessfully attempts to repair through the process of "rehabilitation." This drama of metaphysical fracture and attempted reparation is scripted in a treatise attributed to Thompson, whose political trajectory in some ways parallels that of Conrad's Kurtz and who will later lose faith in the civilizing mission he articulates in *Prospero in Africa*. This manuscript presents the colonial project as the inclusive exclusion of the bare life of the African in the polis of the British empire-as-one-nation. Imperial nationalism's goal of "stretching the short, tight, skin of the nation over the gigantic body of the empire"[31] finds expression in the novel through Thompson's treatise. The treatise maintains that although the African is atavistic and animalistic, these aspects can be excluded so she (or he, more exactly; the African woman's capacity for rehabilitation would be less visible to the imperial focalizer here) can be included as a British subject, a member of the far-flung "British nation" (62). What must be politicized is bare life. Upon discovering "two Africans who in dress, speech, and in intellectual power were no different from the British," and in which "the irrationality, inconsistency, and superstition so characteristic of the African and Oriental races" has been replaced by "the three principles basic to the Western mind: ie, the principle of Reason, of Order, and of Measure" (62), Thompson has an epiphany. "In a flash I was convinced that the growth of the British Empire was the development of a great moral idea: it means, it must surely lead to the creation of one British nation, embracing peoples of all colours and creeds, based on the just proposition that all men were created equal" (62). The great equivalent of all peoples is life as such, which can be transformed into the good life, here British subjecthood. *Prospero in Africa* argues "to be English was basically an attitude of mind: it was a way of looking at life, at human relationship, at the just ordering of human society. Was it not possible to reorientate people into this way of life by altering their social and cultural environment" (63)? That the posited bare life of an entire people must be separated from and opposed to it is clear from the way Thompson distinguishes British from French imperialism:

> He was influenced by the French policy of Assimilation, but was critical of the French as he was of what he called Lugard's retrograde concept of Indirect Rule. "We must avoid the French mistake of assimilating only the educated few. The peasant in Asia and Africa must be included in this moral scheme for rehabilitation. In Great Britain we have had our peasant, and now our worker, and they are no less an integral part of our society."
>
> (63)

By disagreeing with Lugard, Thompson declares a continuity between African and British peoples based on the capacity to be transformed from bare life through "rehabilitation," by which Africans will be administered souls, be given that certain British "attitude toward life." One sentence summarizes concisely the biopolitical project: "his faith in British Imperialism had once made him declare: To administer a people is to administer a soul" (63).

Thompson uses the African soldier during World War II as an example to distinguish British imperial nationalism also from Hitler's German nationalism: "Transform the British Empire into one nation: didn't this explain so many things, why, for instance, so many Africans had offered themselves up to die in the war against Hitler?" (63). The world of detention under the Emergency that the novel constructs, however, creates parallels between British and Nazi power over bare life. The terms with which *Prospero in Africa* sets an agenda for managing bare life, "assimilation" and "rehabilitation," appear to belong to civil and cultural orders, but during the Emergency they belong to the order of the state. These words are hinges connecting Britain's civilizing mission to the colonial totalitarian regime created through a state of exception that compromises the empire's self-image as a benevolent liberal democracy.

In recent years, historians have exposed the violence underpinning the British "counterinsurgency myth," the myth that British policy in the colonies was guided by the goal of winning hearts and minds.[32] In her extensive study of the period, the historian Caroline Elkins argues that lacunae in the official archives enabled the British to maintain the myth of the Emergency, a myth that continues into the twenty-first century. That myth is that Britain carried out a liberal democratic mission of rehabilitation of civilian Kikuyu society allegedly torn apart by the military wing, Mau Mau. Elkins reveals that this announced aim of rescue or rehabilitation was a justification and cover for wide-scale eliminationist policies, which were expunged from Britain's historical records—it was only in 2011, in fact, that Britain began to release the documents to the High Court under pressure from the Kenyan government. By reconstructing these years from the other side of official history through interviews, archival fragments, and fieldwork, Elkins establishes that eliminationist policies were executed through the capricious screening of hundreds of thousands of civilians and indefinite detention without trial of tens of thousands of suspects in concentration camps, where torture and other breaches of human rights regularly occurred. Screened civilians moved through transit camps, then were sent to detention villages enclosed by barbed-wire fences overseen by homeguards; these were populated mostly by women and children. An extralegal act under General Lieutenant Baring, what we can call (though Elkins does not) the implementation of a state of exception, institutes all this. "Before Baring and his government were prepared to embark on the campaign for Kikuyu hearts and minds, they needed first to contain and control the entire oath-taking population," Elkins explains. "To this end, the government armed itself with a series of wide-ranging Emergency regulations. Between January and April 1953, Nairobi transformed itself into a totalitarian state."[33]

Although they were certainly sites of torture, and although, as scholars from Hannah Arendt to Enzo Traverso to Achille Mbembe have argued, imperial techniques in Africa and throughout the world predated and provided templates for Nazi orchestrations of power,[34] the camps in Kenya were not deployed in the same ways as the camps in Nazi Germany. The latter were implemented to constitute a pure, uncontaminated German national body through the liquidation of part of that body, the systematic exterminating of peoples who were first systematically stripped of citizenship and all rights. Yet *A Grain of Wheat* suggests that a fear of contamination that drives biopolitics to the center of state politics and transforms the detainee into bare life also inhabits British policy in Kenya. The colonial government attempted to eliminate what it posited as animal, biological life contained within human beings, which was figured by the Mau Mau. "Mau Mau adherents were *scarcely part* of humanity's continuum . . . had to be gotten rid of, regardless of how it was done," Elkins asserts.[35] Thompson's notes on the insurgency and chants of "eliminate the vermin" (a translation of Kurtz's "exterminate all the brutes!") reflect these sentiments while expressing fear that the imperial-national body will be contaminated by the African insurgent:

> *One must use a stick. No government can tolerate anarchy, no civilization can be built on this violence and savagery. Mau Mau is evil: a movement which if not checked will mean complete destruction of all the values on which our civilization has thriven.*
>
> *"Every whiteman is continually in danger of gradual moral ruin in this daily and hourly contest with the African." Dr. Albert Schweitzer.*
>
> (64–65)

Thompson plans to "incorporate" these notes so as to produce a "coherent philosophy in *Prospero in Africa*" (64). By having them contend that the African as "savage" threatens the "white man's" regression from politicized life ("civilization") into bare life after having shown that *Prospero in Africa* also articulates the colonial mission as the inclusive inclusion of bare life through assimilation and rehabilitation, the novel suggests that Thompson's two seemingly oppositional positions can be synthesized into a single colonial treatise because between democratic and totalitarian regimes, "the only real question to be decided was which form of organization would be best suited to the task of assuring the care, control, and use of bare life."[36] Because they illuminated the precarious boundary between civilization and violence, the effects of anticolonial struggle also provoked a fear of contamination in England, where many worried that clashes with Mau Mau were compromising the empire's (mythic) image. Some English newspapers portrayed the counterinsurgency as a manifestation of regressive savagery; others projected these images back onto the insurgents.[37]

Ngũgi writes against the colonialist claims that bare life is the de facto defining feature of the African by exposing that it is a de jure result of the state of exception. The text depicts the detention camp as the place where law and fact enter into a zone of indistinction, creating *homo sacer*, a detainee neither living nor existing as a political animal, nor dead and therefore outside the law. In the camp, "the possibility of deciding on which founds sovereign power . . . is realized normally"[38] because the sovereign no longer refers back to legal codes in order to apply them to a fact. The colonial authorities, however, disavow that they suspend law and fact by invoking the language of law: "They took us to the roads and to the quarries even those who had never done anything," Mugo comments. "They called us criminals. But not because we had stolen anything or killed anyone" (76). Referencing breaches of human rights under the Geneva Convention such as Article 5, which prohibits detention without trial,[39] Gikonyo asks, "Do you know what it was like to live in detention? It was easier, perhaps, with those of us not labeled hardcore, but Mugo was. So he was beaten, and yet would not confess the oath. It was not like prison. . . . In prison, you know your crime. You know your terms. So many years, one, ten, thirty—after that you get out" (32–33). A scene focalized on Gikonyo at Yala camp dramatizes the emergence of *homo sacer*, a subject suspended between life and death:

> He blankly stared into the wire one evening. . . . Slowly and deliberately (he stood outside himself and watched his actions as if from a distance) he pushed his right hand into the wire and pressed his flesh into the sharp metallic thorns. Gikonyo felt the prick into the flesh, but not the pain. He withdrew the hand and watched the blood ooze. . . . In his cell, Gikonyo found that everything—the barbed wire, Yala camp, Thabai—was dissolved into a colourless mist. He struggled to recall the outline of Mumbi's face without success. Was he dead? He put his hand on his chest, felt the heart-beat and knew he was alive. Why, then, couldn't he fix a permanent outline of Mumbi in his mind? . . . He tried to relive the scene in the wood and was surprised to see he could not experience anything; the desire, the full manhood, the haunting voice of Mumbi, the explosion, no feeling came even as a thing of the past. And all this time, Gikonyo watched himself act—his every gesture, his flow of thought. He was both inside and outside himself.
>
> (128–129)

The dissolution of boundaries between inside and outside that the camps spatialize and engender are elucidated as the passage narrativizes the progressive fragmentation of the detainee, the splitting of biological life from social/political life. "Hands" and "blood" are minimally integrated with the subject through use of the possessive pronoun "his" in the first sentence; by the third sentence, the replacement of the pronoun with the article "the" stages a subject separated from his body, to which he relates as detached objects. His failure to recall his wife and their first sexual encounter shows his disconnections from history, desire, and social existence. The interrogative "was he dead?" indexes this social death. By detailing the splitting and suspension between social life and death as a process that unfolds in time in the camp, the passage undermines the colonialist axiom that the detainee is always first bare life, a "fact" that justifies either her forced entry into politicized life through rehabilitation or her exclusion from it. The transformation of the traitor-homeguard Karanja displays the mirror image of this process that occurs in the camp, demonstrating that the constitution of politicized life relies upon the simultaneous positing of bare, or animal, life: "When he shot them ['the many men, terrorists'] they seemed less like human beings and more like animals" (260), an experience that "thrilled Karanja and made him feel a new man, a part of an invisible might whose symbol was the whiteman" (260). Violently creating bare life while trying to eliminate it enables the Kikuyu collaborators to transcend what is portrayed here as the materiality of the animal or biological lifeworld—they accede to British politicized life, "invisible might."

The novel's depiction of the administration of this "invisible might," however, also marks the limits of Agamben's theory of sovereignty for understanding how power operates in the colonial state. *A Grain of Wheat* does portray imperial power as sovereign and exceptional, often by highlighting its mysticism in ways that also echo Conrad's descriptions of the mystical character of Russian autocracy in *Under Western Eyes*. The Mahee police station, for example, is "a symbol of that might which dominated Kenya to the door of every hut" (111); in the camps, "some detainees were beaten, all of them were rigorously questioned by the government agents whose might lay in the very mystery of their title—Special Branch" (121). But the novel also demonstrates that sovereign power is actually entangled with its apparent other: a Kafkaesque bureaucracy. The relationship between sovereignty, power centered and localized in the One, and bureaucracy, power diffused and decentered, is not addressed by Agamben in *Homo Sacer*, but it is by Judith Butler.

Butler argues that in specific situations of counterinsurgency, sovereign power operates through what Foucault calls tactics of governmentality. Foucault asserted that an episteme of governmentality, "understood as the way in which political power manages and regulates populations and goods,"[40] historically replaces that of sovereignty. Agamben, by contrast, locates a renewal of sovereignty in modernity. Revising both positions in her analysis of indefinite detention at Guantanamo Bay after September 11, 2001, Butler proposes that sovereignty and governmentality coexist and reinforce each other: sovereignty reemerges within governmentality to manage bare life. "The suspension of the life of a political animal, the suspension of standing before the law, is itself a tactical exercise, and must be understood in terms of the larger aims of power," she contends. "Governmentality operates through state and non-state institutions and discourses that are legitimated neither by direct elections nor through established authority. . . . Governmentality gains its meaning and purpose from no single source, no unified sovereign subject . . . the tactics operate diffusely . . . in relation to specific policy aims."[41] In the case of the U.S. counterinsurgency, sovereignty reemerges within governmentality under a state of exception primarily in the exercise of prerogative power. Prerogative power is reserved either for the executive branch of government or given to managerial officials with no clear claim to legitimacy, and the policy codeword that often defines this kind of power is "deeming." Deeming refers to discretionary judgments, which take the place of legal protocols requiring the burden of proof. These "procedures of governmentality, which are irreducible to law, are invoked to extend and fortify forms of sovereignty that are equally irreducible to law."[42]

The novel's staging of the British response to resistance during the Kenyan Emergency elaborates how sovereignty and governmentality reinforce each other. Policing and law enforcement in Africa in general was decentralized. This governing model was shorthanded as "always trust the man on the spot." During the Emergency, this model afforded enormous prerogative power to diffuse functionaries.[43] The novel's handling of the imperial response to the detainees' hunger strike at Rira conveys the diffusion of sovereign power. It clarifies that it is not the sovereign Lieutenant Baring whose decides on life and death, and it indicates that it might not even be the ersatz sovereign, Thompson, who decides. At Rira, the detainees "came together and wrote a collective letter listing complaints. . . . They wanted to be treated as political prisoners not criminals. Food rations should be raised. Unless these things were done, they would go on hunger-strike. And indeed on the third day, all the detainees, to a man, sat down on strike" (152). Colonial authorities confront the detainees' use of legal language and demands to occupy the space of law by suspending international law, creating the "Rira disaster." Textual ambiguities make locating the precise source of this suspension challenging if not impossible, however. Although we know that Thompson "set the white officers and warders on the men" (152) in response to the strike, we don't know exactly what this means. What makes things more confusing is that the novel implies this initial response was not the same as the response to the "riot," which causes the deaths:

> Thompson was on the edge of madness. Eliminate the vermin, he would grind his teeth at night. He set the white officers and warders on the men. Yes—eliminate the vermin. But the thing that sparked off the now famous deaths, was a near-riot act that took place on the third day of the strike. As some of the warders brought food to the detainees, a stone was hurled at them and struck one of them on the head. They let go the food and ran away howling murder! Riot! The detainees laughed and let fly more stones. What occurred next is now known to the world. The men were rounded up and locked in their cells. The now famous beating went on day and night. Eleven men died.
>
> (152)

Here and previously, the text suggests that when "the fact leaked out" (46) this bureaucrat might have been scapegoated for force he did not authorize: "*Because he was the officer in charge*, Thompson's name was bandied about in the House of Commons and the world press. . . . He was whisked off to Githima, an exile from the public administration he loved" (54, my emphasis). The orchestration of the event through the use of passive constructions when the novel first mentions it—"a hunger strike, a little beating, and eleven detainees died" (54)—and again in the later scene cited above further allows for the possibility that the warders and white officers acted as sovereigns. The novel also relates elsewhere that power in Kenya is defined by discretionary judgments that consolidate sovereign exception: "What's power? A judge is powerful: he can send a man to death, without anyone questioning his authority, judgment, or harming his body in return. Yes—to be great you must stand in such a place that you can dispense pain and death to others without anyone asking questions. Like a headmaster, a judge, a Governor" (224). During the Emergency, the most widely used practice of prerogative power was the process of screening. This process was a quintessential act of "deeming" as Butler describes it.

The novel's representation of screening leads to an explanation for why the text employs the elliptical strategy. The work relates that not only was the Emergency a crisis of the juridical order, the norming of sovereign exception and management of bare life through tactics of governmentality, but that it was impelled by, and in turn generated, a crisis of testimonial language. Though *A Grain of Wheat* has inspired many debates about its fictional renderings of history, its rendering of the historical deployment of testimony has not been a focus of any.[44] Yet this deployment was a driving force of both the insurgency and the counterinsurgency. The Gikuyu oath founded, bound, and sustained the anticolonial movement; confession to having taken that oath was what the British used to break the insurgency. Screening was the theater in which the conflict between these testimonial modes was dramatized. "Screening" is an English abscess in Gikuyu, an inassimilable term; the Kikuyu never attempt to translate the word.[45] The absence of accountability to rule of law and normative procedures that characterizes prerogative power is strikingly figured in the novel's choreography of screening, where a hidden subject deems whether or not one is an insurgent under no burden of proof: Karanja's "first job was in a hood. The hood—a white sack—covered all his body except the eyes. During the screening operations, people would pass in queues in front of the hooded man. By a nod of the head, the hooded man picked out those involved in Mau Mau" (261). Once screened, the Kikuyu were directed to confess to having taken the Mau Mau oath. Their willingness to do so often determined whether they went to detention villages or to camps and to which type of camp they would be sent. Confessing determined whether they were candidates for rehabilitation or elimination. As Elkins points out, confession was the main technique through which the fate of insurgents was decided. Because the extracting of confession is a central tactic of the counterinsurgency, the elliptical strategy, which asks us to notice that the novel refuses to allow information to be framed this way, can be read as a textual and political act of resistance.

In *Detained: A Writer's Prison Diary*, Ngũgi analyzes the history of detention in Kenya while reflecting on his own detention during the 1970s. He comments on the mysticism the scene of Karanja's hooded screening evokes, arguing that detention shared much in common with Christian ritual, specifically, its use of confession as a pathway to salvation. "It was precisely to deal a blow to the infectious role of those patriotic Kenyans who had rejected a slave consciousness that detention without trial was first introduced in Kenya by the colonial authorities,"[46] he maintains, and he notes that it persists after colonial rule ends. "Unfortunately it is the repressive features of colonial culture . . . that seem to have most attracted the unqualified admiration of the compradors," he writes. "How else can it be explained that the 1966 laws of detention, sedition, and treason, reproduce, almost word for word, those in practice between 1951 and 1961 during the high noon of colonial culture."[47] The "high noon of colonial culture" includes the Emergency, of course. "Detention without trial is not only a punitive act of physical and mental torture of a few patriotic individuals, but it is also a calculated act of psychological terror against the struggling of millions," Ngũgi explains. "It is a terrorist programme for the psychological siege of the whole nation. That is why the practice of detention from the time of arrest to the time of release is deliberately invested with mystifying ritualism."[48] Throughout, *A Grain of Wheat* comments upon this mysticism to criticize confession, which, in *Detained*, Ngũgi confirms was crucial to breaking the anticolonial movement:

> Political detention, not disregarding its punitive aspects, serves a deeper, exemplary ritual symbolism. If they can break such a patriot, if they can make him come out of detention crying, "I am sorry for all my sins," such an unprincipled about-turn would confirm the wisdom of the ruling clique in its division of the populace into the passive innocent millions and the disgruntled subversive few. The "confession" and its corollary, "Father, forgive us for our sins," becomes a cleaning ritual for all the past and current repressive deeds of such a neocolonial regime. . . . such an ex-detainee might even happily play the role of a conscientious messenger from purgatory sent back to earth by a father figure more benevolent than Lazarus's Abraham, "that he may testify unto them (them that dare to struggle), lest they also come into this place of torment."[49]

The depiction of detention under the state of exception is one way the novel accounts for its elliptical strategy. There are two other ways it does so. It relates that not only does confession fail to save one from, or redeem, the past, but that it is also incapable of translating into meaningful terms what the counterinsurgency demands it provide. How the novel makes these points illustrates that confession does not dispel irony in the narrative, as critics maintain it does, but rather is the object of irony.

The Irony of Salvation and the Case of the Differend

A Grain of Wheat emphasizes that confession is wedded to a discourse of salvation that operates not only in secular but religious domains to crush anticolonial resistance throughout Kenyan history. The text is ambivalent toward Christianity; for example, it endorses the language of Christian sacrifice because it forms an alternative to individualism: "In Kenya we want a death which will change things . . . we want a true sacrifice. But first we have to be ready to carry the cross. . . . I die for you, you die for me, we become a sacrifice for one another. . . . Everybody who takes the Oath of Unity to change things in Kenya is a Christ" (110), Kihika claims. Yet the Christian logic of confession comes under attack in various ways. The goal of the revivalist movement, "the only organization allowed to flourish in Kenya by the government during the Emergency" (99) is conversion through confession; "by publically confessing their sins, they became the saved ones" (98). The transformation of its leader in the novel, Reverend Jackson Kigondu, from respected to reviled after he "confessed how he used to minister unto the devil: by eating, drinking and laughing with sinners; by being too soft with the village elders and those who had rejected Christ" (98) suggests that not only is it impossible to separate confession from politics but that attempting to do so only serves imperialism's ends. The insurgents kill this "Christian soldier, marching as to war," who solicits them to confess and see "the light"—that "politics was dirty, worldly wealth a sin" (98). In *Detained*, Ngũgi comments on the legacy of Christianity in Kenya, asserting, "all these eruptions of brutality between the introduction of colonial culture in 1895 and its flowering with blood in the 1950s were not aberrations of an otherwise humane Christian culture," but rather, "they were its very essence, its law, its logic, and the Kenyan settler with his sjambok, his dog, his horse, his rickshaw, his sword, his bullet, was the true embodiment of British imperialism."[50] The novel ironizes the proposition that confession saves in a series of passages that lead to Mugo's revelation of Kihika's whereabouts to Thompson:

> In bed that night, he dreamed that he was back in Rira. A group of detainees were lined up against the wall, naked to the waist. Githua and Gikonyo were among them. From another corner, John Thompson came holding a machine-

> gun at the unfortunate men against the wall. He was going to shoot them—unless they told what they knew about Kihika. All at once, Githua shouted: Mugo save us. The cry was taken by the others: Mugo save us. The suppliant voices rose to a chanting thunder: Mugo save us. And John Thompson had joined the condemned men and he was crying louder than all the others: Mugo save us. How could he refuse, that agonized cry. Here I am, Lord. I am coming, coming, coming, and riding in a cloud of thunder. And the men with one voice wept and cried: Amen.
>
> (146)

While the dream projects that confessing to Thompson will save others, later we learn that Mugo actually believes it will save him from the "burden" of Kihika. In the instant following his confession to Thompson, Mugo feels freed: "This confession was his first contact with another man. He felt deep gratitude to the whiteman, a patient listener, who had lifted his burden from Mugo's heart, who had extricated him from the nightmare" (199). The results are not what Mugo expected, however. Thompson is not a patient listener who can extricate Mugo from this nightmare; he responds to Mugo's confession by spitting in Mugo's face, slapping him, and accusing him of giving false information. The scene concludes with a fearful Mugo regretting having confessed to knowing Kihika's location, for "he did not want to know what he had done" (227). The "burden" of Kihika not only remains but becomes heavier as a consequence of Mugo's confession to Thompson. This is evinced by the fact that Mugo is compelled to confess his betrayal to Mumbi and the village.

The novel also ironizes Mugo's supposedly sacrificial act of confession at the Uhuru celebrations that it claims "saves" Karanja, whom many suspect as Kihika's betrayer. After "the traitor" is called upon to reveal himself, fear prevents Karanja from publicly denying his guilt. He is about to be killed for keeping silent, when suddenly Mugo "had appeared with a confession which relieved Karanja. Mwaura turned to Karanja with eyes tense with malice. 'He has saved you,' Mwaura said" (260). But the salvation Mugo's confession provides is more curse than gift, for Karanja no longer holds the power he held during the Emergency, possesses no family, nor the love of Mumbi. "For what, then, had Mugo saved Karanja? . . . Life was empty and dark like the mist that enclosed the earth" (261). The salvation it promises Mugo is equally deceptive: "as soon as the first words were out, Mugo felt light. A load of many years was lifted from his shoulders. He was free, sure, confident. Only for a minute" (267). Afterward, the novel implies, Mugo is killed by General R. and Lieutenant Koinandu, but even if he is not, he disappears from the community and social existence following his confession.

While other confessions do not result in actual death, they iterate the fracturing experiences of social death in detention. Rather than saving detainees from this past under the Emergency, these "confessions"—never represented in uninterrupted form—make it reemerge. The interrupted and censored treatment of these speech acts, and the figurations of the confessors, emphasize their coercive dimensions and traumatic effects. By eliciting Mugo's confession when she asks "what is wrong?", Mumbi, to whom Mugo confesses as "a submissive penitent," becomes one with the world of detention: "That night he hardly closed his eyes. The picture of Mumbi merged with that of the village and the detention camps" (266). Gikonyo's confession to Mugo that he confessed the oath in the camp also summons the scene it should save him from having to relive: "Gikonyo searched Mugo's face. He could not discern anything. The silence made him uncomfortable. It seemed as if the whole thing was a repetition of a familiar scene" (141). The shame caused by confessing the oath is reactivated and strengthened when Gikonyo confesses to having confessed:

> The weight had been lifted. But guilt of another kind was creeping in. He had laid himself bare, naked, before Mugo. Mugo must be judging him. Gikonyo felt the discomfort of a man standing before a puritan priest. Suddenly he wanted to go, get away from Mugo, and cry his shame in the dark. . . . Mugo's purity, Mumbi's unfaithfulness, everything had conspired to undermine his manhood, his faith in himself, and accentuate his shame at being the first to confess the oath in Yala camp.
>
> (141)

That the passages figure the confessor Mugo alternately as colonial officer and priest insinuates that Christian discourse parallels, and is even complicit with, the Emergency state that harnesses confession to break the insurgency. Moreover, when quasi-confessions are claimed to have occurred, whether Dr. Lynd's recounting of assault and rape to Thompson, Gikonyo's recounting of his anger at the betrayals of Karanja and Mumbi to Mugo, or Mugo's recounting of betraying Kihika to Mumbi, the reaction each time is identical. A single word is used to describe it: a "recoiling" (53, 141, 236, 266) from the confessant, which makes Mugo cave in on himself in turn, "coil with dread" (266).

Confession does not only make the past return rather than unburden one from it while repelling others instead of drawing them closer. It also fails to render the specific experience it must bring forth in order for the confessant to achieve salvation, in the form of release from—and "rehabilitation" by—the colonial state. That experience is embodied in the Mau Mau oath. The demand to confess the oath produces an instance of what Jean-François Lyotard calls the differend, a "case where the plaintiff is divested of the means to argue and for that reason becomes a victim."[51] Lyotard elaborates: "A case of the differend between two parties takes place when the 'regulation' of the conflict that opposes them is done in the idiom of one of the parties while the wrong suffered by the other is not signified in that idiom."[52] *A Grain of Wheat* articulates that a differend is generated in the juridico-legal spaces of Emergency, its screening centers, camps, and detention villages. This is because there the conflict opposing the colonial government and the Kikuyu is regulated in the idiom of the former, who demand testimony to colonial experience in the form of confession, while for the Kikuyu, the wrongs suffered under colonialism are expressed in another, insurgent idiom incompatible with confession.

By eliciting confessions, the state aims to capture and translate into supposedly rational discourse the supposedly irrational behavior of the Kikuyu and enable them to be saved from Mau Mau and themselves, "rehabilitated." The irrationality of the Kikuyu was thought to be crystallized in the Mau Mau oath, derided by the British as "barbaric mumbo jumbo."[53] But while the state claimed the oath was more evidence of "backwardness and savagery of the Kikuyu, the practice had logic and purpose," Elkins explains. "It was the rational response of a rural people seeking to understand the enormous socio-economic and political changes taking place around them while attempting to respond collectively to new and unjust realities."[54] Yet the oath remains shrouded in mystery, in part because what is pledged went beyond the stated goals of the movement: "For those Kikuyu who pledged themselves to Mau Mau, the meanings of land and freedom were less defined and much more complex than merely tossing off the British yoke and reclaiming the land of their ancestors."[55] Indeed, "it was as much the ambiguity as the specificity of Mau Mau's demand for land and freedom that made it so appealing to the Kikuyu masses and such a powerful and difficult movement for the British to suppress."[56] The oath is mysterious also because, although it is not "barbaric," its force defies logic, or, more precisely, it defies the logic underlying the colonial deployment of testimony, which assumes that witnesses control their speech and not vice versa. Many who underwent the oathing ritual and thereby swore allegiance to the insurgency in fact were perjuring themselves: they felt and intended no commitment to the movement. Yet they were still bound by the oath. Oathing was often not chosen but forced, and even brutally so, but "forced oathing did not make the pledge less binding, and in fact the bind of the oath often prevented them—even under torture or threat of death—from betraying the movement."[57] Testimonial discourse here does not obey the laws that the colonial state assumes it does. Committing witnesses beyond and even against their will, the oath relates that this testimony is uncontainable by conscious intention.

The novel demonstrates that the oath cannot be translated into the idiom of colonial regulation of the conflict. Its complexity makes it exceed the frame of confession the state insists it must appear within: "The detainees had agreed not to confess the oath, or give any details about Mau Mau: how could anybody reveal the binding force of the Agikuyu in their call for African freedom?" (121). Delivering this point as a question suggests that it might very well be impossible to reveal this force, that the oath remains outside of the control of anyone who might try to do so. *A Grain of Wheat* not only describes the differend, however. Because it does not offer a single scene in which a confession of oath taking to colonial authorities is represented in narrative time or space, the novel critically enacts the effects of the differend—the impossibility of translating wrongs suffered under colonialism into the terms in which the conflict was regulated.

Together, the elliptical strategy, the exposure of sovereign exception and tactics of governmentality, the ironization of salvation, and the illustration and enactment of the differend challenge received ideas about the novel. Considered in the context of these textual features, ellipsis is not, as some argue, an unmediated reflection of the world of the concentration camp and its silencing of witnesses. But nor is it true that "it is one of the unconscious ironies of *A Grain of Wheat* that its vision of Kenyan national identity relies upon the same confessional logic as that of the colonial torture chamber in the detention camps."[58] The silences that ellipses produce should not be understood exclusively as repressive.[59] By replacing confession, these silences constitute an active critique of imperial law and discourse under the Emergency. This same discourse recurs postindependence when the neocolonial state creates "laws of detention, sedition, and treason [that] reproduce, almost word for word, those in practice between 1951 and 1961"[60] and equally invests detention with "mystifying ritualism" of which confession is a crucial part.[61]

Because the experiences of colonial struggle cannot fit within the discursive frame the dominant establishes and through which it regulates the conflict, it would seem that these experiences are destined to be left unrepresented. The novel, however, passes through the impasse of witnessing it stages. It rejects confession for other formal tactics that it levers against the repressions that create collective amnesia, foment endless cycles of betrayal, and prevent the nation from learning from the past. These tactics attempt to "give the differend its due," as Lyotard puts it. Lyotard asserts that "what is at stake in a literature, in a philosophy, in a politics perhaps . . . is to bear witness to differends by finding idioms for them."[62] Through this alternative, insurgent idiom, the textured and uneven experience of Emergency breaks through the structural containments that organize confessional discourse.

Uncanny Rhetoric and Orature

Writing against the neocolonial policy of national amnesia and the colonial and Christian deployments of confessions, *A Grain of Wheat* illustrates why the Emergency cannot be accessed through the main formal tactic Conrad uses in *Under Western Eyes*. Ngũgi does, however, employ other strategies he attributes to Conrad to address and coax it into narrative. These strategies include "shifting points of view in time and space; the multiplicity of narrative voices; the narrative-within-a-narration; the delayed information that helps the revision of previous judgments so that only at the end with the full assemblage of evidence, information and points of view can the reader make a full judgment."[63] The replacement of a single, unified narrative perspective with multiple perspectives has stood out to readers,[64] but another, less obvious strategy does a different kind of work. What distinguishes this strategy from the well-documented polylogic structure of the novel is that it maps a criticism of violence, both colonial and anticolonial, onto an elaboration of uneven gendering under colonialism and decolonization. This strategy, which I will call uncanny rhetoric, also exposes the limits of confessional discourse for addressing the Emergency.

This textual strategy launches the novel. The opening scene indicates that the history the novel addresses will not lend itself easily to confessional discourse. The events the first paragraph relates resist temporal distinctions between past, present, and future and displace boundaries between fiction and reality and between figural and literal speech—all determinations confession requires if it is to function according to the ends to which Christianity and the colonial state put it.

> Mugo felt nervous. He was lying on his back and looking at the roof. Sooty locks hung from the fern and grass thatch and all pointed at his heart, a clear drop of water was delicately suspended above him. A drop fattened and grew dirtier as it absorbed grains of soot. Then it started drawing towards him. He tried to shut his eyes. They would not close. He tried to move his head: it was firmly chained to the bed-frame. The drop grew larger and larger as it drew closer and closer to his eyes. He wanted to cover his eyes with his palms; but his hands, his feet, everything refused to obey his will. In despair, Mugo gathered himself for a final heave and woke up.
>
> (3)

This passage trembles between past and present, dream and reality, literal and figural dimensions of language, even after the final sentence seems to clear things up. The use of the preterite without additional framing suggests that the events described occur in the narrative present, which the imagery indicates is the time of the Emergency and the space of the detention camp: The drop of water and the chains that fasten Mugo to his bed evoke a cell or even torture chamber, his paralysis the aftereffects of a beating by camp guards. When the passage eventually relates that we are witnessing sleep rather than waking life, it raises more questions. First, are these "literal" dream references to a cell in which Mugo was detained in the past or figurations of the hut while he is sleeping—is sleep what "chains" him to the bed and "paralyzes" him as he semiconsciously registers water dropping from the ceiling before the "final heave" that pulls him out of the last vestiges of sleep? Second, did the violent scene the literal reading of chains, paralysis, and water evokes actually occur in the past, or is it a figure created by dream-work, a condensation or displacement of a moment that never was? Finally, should we jettison this either/or logic altogether and read the episode as a double staging in which past and present and literal and figural and dream and reality coincide: sleep (figuratively) chains him to the bed because chains once also (literally) chained him to the bed, and he fears the drop of water in his semiconscious state because it mimics the waterboarding he experienced in a cell? That "he remained unsettled fearing, as in the dream, that a drop of cold water would suddenly pierce his eyes" (3) and that "he knew that it was only a dream: yet he kept on chilling at the thought of a cold drop falling into his eyes" (4) does not resolve the uncertainty. It does not tell us what to read as literal and what as figural because we do not know quite what "it," the dream, encompasses, beyond the drop of water. Because this passage vacillates between literal and figural, reality and fiction, and various temporalities while settling into none, its referent overflows grammatical and logical constraints imposed by confession as it is deployed in governmental and Christian contexts.

This scene does not merely indicate that confession is inadequate to the task of portraying the history *A Grain of Wheat* addresses; it establishes an idiom through which obscured events will erupt throughout. This idiom is an uncanny rhetoric, a double staging of repression under colonialism and a textual insurgency that breaks through it. I take the definition of rhetoric here from Paul de Man, who defines it as expression that produces an irreducible undecidability between literal and figural dimensions of language and therefore preserves what is said from any single or exhaustive interpretation, any logic that opposes truth with falsity.[65] I take the definition of the uncanny from Freud, who asserts that "this uncanny is in reality nothing new or alien, but which is familiar and old-established in the mind and which has become alienated from it only through the process of repression."[66] This novel's opening scene is uncanny not only because it might describe the return of a repressed in Mugo's mind but, more importantly, because, when the novel rhetorically disarticulates limits between the figural and literal, it both indexes an act of repression under colonialism and translates such events *as* the defamiliarized familiar. By maintaining events' resistance to chronological time even as it places them into the narrative, formally locating them between past, present, and future and as displacing the limits separating these, uncanny rhetoric preserves the alterity of these unexperienced or not fully experienced moments as it texts them. Rather than "recovering" the "true history," therefore, uncanny rhetoric shows that this history defies the logic of truth recovery and portrays it instead as disrupting dominant processes such as confession, which would claim to recover it but instead reduces its complexity and its alterity.

The uncanny also functions as a *theme*, however, and one that is regularly associated with women in the novel, who operate as portals to a past discontinuous with reason. By thematizing women as objects that mediate compulsive returns of the repressed, the text enforces colonialist, patriarchal narratives of modernity and the psyche even while it motivates uncanny rhetoric toward a critique of the cultural logic of imperial modernity.[67] The *Unheimlich*, as Freud describes it, is a feeling that overtakes reason by which the familiar or homey becomes unhomey, defamiliarized. This happens when a past never experienced in the strict sense "reemerges." In Freud's narrative, the privileged example of the theater of the uncanny is the mother's vagina, "the entrance to the former *Heim* of all human beings." While in Freud's case, as in Conrad's and others, the uncanny is aligned with woman-as-mother, Gayatri Spivak has demonstrated that the uncanny's morphology as an othering of the familiar exceeds normative, and norming, narratives that embed it. It can be lifted from such narratives to function as a critical tool that delinks it from patriarchal and colonial axiomatics.[68] The novel both expresses these colonialist and patriarchal narratives of the uncanny and, through rhetoric, delinks its morphology of the defamiliarized familiar from them, providing a countermode to colonial forms of attestation that allows repressed, unauthorized histories to fulminate as narrative ruptures.

The uncanny as a thematic (rather than as an enactment of rhetoric) subjects characters to a compulsive return of a history outside of their control. This is especially true of Mugo, who "allowed himself to drift into things or be pushed into them by an uncanny demon; he rode on the wave of circumstance and lay against the crest, fearing but fascinated by fate" (24). By making women the vehicles of these returns, as well as "uncanny demons" themselves, the novel, as Brendon Nicholls asserts, "articulates Mau Mau at the expense of female articulation and gender-political agency."[69] As sites and midwives of the uncanny, women activate and perpetuate characterological trauma. The old woman of Thabai, Gitogo's mother, occasions Mugo's first encounter with the uncanny. She is at once outside of time yet familiar: "Nobody knew her age: she had always been there, a familiar part of the old and the new village" (6). The text dramatizes the defamiliarization of the familiar by positioning her as mother/not mother to Mugo, whom she mistakes for the ghost of her son, a young man shot when he is misrecognized as an insurgent. Her portrayal invokes the Freudian narrative of the maternal become frightening, *Unheimlich*, "'the name for everything that which ought to have remained secret and hidden . . . but has come to light' (Schelling)."[70] Freud-via-Schelling's sentiment is paraphrased by a proverb voiced through Warui after the alleged return of the old woman's dead son: "those buried in the earth should remain in the earth. Things of yesterday should remain with yesterday" (198). It is the mother, however, not the son, who is the catalyst for disinterment of Mugo's past, for "it was her eyes that most disturbed Mugo. He always felt naked, seen. . . . Mugo felt the woman fix him with her eyes, which glinted with recognition. Suddenly he shivered at the thought that the woman might touch him. He ran out, revolted" (8). Condensing this particularly Freudian formulation of the uncanny as revulsion inspired by contact with the maternal genitals, here metonymized as the eyes, is the equally Freudian formulation of it as confusion of repression for fate: "Perhaps there was something fateful in his contact with the old woman" (8). This "fateful" contact disturbs Mugo "in a way he could not explain. He wandered through the streets thinking about the old woman and that thrilling bond he felt existed between them. Then he tried to dismiss the incident. But as he went on, he found himself starting at the thought of meeting a dead apparition" (198). When Mugo seeks out the old woman for shelter after he confesses to the community, she "claims him" (269) as her own but then transforms into another woman, his dead aunt, also a mother surrogate from Mugo's past: "Suddenly her face had changed. Mugo looked straight into the eyes of his aunt. A new rage moved him. Life was only a constant repetition of what happened yesterday and the day before" (269). The buried past raised through Mugo's encounter with the old woman, along with a past Mumbi raises by recounting it to Mugo, results in madness. "Mugo saw thick blood dripping from the mud walls of his hut . . . he walked to his hut, resolved to find out if the blood was really there" and discovers that "he saw nothing on the walls. . . . Was he cracking in the head? He started at the thought and again looked at the walls" (199).

The novel thematizes women as the return of the repressed in wider, historical terms, to castigate political arrangements in precolonial Kenya as anachronistic instances of British imperialism. Queen Elizabeth is the uncanny repetition of Kikuyu precolonial matriarchs. In both cases, the Law of the Mother is castrating. The earliest missionaries tell of "another country beyond the sea where a powerful woman sat on the throne," whose "shadow of . . . authority and benevolence" (13–14) will soon cover the Agikuyu. The words of the missionary "echoed something in the heart, deep down in their history. It was many, many years ago. The women ruled the land of the Agikuyu. Men had no property, they were only there to serve the whims and needs of the women" (14). The novel places a narrative of female sexual dominance over men onto a narrative of colonial dominance over Africa in order to justify biopolitical domination through the phallus as a form of political resistance. "They waited for women to go to war, they plotted a revolt, taking an oath of secrecy to keep them bound to each in the common pursuit of freedom. They would sleep with all the women at once, for didn't they know the heroines would return hungry for love and relaxation" (14)? The reference to oath-taking in the name of freedom also figures the matriarchy not merely as precursor to, but earlier versions of, imperialism. The plan works, for "Fate did the rest; women were pregnant; the takeover met with little resistance" (14). That matriarchy is traumatic and thus returns is articulated in the next sentence, when it is revealed that "that was not the end of a woman as a power in the land" nor the end of a threatening power. "Years later a woman became a leader and ruled over a large section in Muranga. She was beautiful" (14) and uses her beauty to maintain power. In the first bid for "freedom," men dethrone women by deploying sex toward reproductive ends, and in the second bid, a woman is dethroned for deploying sex toward nonpatriarchal ends—to seduce, rather than reproduce, her male subjects. At one of the dances, the leader disrobes; "for a moment, men were moved by the power of a woman's naked body. The moon played on her: an ecstasy, a mixture of agony and joy hovered on the woman's face . . . a woman never walked or danced naked in public. Wangu Makeri, the last of the great Gikuyu women, was removed from the throne" (14–15). The next manifestation of this ruler will be Queen Elizabeth, who will also castrate her male (colonial) subjects. The Emergency "was all because of a woman—a new Wangu—in England—had been crowned: what good ever came from a woman's rule?" (160), the men ask. When the women retort that, after all, "Governor Baring, who rules Kenya, has a penis" (161), the men have the last word. Colonial domination is once again rewritten as perverse sexuality, an unholy marriage that subverts the Law of the Father by putting the wife in control. "Ah, it's still the woman's shauri. See how all you women have sent the men to detention for their penises to rot there, unwilling husbands to Queen Elizabeth?" (161). The women capitulate to the masculinist interpretation of history: "'And to the forests, too,' the women would burst out, the raillery turning into bitterness" (161). Critics' commendation of the novel's positive depiction of women based on strong female characters[71] must therefore be measured against this thematization of the uncanny, through which women re-present historical trauma and characterological trauma, both coded as the castrating of the African man.

In counterpoint to this repressive thematization of women and the uncanny is uncanny rhetoric, a mode through which women become subjects of attestation and historical change rather than objects of compulsive repetitions that create silences. In a crucial episode, the novel transforms Mumbi from a would-be confessant into a disruptive force whose testimony generates what confessing cannot. The story that interrupts Mumbi's long quasi-confession to Mugo of her marital infidelity—a disclosure that replaces declarations of responsibility with questions and uses a passive verb to displace agency ("I let Karanja make love to me" [171])—forces the impossible to occur. Mumbi relates to Mugo what happens after he is arrested for attempting to save the villager Wambuku from being beaten to death by homeguards as the villagers build a trench. "Mumbi had stopped her narrative to hum the tunes for Mugo" (164), songs the villagers sang defiantly at the trench to reject conditions under the Emergency. The songs inspire the homeguards to beat the Kikuyu with more force. The songs are not only an interruption in Mumbi's process of "confessing" without confessing but produce an interruption in homogenous temporality: "Mugo was rooted to his seat, painfully reliving a scene he never saw, for by that time he had been detained" (164). The oxymoron of the final sentence states precisely the need for what the novel relates confession cannot give: the capacity to "re-live" a past never lived the first time as a future yet to come.

Mumbi's attestation crystallizes what Ngũgi theorizes elsewhere as orature. It performs a collective past as living in self-differentiation rather than frozen into a moment in a linear historical trajectory. The novel's treatment of Gikuyu song does not imply, however, that only "traditional" Gikuyu orality can translate the trauma of the Emergency. Rather than fetishizing custom as culture and divorcing precolonial discursive practices from their endless reworkings throughout time—gestures of the colonized intellectual Fanon famously criticized in *The Wretched of the Earth*[72]—orature performs culture as what attacks constructed barriers between aesthetics and politics as well as between tradition and modernity. In *Globalectics*, Ngũgi explains,

> Performance is the central feature of orature. . . . Performance involves the performer and audience, and in orature, the performer and audience interact. . . . Anywhere from the fireside, village square, and market place to the shrine can serve as the performance space and mise-en-scène. . . .
>
> Orature is not pure metaphysics or a zombie that comes alive only when inhabiting the body of the written and other recorded forms. It is a dynamic living presence in all cultures. In the case of Africa, the authors of the "On the Abolition of the English Department" stressed the fact that "the art did not end yesterday; it is a living tradition," is a presence in religious functions, births, funerals. . . . In the anti-colonial resistance, song and dance played a pivotal role in recruiting, rallying, and coding the social vision. The colonial authorities feared orature more than they did literature.[73]

As orature, Mumbi's performance bears witness to the impossible time of a trauma whose force erupts into an already disrupted quasi "confession" to Mugo. Because it has Mumbi occupy the role of a witness that makes the Emergency signify in a way that interrupts the compulsive returns that victimize Mugo and others, the novel's deployment of orature intercepts the thematic staging of the uncanny that denies both women and men agency to create a future nation that can reverse the social, political, and economic stratifications that structured its past.

Mumbi's performance spurs the staging of uncanny rhetoric, forcing into the narrative what has been repressed—an irreducible bond to others, attachments to the socius of the present and past, which confession fails to illuminate or create. The effects of Mumbi's performance rejects the atomistic and individualist ethos of neocolonial Kenya, for "before Mumbi told her story" Mugo had "seen these huts as objects that had nothing to do with him. . . . Now they were different: the huts, the dust, the trench, Wambuku, Kihika, Karanja, detention-camps, the white fence" (195). Although Mugo "wanted to resume that state, a limbo, in which he was before he heard Mumbi's story and looked into her eyes" (197), orature refuses Mugo's, and Kenyatta's, desires to suppress that past and those connections. The novel relates that "Mumbi's story had cracked open his dulled inside and released imprisoned thought and feelings. . . . Previously, he liked to see events in his life as isolated. Things had been fated to happen at different moments. One had no choice in anything as surely as one had no choice in one's birth. . . . Numbed, he ran without thinking of the road, its origin or its end" (195). This episode and another that follows enact the comingling of past and present, literal and figural dimensions of language shaping the novel's opening scene. Here, it is unclear whether the "road" is literal or a figure for time and history. This turning of time into space and vice versa continues as a topography of mixed temporalities makes it increasingly difficult to determine literal descriptions of the external landscape in the present from figural stagings of mental theaters and the past.

> Mugo abruptly stopped in the middle of the main village street, surprised that he had been walking deeper and deeper into the village. Incidents tumbled on him. He stirred himself with difficulty, to cut a path through the heap. He was again drawn to the trench and seemed impotent to resist this return to yesterday. The walls of the trench were now battered: soil had fallen to the bottom. . . . The whole scene again became alive and vivid. He worked a few yards from the woman. He had worked in the same place for three days. Now a homeguard jumped into the trench and lashed the woman with a whip. Mugo felt the whip eat into his flesh, and her pained whimper was like a cry from his own heart. Yet he did not know her, had for three days refused to recognize those around him as fellow sufferers. Now he only saw the woman, the whip, and the homeguard. Most people continued digging, pretending not to hear the woman's screams, and fearing to meet a similar fate. . . . In terror, Mugo pushed forward and held the whip before the homeguard could hit the woman a fifth time.
>
> (196)

Mumbi's performance coaxes the repressed event to light, which a compelled confession to the colonial officers immediately following the episode in the ditch fails to accomplish: "To Mugo the scene remained a nightmare whose broken and blurred edges he could not pick or reconstruct during the secret screening that later followed" (196). Just as important is how orature summons this event. Neither fully past nor present, it emerges a struggle between two times. Although the passage is delivered in the past tense, the regular interruption of "nows" demonstrates the past fighting to erupt into the present.

Women figure as potentiates of historical change not only because they force a confrontation with history in crisis while answering the demands of the insurgency in various ways but also because they expose and disrupt the repetition of colonial violence haunting anticolonial struggle. The novel departs from ways that Ngũgi claims Fanon's *The Wretched of the Earth* has been misread and misappropriated.[74] "The violence which governed the ordering of the colonial world, which tirelessly punctuated the destruction of the indigenous social fabric, and demolished unchecked the systems of reference of the country's economy, lifestyles, and modes of dress," Fanon writes, "this same violence will be vindicated and appropriated when taking history into their own hands, the colonized swarm into the forbidden cities."[75] Both the plotting of women and their figuration through uncanny rhetoric insinuate that retributive violence connects the anticolonial movement too closely to the orders it opposes and reject violence as a method with which to manage betrayals.

By demanding one speak in the idioms of law, confessions, and trials, the Mau Mau justify retributive violence by attaching its orchestration to the legal process, thereby raising the specter of British deployments of law and violence under the Emergency. Women highlight, question, and interrupt acts of retributive violence in response to betrayal. Mumbi, for example, warns her enemy Karanja to stay away from the Uhuru celebration where his life will be threatened unless he confesses (and if he confesses), and she also declines to publicize Mugo's confession in an attempt to stop the cycle of violence: "I did not want anything to happen. I never knew that he would later come to the meeting" (275). Mugo's trial at the end of the novel also functions as means of retribution, and as such, it invokes the trial of Jomo Kenyatta.[76] Like confessions throughout the work, the trial is replaced by an ellipsis. After General R. and Lieutenant Koinandu announce the "trial will be held tonight" and assure Mugo, "your deeds alone will condemn you" (270), as they lead him out of the hut, the next we hear of the trial is after Mugo has gone missing. Only General R. and Lieutenant Koinandu are said to have been present at the trial over which the elder woman Wambui presides. This judge, whose "fighting spirit" (204) is legendary for maintaining that "women had to act. Women had to force the issue" (204), and for unifying the workers at the party meeting for the worker's strike in 1950, questions whether the trial should have taken place at all, in light of Mugo's subsequent disappearance and probable execution. Wambui was "lost in a solid consciousness of a terrible anti-climax to her activities in the fight for freedom. Perhaps we should not have tried him, she muttered" (275–276). By suggesting that the protocols of law provide a cover or even justification for killing, Wambui's statement connects the violence of the anticolonial movement to that of the Emergency state.

While the original version of the novel warns against the repetition of colonial violence in the future in various ways, the revised version makes heavy changes to two successive passages, which suggests that Ngũgi responded to criticism of his initial portrayal of Mau Mau while maintaining and highlighting a critique of violence against women the original version delivers. These changes make these passages reflect on each other, and in so doing, they hold colonialism as well as anticolonial movements accountable for violence and indicate that the new nation must interrupt this cycle of violence to cast off a colonial legacy. In the 1967 text, General R., whose real name is Muhoya, defended his mother from beatings by his father, "a petty tyrant" (241), but his mother "took a stick and fought on her husband's side" (241), insisting that patriarchal order must be maintained: "He is your father, and my husband" (241). Changes to three sentences connect African patriarchal violence to colonial violence against an entire people. In the revised edition of the novel, Muyoha's father "graduated from an ordinary colonial messenger into petty assistant chief" (211), and when they are locked in battle, he is described not as a "petty tyrant" but "a petty colonial tyrant" (212). The final sentence Ngũgi adds to this paragraph picks up on the reconfigured descriptions of the father, conveying that that instance of submission to patriarchy, depicted as pathological, becomes an allegory of colonial submission: "It was only later when he saw how so many Kenyans could proudly defend their slavery that he understood his mother's reaction."[77] Read as a response to criticisms of Ngũgi's exaggeration of excessive Mau Mau violence, these amendments indicate that there is a structural nature to it, and its source is colonialism. Turning violence toward women into the privileged metaphor through which to represent both colonial violence and the stymieing of the anticolonial spirit insinuates an ironic critique of the episode that follows. That episode justifies anticolonial violence expressed specifically in terms of violence against women and imagines the postcolony's new order as African patriarchy.

Here, the uncanny operates not within the patriarchal and colonial narrative but as a rhetorical defamiliarization of the familiar that indicates that anticolonial violence reinstates colonialism as patriarchy. Lieutenant Koinandu reflects with satisfaction on his assaults on his former employer Dr. Lynd, the white woman he rapes and whose beloved dog he hacks to death after leading insurgents into her house to steal her guns. The revised version of the novel suggests again that Ngũgi responds to critics by rewriting the scene in a way that leaves unclear whether a rape occurs, although most read this rape as entirely absent.[78] But both versions' treatments of this episode suggest that Mau Mau violence reflects Kikuyu patriarchal violence against women, itself a reflection of colonial power, as the preceding episode cited above relates. The revised version adds a staging of uncanny rhetoric that substitutes for the rape scene in the original. After adding into the text Koinandu's claim that "Independence, when finally won, would right all the wrongs, would drive the likes of Dr. Lynd and her dogs from the country. Kenya after all was a black man's country . . . he was going to enter the forest in triumph over Dr. Lynd" (213), in order to substitute for the rape, the revised version also troubles this vision of a patriarchal future by establishing that it conditions the compulsive repetition of the past.

> In the years of hardships and deaths on the battlefield he had almost forgotten the incident, until the other day when he went to Githima to see Mawaura about plans to lure Karanja into attending Uhuru celebrations. And there in front of him was Dr. Lynd and her dog. She stood there as if mocking him: See me, I have still got the big house, and my property has even multiplied. Githima had not in fact changed much. The exclusive white settlement seemed to have grown bigger instead. . . . Why were all these whites still in Kenya despite the ringing of the Uhuru bells? Would Uhuru really change things for the likes of him and General R? . . . Dr. Lynd's unyielding presence became an obsession. It filled him with fear, a kind of premonition. He had tried to share those thoughts with General R. but he could not find the words. . . . Even now, as he ran, the

> thought of the unexpected encounter made him shudder. The ghost had come to eat into his life.
>
> (214)

This scene, like the others, oscillates between literal and figural, past and present, memory and delusion. We cannot determine if Lynd's "unyielding presence" is literal or figural and whether Lynd literally appeared before Koinandu with her dog in Githima or figuratively appears in his mind as a "ghost." For it is disclosed earlier in the revised version of the novel that Koinandu killed the dog and that Lynd has a new pet. Mau Mau violence against Lynd, and the colonizer generally, seems only to have strengthened the latter's control and increased their domains. Uncanny rhetoric, the spectral return of Dr. Lynd, enables these fears to be represented, which confession to General R., the passage implies—again by invoking ellipsis—cannot. That the specter of Lynd appears when another act of retributive violence is planned, the killing of Karanja, underscores the role of women through, and as, uncanny rhetoric in disrupting the compulsive repetitions of violence. Ngũgi's rewriting of this scene and the one cited above demonstrates his desire to link anticolonial violence to the oppression of women as well as elucidates that it repeats and strengthens a colonial legacy.

By finding a new idiom for the Emergency through uncanny rhetoric, *A Grain of Wheat* does not only pass through the impasse generated by the differend by bearing witness to the Emergency; it also elaborates that in order for a postcolonial Kenya to emerge, the cycles of patriarchy and violence must be disrupted. Moreover, by detaching the uncanny from the colonial and heteronormative narratives of psychoanalysis the work references in its presentation of character, the text's formal tactics bestow ethical and political value on a discourse of the unverifiable. Form highlights the value of testimony as an act discontinuous with proof. Uncanny rhetoric cannot capture the event in itself, a project the novel's polylogic structure rejects from the outset, just as it suggests that the past attains value and meaning through its multiple retellings.[79] Instead, this spectral orchestration that suspends temporal, spatial, external, and internal indices instructs us that there is no event "in itself" that fits into a chronology. It preserves the unexperienced experience of the trauma in its alterity. But most important, the novel procures the hazy, secluded, secretive scenes of this era without either retreating from bearing witness and lapsing into silence, which the elisions of confession suggest it will, or capitulating to, even negotiating with, the colonial language of confession. The novel "institute[s] new addresses, new addressors, new significations, and new referents in order for the wrong to find an expression and for the plaintiff to cease being a victim."[80] Through formal tactics motivated toward restoring agency for those denied it under colonialism, insurgency, and counterinsurgency, *A Grain of Wheat* finds a way to give the differend its due.

NOTES

INTRODUCTION. CHALLENGING RUPTURES: TESTIMONIAL INSURGENCIES, SPECTRAL WITNESSES

1. The epigraph to this chapter is from Walter Benjamin, "Theses on the Philosophy of History," in *Illuminations*, trans. Harry Zohn (New York: Schocken, 1968), 255.

2. There are very few investigations into modernism and testimony, and those that exist have focused mostly on censorship trials or copyright law. The two most significant contributions are Paul K. Saint-Amour's *The Copywrights: Intellectual Property and the Literary Imagination* (Ithaca, N.Y.: Cornell University Press, 2003) and *Modernism and Copyright*, ed. Paul K. Saint-Amour (Oxford: Oxford University Press, 2010). Two important exceptions are Ravit Reichman's analysis of Virginia Woolf, Hannah Arendt, and Rebecca West, which addresses questions of trauma through the legal category of injury: *The Affective Life of Law: Legal Modernism and the Literary Imagination* (Stanford, Calif.: Stanford University Press, 2009) and Rex Ferguson's examination of how criminal law shapes the modernism of E. M. Forster, Ford Maddox Ford, and Marcel Proust in *Criminal Law and the Modernist Novel: Experience on Trial* (Cambridge: Cambridge University Press, 2013).

3. Among the most canonical studies that constituted the field of trauma and memory studies are Shoshana Felman and Dori Laub, *Testimony: Crises of Witnessing in Literature, Psychoanalysis, and History* (New York: Routledge, 1992); Cathy Caruth, *Unclaimed Experience: Trauma, Narrative, and History* (Baltimore, Md.: Johns Hopkins University Press, 1996); Geoffrey H. Hartman, *The Longest Shadow: In the Aftermath of the Holocaust*, Helen and Martin Schwartz Lectures in Jewish Studies (Bloomington: Indiana University Press, 1996); Dominick LaCapra, *Writing History, Writing Trauma* (Baltimore, Md.: Johns Hopkins University Press, 2001); and Giorgio Agamben, *Remnants of Auschwitz: The Witness and the Archive*, trans. Daniel Heller-Roazen (New York: Zone, 2000).

4. Paul Fussell, *The Great War and Modern Memory* (New York: Oxford University Press, 1975); Modris Eksteins, *Rites of Spring: The Great War and the Birth of the Modern Age* (Boston: Houghton Mifflin, 1989); Samuel Lynn Hynes, *A War Imagined: The First World War and English Culture* (London: Bodley Head, 1990); Sandra M. Gilbert, "Soldier's Heart: Literary Men, Literary Women, and the Great War," in *No Man's Land: The Place of the Woman Writer in the Twentieth Century*, ed. Sandra M. Gilbert and Susan Gubar (New Haven, Conn.: Yale University Press, 1989); Margaret R. Higonnet, *Nurses at the Front: Writing the Wounds of the Great War* (Boston: Northeastern University Press, 2001); Vincent Sherry, *The Great War and the Language of Modernism* (Oxford: Oxford University Press, 2003); Trudi Tate, *Modernism, History, and the First World War* (Manchester: Manchester University Press, 1998).

5. Fussell, *The Great War and Modern Memory*, 21–23.

6. Carl Krockel, *War Trauma and English Modernism: T. S. Eliot and D. H. Lawrence* (Basingstoke: Palgrave Macmillan, 2011).

7. Although Lecia Rosenthal also focuses on World War I in her chapter on Virginia Woolf's *To the Lighthouse* in *Mourning Modernism: Literature, Catastrophe, and the Politics of Consolation* (New York: Fordham University Press, 2011), she argues that modernist periodization is disrupted by the aesthetics of the late sublime: "Reading Kant's elaboration of the war sublime alongside the anticipatory finality of a 'war to end all war,' I situate the emergence of modernism within the competing discourses of violence and the end of violence, fragmentation and privative totality, individual death and species survival" (5).

8. Jay Winter, *Sites of Memory, Sites of Mourning: The Great War in European Cultural History* (Cambridge: Cambridge University Press, 1995), 3–5.

9. Fredric Jameson, *A Singular Modernity: Essays on the Ontology of the Present* (London: Verso, 2002), 24.

10. Fredric Jameson, "Modernism and Imperialism," in *Nationalism, Colonialism, and Literature*, ed. Fredric Jameson, Edward Said, and Terry Eagleton (Minneapolis: University of Minnesota Press, 1990).

11. Among these see, for example, Simon Gikandi, *Maps of Englishness: Modernism and National Culture in England* (Princeton, N.J.: Princeton University Press, 1996); Jed Esty, *A Shrinking Island: Modernism and National Culture in England* (Princeton, N.J.: Princeton University Press, 2003); Nicholas Brown, *Utopian Generations: The Political Horizon of Twentieth-Century Literature* (Princeton, N.J.: Princeton University Press, 2005); Peter J. Kalliney, *Cities of Affluence and Anger: A Literary Geography of Modern Englishness* (Charlottesville: University of Virginia Press, 2006); Laura Winkiel, *Modernism, Race, and Manifestos* (Cambridge: Cambridge University Press, 2008); Mary Lou Emery, *Modernism, the Visual, and Caribbean Literature* (Cambridge: Cambridge University Press, 2009); Matthew Hart, *Nations of Nothing but Poetry: Modernism, Transnationalism, and Synthetic Vernacular Writing* (Oxford: Oxford Univer-

sity Press, 2010); Christopher GoGwilt, *The Passage of Literature: Genealogies of Modernism in Conrad, Rhys, and Promoedya* (New York: Oxford University Press, 2010); and Urmila Seshagiri, *Race and the Modernist Imagination* (Ithaca, N.Y.: Cornell University Press, 2010).

12. Jameson, *A Singular Modernity*, 34.

13. Ibid., 12–13.

14. Ibid., 40.

15. Ibid., 15.

16. An exhaustive analysis of how trauma returns throughout Freud's works is offered in Ruth Leys, *Trauma: A Genealogy* (Chicago: University of Chicago Press, 2000).

17. On the former, see Irene Visser, "Trauma Theory and Postcolonial Literary Studies," *Journal of Postcolonial Writing* 47, no. 3 (2011): 170–182; on the latter, see Lauren Berlant, *Cruel Optimism* (Durham, N.C.: Duke University Press, 2011).

18. Benjamin, *Illuminations*, 262–263.

19. Walter Benjamin, *The Arcades Project*, trans. Howard Eiland and Kevin McLaughlin (Cambridge, Mass.: Harvard University Press), 458.

20. Benjamin, *Illuminations*, 255.

21. For a critical assessment of the debates about the Shoah as singular traumatic event see Michael Rothberg, *Multidirectional Memory: Remembering the Holocaust in the Age of Decolonization* (Stanford, Calif.: Stanford University Press, 2009), 1–29.

22. Rothberg, *Multidirectional Memory*, 11.

23. *Rebecca West Today: Contemporary Critical Approaches*, ed. Bernard Schweizer (Newark: University of Delaware Press, 2006), 26.

24. For a thorough reading of these topics in West's work, see Marina MacKay, *Modernism and World War II* (Cambridge: Cambridge University Press, 2007).

25. http://www.theatlantic.com/politics/archive/2013/02/obamas-memo-on-killing-americans-twists-imminent-threat-like-bush/272862/.

26. On the contact zone as site of transcultural encounter, see Mary Louise Pratt, *Imperial Eyes: Travel Writing and Transculturation* (London: Routledge, 1992). The scholar who has made "missed encounter" the central term by which to understand trauma is Cathy Caruth, in *Unclaimed Experience*.

27. This is particularly pronounced in explorations of modernist and postmodernist works and trauma. For example, Anne Whitehead analyzes formally experimental contemporary works and argues that "novelists have frequently found that the impact of trauma can only adequately be represented by mimicking its forms and symptoms, so that temporality and chronology collapse, and narratives are characterized by repetition and indirection" *Trauma Fiction* (Edinburgh: Edinburgh University Press, 2004), 3. In *The Edge of Modernism:*

American Poetry and the Traumatic Past (Baltimore, Md.: Johns Hopkins University Press, 2006), Walter Kaladjian distinguishes between "banal" language and the figural language he associates with the American poets whose work he examines: "The ways in which the formal resources of the poet's craft—its figurative language, its reliance on catachresis (mixed and contradictory metaphors), aposiopesis (or invoked interruptions of absence and silence, often through ellipsis), anacoluthon (non sequiturs and shifting patterns of syntax), its grammatological techniques and the spatial arrangement on the page—together forge a salutary medium for staging traumatic histories in ways that resist the banal spectacle of the image world otherwise governing contemporary consumer society" (11).

28. Raymond Williams, "Metropolitan Perceptions and the Emergence of Modernism," in *The Politics of Modernism: Against the New Conformists*, ed. Tony Pinkney (London: Verso, 1989), 37–48.

29. This model informs not only Pascale Casanova's argument in *The World Republic of Letters* (Cambridge, Mass.: Harvard University Press, 2007) but also David Damrosch's in *What Is World Literature* (Princeton, N.J.: Princeton University Press, 2003).

30. Jessica Berman, *Modernist Commitments: Ethics, Politics, and Transnational Modernism* (New York: Columbia University Press, 2011), 7. The terms ethics and "politics" that animate my readings, even when these terms are not explicitly used, derive from a less pluralistic philosophico-theoretical grouping than that of Berman's *Modernist Commitments*, which employs a language of reciprocity and selfhood in a critical project that attempts to create a "transition to politics and action from ethics" (21). My approach to the ethical and political is influenced by critiques of this language. I am inspired by and share Berman's desire to avoid totally disassociating the ethical and the political, but in place of searching for a transition between them managed through narrative, I will argue that testimony, as what occurs in narrative, also interrupts narrative.

31. For an excellent, sustained complication of these two positions, see the collection *Modernism and Colonialism: British and Irish Literature, 1899–1939*, ed. Richard Begam and Michael Valdez Moses (Durham, N.C.: Duke University Press, 2007).

32. Brown, *Utopian Generations*.

33. Paul K. Saint-Amour, "Weak Theory and Global Modernism," keynote delivered at Global Modernisms: A Symposium, Ithaca College, April 2014.

34. Casanova, *The World Republic of Letters*.

35. On modernism and transnationalism, in addition to Berman, *Modernist Commitments*; and Hart, *Nations of Nothing But Poetry*; see also Laura Doyle and Laura Winkiel, eds., *Geomodernisms: Race, Modernism, Modernity* (Bloomington: Indiana University Press, 2005); Rebecca Walkowitz, *Cosmopolitan Style: Modernism Beyond the Nation* (New York: Columbia University Press, 2006); Jahan Ramazani, *A Transnational Poetics* (Chicago: University of Chi-

cago Press, 2009); Pamela L. Caughie, ed., *Disciplining Modernism* (New York: Palgrave, 2010); Paul Jay, *Global Matters: The Transnational Turn in Literary Studies* (Ithaca, N.Y.: Cornell University Press, 2010); Susan Stanford Friedman, "Why Not Compare?" *PMLA* 126, no. 3 (May 2011): 753–762; Susan Stanford Friedman, "Planetarity: Musing Modernist Studies," *Modernism/ Modernity* 17, no. 3 (September 2010): 471–499; Saikat Majumdar, *Prose of the World: Modernism and the Banality of Empire* (New York: Columbia University Press, 2013). On world literature, see David Damrosch, *What Is World Literature*; Pascale Casanova, *The World Republic of Letters*; Franco Moretti, *Graphs, Maps, Trees: Abstract Models for Literary History* (New York: Verso, 2007). On world literature and postcoloniality, see Natalie Melas, *All the Difference in the World: Postcoloniality and the Ends of Comparison* (Stanford, Calif.: Stanford University Press, 2007); Peter Hitchcock, *The Long Space: Transnationalism and Postcolonial Form* (Stanford, Calif.: Stanford University Press, 2009); Andrew Rubin, *Archives of Authority: Empire, Culture, and the Cold War* (Princeton, N.J.: Princeton University Press, 2012); and Emily Apter, *Against World Literature: On the Politics of Untranslatablilty* (London: Verso, 2013).

36. Others have challenged the transnational or global turn in recent literary studies in various ways. Pheng Cheah argues that the privileging of cosmopolitanism over nationalism in literary and cultural studies is premised on a false opposition between the two modes of sociality and on a reduction of the nation to an epiphenomenon of the state. This reduction, along with the postnationalist reception of the "distending of the hyphen in contemporary globalization as a sign of the disintegration of both nation and state" overlooks the contingencies that determine what ethical and political work either cosmopolitanism or nationalism can perform at a given historical moment, especially in the context of imperial and neoimperial world orders. Pheng Cheah, *Inhuman Conditions: On Cosmopolitanism and Human Rights* (Cambridge, Mass.: Harvard University Press, 2007), 36. From another perspective, Étienne Balibar has shown that the emergence of transnational economic alliances such as the European Union have actually inspired a closing of national borders within Europe along with the development of new nationalisms that deploy the language of ethnic belonging to stigmatize immigration and multiculturalism. Étienne Balibar, *We, the People of Europe? Reflections on Transnational Citizenship*, trans. James Swenson (Princeton, N.J.: Princeton University Press, 2004). And Peter Hitchcock criticizes the growth of "world literature" studies as another form of homogenizing global capitalism; it allows one to "consume postcolonialism without that nasty taste of social struggle in which a reader's own cosmopolitanism may be at stake." Hitchcock, *The Long Space*, 5.

37. In addition to Michael Rothberg's *Multidirectional Memory*, see Victoria Burrows, *Whiteness and Trauma: The Mother-Daughter Knot in the Fiction of Jean*

Rhys, Jamaica Kincaid, and Toni Morrison (Basingstoke: Palgrave Macmillan, 2004); Anne Whitehead, *Trauma Fiction*; Sam Durrant, *Postcolonial Narrative and the Work of Mourning: J. M. Coetzee, Wilson Harris, and Toni Morrison* (Albany: State University of New York Press, 2004); Gabriele Schwab, *Haunting Legacies: Violent Histories and Transgenerational Trauma* (New York: Columbia University Press, 2010); and Stef Craps, *Postcolonial Witnessing: Trauma out of Bounds* (New York: Macmillan, 2013).

38. Schwab, *Haunting Legacies*, 29.

39. The first is "Violence and Metaphysics: An Essay on the Thought of Emmanuel Levinas," in *Writing and Difference*, trans. Alan Bass (Chicago: University of Chicago Press, 1978), 79–195.

40. Jacques Derrida, *Adieu: To Emmanuel Levinas*, trans. Pascale-Anne Brault and Michael Naas (Stanford, Calif.: Stanford University Press, 1999), 33.

41. Joseph Slaughter, *Human Rights, Inc.: The World Novel, Narrative Form, and International Law* (New York: Fordham University Press, 2007), 10.

42. Felman and Laub, *Testimony*, 5.

43. As Étienne Balibar writes, "Every social community reproduced by the functioning of institutions is imaginary, that is to say, based on the projection of individual existence into the weft of a collective narrative, on the recognition of a common name and on traditions lived as the trace of an immemorial past (even when they have been fabricated and inculcated in the recent past)." "The Nation Form: History and Ideology," in Étienne Balibar and Immanuel Wallerstein, *Race, Nation, Class: Ambiguous Identities* (London: Verso, 1992), 93–94. Benedict Anderson's definition is of the nation "as an imagined political community, both inherently limited and sovereign. It is imagined because the members of even the smallest nation will never know most of their fellow-members, meet them, or even hear of them, yet in the minds of each lives the image of their communion." Benedict Anderson, *Imagined Communities: Reflections on the Origin and Spread of Nationalism*, rev. ed. (London: Verso, 2006), 6.

44. For example, see Sinkwan Cheng, "The Female Body as a Post-Colonial Site of Political Protest: The Hunger Strikers Versus the Labor Strikers in Forster's *A Passage to India*," in *Law, Justice, and Power: Between Reason and Will*, ed. Sinkwan Cheng (Stanford, Calif.: Stanford University Press, 2004), 115–136; Kieran Dolin, *Fiction and the Law: Legal Discourse in Victorian and Modern Literature* (Cambridge: Cambridge University Press, 1999); Richard Clarke Sterne, "The Trial in *A Passage to India*: 'Justice' Under Colonial Conditions," in *Un-Disciplining Literature: Literature, Law, and Culture*, ed. Kostas Myrsiades and Linda Myrsiades (New York: Peter Lang, 1999); and Ferguson, *Criminal Law and the Modernist Novel*, 51–82.

45. Giorgio Agamben, *State of Exception*, trans. Kevin Attell (Chicago: University of Chicago Press, 2005), 6–7.

46. Ibid., 7.

47. Ibid.

48. Agamben does point to England's passage of the Emergency Powers Act in October 1920 but does not discuss the Rowlatt Acts in India as an effect of a wider shift in modernity's deployment of states of exception.

49. E. M. Forster, *A Passage to India* (New York: Harvest, Harcourt, 1984), 22. Hereafter cited in the text.

50. Edward W. Said, *Culture and Imperialism* (New York: Knopf, 1993); and Sara Suleri, *The Rhetoric of English India* (Chicago: University of Chicago Press, 1992).

51. See Brian May, who argues against the charges by formative readings such as that of Said's and Suleri's that the novel's symbolic strategies underwrite imperialism. May's reading of the countersymbolic complicates the relationship between modernism and colonialism. "The three competing modes of putatively imperialist representation at work in *A Passage to India*, the trio that I will distinguish and whose conflictual relationships I will examine—impressionism, elementalism, apocalypticism—are significantly 'modernist' modes of representation. To distinguish these modes as such, and to identify the kinds of work that they do, severally and together, is to begin to redefine the relationship between modernism and colonialism as intricate and conflicted. And certainly, this is a worthy task, given how often the complexities in this relationship have been overlooked." "Romancing the Stump: Modernism and Colonialism in Forster's *A Passage to India*," in *Modernism and Colonialism*, 137.

52. Jenny Sharpe, *Allegories of Empire: The Figure of Woman in the Colonial Text* (Minneapolis: University of Minnesota Press, 1993).

53. Conrad, *Heart of Darkness* (New York: Norton, 2005), 12.

54. Forster wrote and deleted the rape scene, a deletion that has produced conflicting commentaries about the text's management of race and gender politics under anticolonial revolt. Jenny Sharpe acknowledges that many feminist critics read this deletion as another instance of repression of female agency, agency expressed in the fact that Adela fights off her attacker. Sharpe argues, however, that reading this novel in relation to discourses of the Indian Mutiny of 1857 indicates that the withdrawal of the rape scene exposes colonial truths about the mutiny as fictions. "By generating its narrative desire through the indeterminate status of a sexual assault, *A Passage to India* drives a wedge of doubt between a colonial discourse of rape and its object . . . when situated within the racial memory of the Mutiny, Adela's extension and withdrawal of the charge interrupt a plotting that establishes a causal relation between the native assault of English women and British suppression of the rebellion." *Allegories of Empire*, 124–125.

55. Pericles Lewis challenges this paradigm: "If the novel is indeed the characteristic art form of secularization, in Lukács's words, 'the representative art form of our age,' and if modernity is indeed a secular age, we might expect

the modernist novel to be doubly secular," but he disagrees by demonstrating that modernists' "quest for a modern form of the 'secular sacred' underwrote many of their experiments with form and technique; in particular, they sought the means to combine naturalistic descriptions of the visible world, such as those that the great realist novelists of the nineteenth century had offered, with spiritual insight of the kind found in the symbolist poets. If God died in the nineteenth century, he had an active afterlife in the twentieth." Pericles Lewis, *Religious Experience and the Modernist Novel* (Cambridge: Cambridge University Press, 2010), 23, 25.

56. See Paul de Man's "Autobiography as De-Facement," in *The Rhetoric of Romanticism* (New York: Columbia University Press, 1984), 67–81.

57. Jacques Derrida, *Specters of Marx: The State of the Debt, the Work of Mourning, and the New International*, trans. Peggy Kamuf (New York: Routledge, 1994), 151.

58. Slaughter, *Human Rights, Inc.*, 10.

59. Dolin, *Fiction and the Law*, 185.

60. Said, *Culture and Imperialism*, 203.

61. On the distinction between the subaltern and the popular, see Gayatri Chakravorty Spivak, "Scattered Speculations on the Subaltern and the Popular," in *An Aesthetic Education in the Era of Globalization* (Cambridge, Mass.: Harvard University Press, 2012): 429–443.

62. R. Radhakrishnan, "Why Compare?" *New Literary History* 40, no. 3 (Summer 2009): 459.

63. Ibid., 465.

64. Ibid., 471.

65. Georges Bataille, Jean-Luc Nancy, and Maurice Blanchot have argued that the peculiar "experience" by which friendship is claimed through a speech that separates each party from themselves and each other and thus questions whether friendship is continuous with determinacy or experience, especially during a time of political conflict, indicates friendship as a sign of the ethical. Georges Bataille, *Guilty*, trans. Stuart Kendall (Albany: State University of New York Press, 2011); Jean-Luc Nancy, *The Inoperative Community*, ed. Peter Connor, trans. Peter Connor, Lisa Garbus, Michael Holland, and Simona Sawhney (Minneapolis: University of Minnesota Press, 1991); Maurice Blanchot, *The Unavowable Community*, trans. Pierre Joris (Barrytown, N.Y.: Station Hill, 1988). On parabola and friendship, see Jacques Derrida, *The Politics of Friendship*, trans. George Collins (London: Verso, 1997).

66. Laura Winkiel, "The Utopian Aspect of Transnational Comparison," *English Language Notes* 49, no. 1 (Spring/Summer 2011): 148.

67. Ibid.

68. Jane Gallop, "The Historicization of Literary Studies and the Fate of Close Reading," *Profession* (2007): 185.

1. COMPELLED CONFESSIONS AND FORCED ATTACHMENTS IN JOSEPH CONRAD'S UNDER WESTERN EYES AND "POLAND REVISITED"

1. Joseph Conrad, *Under Western Eyes*, ed. Jeremy Hawthorn (Oxford: Oxford University Press, 2003), 3. Hereafter cited in the text.

2. Joseph Conrad, *A Personal Record* (Garden City, N.Y.: Doubleday, 1925), 94–95.

3. Ibid., 95.

4. Christopher GoGwilt, *The Invention of the West: Joseph Conrad and the Double-Mapping of Europe and Empire* (Stanford, Calif.: Stanford University Press, 1995), 27.

5. See Eloise Knapp Hay, *The Political Novels of Joseph Conrad: A Critical Study* (Chicago: University of Chicago Press, 1963).

6. Stephen Ross, *Conrad and Empire* (Columbia: University of Missouri Press, 2004), 187. Ross argues that Conrad presciently sees through "the field of imperialism," still organized under the authority of nation-states, to expose the homogenizing system of deterritorialization and commercialization that exceeds its scope, "the larger, incipiently global, movement of Imperial modernity itself" (6).

7. GoGwilt, *The Invention of the West.*

8. Rebecca Walkowitz, *Cosmopolitan Style: Modernism Beyond the Nation* (New York: Columbia University Press, 2006).

9. John Marx, *The Modernist Novel and the Decline of Empire* (Cambridge: Cambridge University Press, 2005), 25–58.

10. Kwame Anthony Appiah, *Cosmopolitanism: Ethics in a World of Strangers* (New York: Norton, 2006), 7–8. Although cosmopolitanism is a concept with many referents, a critical attitude toward a perceived narrowness of belonging associated with nationalism tends to be a common feature of many conceptualizations. Scholars have explored how British modernist writing is informed by versions of this paradigm, including Conrad's. In addition to Walkowitz, *Cosmopolitan Style*; and Marx, *The Modernist Novel and the Decline of Empire*, see also Laura Doyle and Laura Winkiel, eds., *Geomodernisms: Race, Modernism, Modernity* (Bloomington: Indiana University Press, 2005); Jessica Berman, *Modernist Fiction, Cosmopolitanism, and the Politics of Community* (Cambridge: Cambridge University Press, 2001); and Andrew John Miller, *Modernism and the Crisis of Sovereignty* (New York: Routledge, 2008). Some works that pressure the rise of the term from postcolonial, feminist, and Marxist perspectives include the collections *Cosmopolitics: Thinking and Feeling Beyond the Nation*, ed. Bruce Robbins and Pheng Cheah (Minneapolis: University of Minnesota Press, 1998); and *Conceiving Cosmopolitanism: Theory, Context, and Practice*, ed. Steven Vertovec and Robin Cohen (Oxford: Oxford University Press, 2003); as well as Timothy Brennan, *At Home in the World: Cosmopolitanism Now* (Cambridge, Mass.: Harvard University Press, 1997).

11. Paul Gilroy, *Postcolonial Melancholia* (New York: Columbia University Press, 2006), 67, 68.

12. Arjun Appadurai, *Modernity at Large: Cultural Dimensions of Globalization* (Minneapolis: University of Minnesota Press, 1996).

13. Zdzislaw Najder, *Joseph Conrad: A Life*, trans. Halina Najder (Rochester, N.Y.: Camden House, 2007), 412.

14. Among the works that established this way of reading are Andrzej Busza, *Conrad's Polish Literary Background and Some Illustrations of the Influence of Polish Literature on His Work* (Rome: Antemurale, 1966); Edward Said, *Joseph Conrad and the Fiction of Autobiography* (Cambridge, Mass.: Harvard University Press, 1966); Edward Said, *Culture and Imperialism* (New York: Vintage, 1993); Ian Watt, *Conrad in the Nineteenth Century* (Berkeley: University of California Press, 1979); Zdzislaw Najder, *Joseph Conrad: A Chronicle* (New Brunswick, N.J.: Rutgers University Press, 1983); Keith Carabine, *The Life and the Art: A Study of Conrad's Under Western Eyes* (Amsterdam: Rodopi, 1996); Geoffrey Galt Harpham, *One of Us: The Mastery of Joseph Conrad* (Chicago: University of Chicago Press, 1996).

15. Joseph Conrad, "Poland Revisited," in *Joseph Conrad: Notes on Life and Letters*, ed. J. H. Stape (Cambridge: Cambridge University Press, 2004), 114. Hereafter cited in the text.

16. Details in this paragraph are drawn from Najder, *Joseph Conrad*, 15–21.

17. Harpham, *One of Us*, 33.

18. J. M. Coetzee, "Confession and Double Thoughts: Tolstoy, Rousseau, Dostoevsky," in *Doubling the Point: Essays and Interviews*, ed. David Attwell (Cambridge, Mass.: Harvard University Press, 1992), 282.

19. Ibid., 257.

20. Conrad, *Heart of Darkness*, 9.

21. Watt, *Conrad in the Nineteenth Century*.

22. On this relationship see Paul de Man, *Allegories of Reading: Figural Language in Rousseau, Nietzsche, Rilke, and Proust* (New Haven, Conn.: Yale University Press, 1979), 278–301.

23. Coetzee, "Confession and Double Thoughts," 273.

24. Coetzee's parenthetical aside, "though he now acknowledges it," and his identification of a confession as "false coin" compromise his otherwise careful argument about truth, deception, and shame. Because Coetzee does not define what it means to "acknowledge" the truth and conflates lie with countertruth uttered by an unwitting subject, his otherwise radical reading of confession conserves the history of a philosophical dualism between testimony and perjury, truth and lie. On this subject see Jacques Derrida, "History of the Lie: Prolegomena," in *Without Alibi*, trans. Peggy Kamuf (Stanford, Calif.: Stanford University Press, 2002), 28–70.

25. De Man, *Allegories of Reading*, 286.

26. Coetzee cites de Man in making this point. De Man explains that "each new stage in the unveiling suggests a deeper shame, a greater impossibility to reveal, and a greater satisfaction in outwitting this impossibility" (de Man, *Allegories of Reading*, 286). Coetzee makes reference to de Man's reading of Rousseau's shame. De Man argues that "what Rousseau really wanted . . . was the public scene of exposure which he actually gets."

27. Nicholas Abraham and Maria Torok, working from Freud's theorization of mourning and melancholia, call this psycholinguistic event the melancholic incorporation of the exquisite corpse, an act that manifests verbally. Instead of mourning the loss by decathecting from the object, the melancholic incorporates it, according to Freud. According to Abraham and Torok, the melancholic identifies with this internal foreigner in the torsions of enunciations, indirect speech and verbal as well as nonverbal practices. Nicholas Abraham and Maria Torok, *The Wolf Man's Magic Word: A Cryptonymy*, trans. Nicholas Rand (Minneapolis: University of Minnesota Press, 1986).

28. Harpham, *One of Us*, 35. The difference in our readings is that Harpham, focusing on Conrad's depiction of the funeral not in "Poland Revisited" but in *A Personal Record*, sees Conrad both accomplishing mourning of the father and at the same time producing a substitute: "With his functional bipaternity, Conrad was able to mourn one father and settle into an ongoing, largely epistolary quarrel that lasted well into adulthood, with another" (34).

29. Conrad, *A Personal Record*, ix–x.

30. Najder, *Joseph Conrad*, 21.

31. As Peter Holquist writes, "In the aftermath of October, 1905, the government moved from concessions to a policy of 'pacification,' dispatching punitive detachments to Siberia, the Baltic, and the Causcasus. The imperial government granted military commanders in charge of such detachments *carte blanche* to operate against civilian populations. Intended to intimidate the population, they were 'a form of state terror directed against its own citizens'." Peter Holquist, "Violent Russia, Deadly Marxism? Russia in the Epoch of Violence, 1905–21," *Kritika: Explorations in Russian and Eurasian History* 4, no. 3 (Summer 2003): 632.

32. Ibid., 636.

33. In addition to *A Personal Record*, see, for example, "A Note on the Polish Problem" (1916) and "The Crime of Partition" (1919) in *Notes on Life and Letters*.

34. See Reynold Humphries, "The Representation of Politics and History in *Under Western Eyes*," *Conradiana: A Journal of Joseph Conrad Studies* 20, no. 1 (1988): 13–32; and Josiane Paccaud, "The Name of the Father in Conrad's *Under Western Eyes*," *Conradiana: A Journal of Joseph Conrad Studies* 18, no. 3 (1986): 204–218. Susan Jones points out that confession comes at a cost not

only to Razumov, the novel's protagonist, who suffers "physical disfigurement and loss of identity," but also to the author, who experienced "physical and psychological breakdown." Susan Jones, *Conrad and Women* (Oxford: Clarendon, 1999), 53.

35. In *Conrad's Political Novels*, Eloise Knapp Hay points out that the writings are inspired by historical acts that challenged the law's authority. Real crimes were the basis for "Gasper Ruiz" and also for *Nostromo*, *Lord Jim*, *The Secret Agent*, and *Under Western Eyes* (148). Conrad's texts call attention to witnessing in their literary form, perhaps most famously through their orchestrations of Marlowe as the framing device that organizes facts and provides judgments in the earlier novels. In his analysis of *Lord Jim*, Kieran Dolin locates Marlowe's narrative in the tradition of forensic rhetoric. He notes that other critics have also employed the term "advocate" to characterize Conrad's most famous framing device. Dolin explains that "although this term refers to the oratory of the law courts, and particularly to the need to persuade a judge or jury, it may be applied to Marlow because he is primarily concerned with obtaining justice for Jim. In this project he examines witnesses and presents their evidence." Kieran Dolin, *Fiction and the Law: Legal Discourse in Victorian and Modern Literature* (Cambridge: Cambridge University Press, 1999), 153.

36. Carabine, *The Life and the Art*, 25.

37. Other essays that also approach confession but do not treat its displacement and generalization throughout the novel are Thomas J. Cousineau, "The Ambiguity of Razumov's Confession in *Under Western Eyes*," *Conradiana: A Journal of Joseph Conrad Studies* 18, no. 1 (1986): 27–40; and Andrew Long, "The Secret Policeman's Couch: Informing, Confession, and Interpellation in Conrad's *Under Western Eyes*," *Studies in the Novel* 35, no. 4 (2003): 490–510.

38. Peter Brooks, *Troubling Confessions: Speaking Guilt in Law and Literature* (Chicago: University of Chicago Press, 2000), 9–10.

39. As Gilroy agues, a cosmopolitan ethics is one that goes beyond tolerance of differences to active cultivation of responsibilities to others.

40. Holquist, "Violent Russia," 628.

41. Holquist, for example, focuses on the period lasting from 1905 to 1921 ("Violent Russia"), and Abraham Ascher looks backward to 1904. Abraham Ascher, "Introduction," in *The Russian Revolution of 1905: Centenary Perspectives* (London: Routledge, 2005), 1–12.

42. Ascher, "Introduction," 3.

43. Joan Neuberger, *Hooliganism, Crime, Culture, and Power in St. Petersburg, 1900–1914* (Berkeley: University of California Press, 1993), 76.

44. Beryl Williams, "1905: The View from the Provinces," in *The Russian Revolution of 1905: Centenary Perspectives* (London: Routledge, 2005), 34–54.

45. Teodor Shanin, *Roots of Otherness: Russia's Turn of the Century*, vol. 2, *Russia, 1905–07: Revolution as a Moment of Truth* (New Haven, Conn.: Yale University Press, 1986), 1–2.

46. Conrad, "Author's Note," in *Under Western Eyes*, 282.

47. Paul Kirschner has noted the precariousness of the boundaries between the Russian and English through the exchange of cultural signifiers and ideologies in the novel, which suggests a compatibility between Western materialism and Russian. Paul Kirschner, "Revolution, Feminism, and Conrad's Western 'I,'" *The Conradian* 10, no. 1 (May 1985): 1920. Christopher GoGwilt contends that the novel's "aesthetic power" is that it adduces that the West is not a historically stable entity but an invention that is "the effect of recent animosities" and that it undermines the ethnographic and racial categories of the Russian against which this invented West is measured. He acknowledges that the novel "does seem to reproduce a characteristic feature of twentieth-century formulations of 'the West' not only as the expression of a long, coherent political history, but as the only coherent version of political history, all others constituting either failed models of political development, caricatures of the 'Western' model, or systems of political organization essentially mythic or ahistorical." Yet, "even as *Under Western Eyes* reproduces this construction of 'the West' as the closure of political history . . . its aesthetic power depends on dramatizing the confusion of European political identity that this idea implies. . . . [It] uses the term 'Western' to make its reader 'see' the set of mistaken political legacies it articulates" (*Invention of the West*, 160).

48. Conrad, "Author's Note," 281.

49. Ibid.

50. Ibid.

51. Ibid., 282–283.

52. Rebecca Walkowitz uses this phrase to define Conrad's strategies in *The Secret Agent*. She argues that literary impressionism resists the rhetoric of individuality that functions as justification for imperialism because it resists the "fact" of identity, demonstrating how "nature" is produced through social processes, how the foreign is at the heart of the nation (*Cosmopolitan Style*, 28).

53. Byron Carmen-Santangelo argues the work's criticism of one empire serves as a foil for a perspective shaped by another.

54. Pheng Cheah explains that Kant's theory of the cosmopolitical as a moral necessity "is formulated too early to take into account the role of nationalism in the age of liberalism. It is more a philosophical republicanism and federalism designed to reform the absolutist dynastic state than a theory opposing the modern theory of nationality." Pheng Cheah, *Inhuman Conditions: On Cosmopolitanism and Human Rights* (Cambridge, Mass.: Harvard University Press, 2007), 23.

55. "Autocracy and War," in *Joseph Conrad: Notes on Life and Letters*. Hereafter cited in the text.

56. See Jacques Derrida, *The Politics of Friendship*, trans. George Collins (London: Verso, 1997).

57. See Jacques Derrida, "Foreigner Question/Coming from Abroad," in *Of Hospitality: Anne Dufourmantelle Invites Jacques Derrida to Respond*, trans. Rachel Bowlby (Stanford, Calif.: Stanford University Press, 2000).

58. GoGwilt argues that because it expresses "a thoroughgoing skepticism about the legitimacy of nineteenth-century European representations of political community . . . 'Autocracy and War' is a revealing hinge text between Conrad's fictions of empire and fictions of revolution, because what is usually taken as his conservative political standpoint poses a key turn-of-the century question: how to imagine an international community beyond the limits of European concepts of nation and race" (*The Invention of the West*, 29). I would argue that the focus on statelessness and rootlessness consolidates older concepts of nation and race and seems to repeat rather than revise previous concepts of nation and race.

59. Étienne Balibar, "Racism and Nationalism," in Étienne Balibar and Immanuel Wallerstein, *Race, Nation, Class: Ambiguous Identities* (London: Verso, 1992), 60.

60. "Anti-Semitism functioned on a European scale: each nationalism saw in the Jew (who was himself contradictorily conceived as both irreducibly inassimilable to others and as cosmopolitan, as members of an original people and as rootless) its own specific enemy and the representative of all other 'hereditary enemies'; this meant, then, that all nationalisms were defined against the same foil, the same 'stateless other,' and this has been a component of the very idea of Europe as the land of modern nation-states, or, in other words, civilization." Ibid., 62.

61. In Conrad's other writings that address Poland, nations are defined through the essential character of a specific people, a character that survives even drastic rearrangements of base and superstructure by imperialism. Insisting on Poland's essential "Western" character enables Conrad to separate Poland from Russia and Europe's "illegitimate" democracies, heirs of revolutions, and to separate his father from the revolutionaries *Under Western Eyes* presents. In "A Note on the Polish Problem" (1916), he argues of the Poles: "In temperament, in feeling, in mind, and even in unreason, they are Western, with an absolute comprehension of all the Western modes of thought, even of those that are remote from their own historical experience" (*Notes on Life and Letters*, 109). Poland is "an outpost of the Western powers" with shared "kinship" if not genealogical ties to the West (110). "The Crime of Partition" (1919) argues that Poland, "deprived of its independence, of its historical continuity, and with its religion and language persecuted and repressed, became a mere geographical expression"; however, "the nation refused to rest therein. It haunted the territories of the Old Republic in the manner of a ghost haunting its ancestral mansion where strangers are making themselves at home . . . never ceasing to inspire a sort of awe, a strange uneasiness in the hearts of the

unlawful possessors" (*Notes on Life and Letters*, 96). Maintaining the opposition between deracinated cosmopolitan states produced through revolutions and rooted nations whose essential character is linked to the West enables Conrad to claim that his father was not a revolutionary but rather one of the "patriots" who, "believing in the spirituality of a national existence could not bear to see that spirit enslaved" (*A Personal Record*, x).

62. My reading of the meaning of translation in the novel differs from that of others who have addressed the framing device. In addition to Hay, *Conrad's Political Novels*; and Dolin, *Fiction and the Law*; see Bruce Henricksen, *Nomadic Voices: Conrad and the Subject of Narrative* (Urbana: University of Illinois Press, 1992); Gail Fincham, "To Make You See: Narration and Focalization in *Under Western Eyes*," in *Joseph Conrad: Voice, Sequence, History, Genre*, ed. Jakob Lothe, Jeremy Hawthorne, and James Phelan (Columbus: Ohio State University Press, 2008); and Carola M. Kaplan, "Conrad's Narrative Occupation of/by Russia in *Under Western Eyes*," *Conradiana: A Journal of Joseph Conrad Studies* 27, no. 2 (1995): 97–114.

63. Lawrence Venuti, *Nation, Language, and the Ethics of Translation*, ed. Sandra Berman and Michael Wood (Princeton, N.J.: Princeton University Press, 2005), 179, 178.

64. Ibid., 179.

65. Walter Benjamin, "The Task of the Translator," in *Illuminations*, trans. Harry Zohn (New York: Schocken, 1968), 69–82.

66. Conrad, *A Personal Record*, vii.

67. On the uneasy relation between Conrad's novel and Russian literature, see Kaplan, "Conrad's Narrative Occupation of/by Russia in *Under Western Eyes*."

68. In Derrida's writings during and after the so-called ethical and political turn (a narrative of development Derrida himself rejects to describe his work), the philosopher examines how the apparently opposed secular and religious traditions, the juridico-legal and Abrahamic discourses of responsibility, actually share a problematic reliance on the autonomous, intending subject as the basis of their articulations of moral decision while suppressing the aporetic structure of responsibility they simultaneously reveal as haunting them. Religious discourses of ethics both Christian (Kierkegaard) and Judaic (Levinas) reproduce this aporia while displacing it, and "this applies all the more to political or legal matters. The concept of responsibility, like that of decision, would thus be found to lack coherence or consequence, even lacking identity with respect to itself, paralyzed by what can be called an aporia or antinomy. That has never stopped it from 'functioning.' . . . On the contrary, it operates so much better, to the extent that it serves to obscure the abyss or fill in its absence of foundation." Jacques Derrida, *The Gift of Death*, trans. David Wills (Chicago: University of Chicago Press, 1996), 84.

69. Jacques Derrida, *Adieu: To Emmanuel Levinas*, trans. Pascale-Anne Brault and Michael Naas (Stanford, Calif.: Stanford University Press, 1999), 23.

70. Pericles Lewis, *Religious Experience and the Modernist Novel* (Cambridge: Cambridge University Press, 2010), 23.

71. Ibid., 25.

72. Jonathan W. Daly, *Autocracy Under Siege: Security Police and Opposition in Russia, 1866–1905* (DeKalb: Northern Illinois University Press, 1998), 149.

73. Ibid., 165.

74. Ibid., 150.

75. Ibid., 145.

76. Daly compares the French and Russian security police and notes that "the watchfulness of modern states seems to depend on the resources available to governments and the range and diversity of social phenomena to be watched. It is not surprising, then, that the French state's capacity to conduct surveillance was relatively greater than that of the Russian state" (ibid., 107). Holquist argues that "colonial *practices* employed by the Russian imperial state and its military must be seen within the spectrum of other European colonial measures. Russian officers knew of, and sought to emulate, the practices of other European powers, devoting particular attention to the French experience in Algeria. This exchange was not entirely in one direction. French officers, such as France's leading theorist of colonial warfare, Herbert Lyautey, studied the Russian conquest of the Caucasus and Central Asia" ("Violent Russia," 634).

77. The veiling of woman as figure for truth has been addressed widely in feminist theory and theories of gender and sexuality.

78. This supports what Andrew Michael Roberts sees in Conrad's works as a shift from a moral code of behavior based in the sovereign subject to an ethics of uncodifiable, unprogrammatic responsibility to the other by a subject that is not an *ipse*, or self. Andrew Michael Roberts, "Conrad and the Territory of Ethics," *Conradiana: A Journal of Joseph Conrad Studies* 37, nos. 1/2 (2005): 133–146.

79. See Avrom Fleishman, *Conrad's Politics: Community and Anarchy in the Fiction of Joseph Conrad* (Baltimore, Md.: Johns Hopkins University Press, 1967); Man-Sik Lee, "Razumov's Moral Growth in Joseph Conrad's *Under Western Eyes*," *Nineteenth-Century Literature in English* 9, no. 1 (2005): 261–280; Jil Larson, "Promises, Lies, and Ethical Agency in *Under Western Eyes*," *Conradiana: A Journal of Joseph Conrad Studies* 29, no. 1 (1997): 41–58; and Sung Ryol Kim, "The Wanderings of Cain: *Under Western Eyes* as Ethical Drama," *Nineteenth-Century Literature in English* 6, no. 2 (2002): 103–130. For a contrasting vision of ethics in Conrad's works, one closer to Roberts's and my own, see Yael Levin, "The Moral Ambiguity of Conrad's Poetics: Transgressive Secret Sharing in *Lord Jim* and *Under Western Eyes*," *Conradiana: A Journal of Joseph Conrad Studies* 39, no. 3 (2007): 211–228.

2. TRAUMAS OF NATION AND NARRATIVE: LEGAL AND LITERARY WITNESSING IN REBECCA WEST'S WARTIME WRITINGS

1. *Rebecca West Today: Contemporary Critical Approaches*, ed. Bernard Schweizer (Newark: University of Delaware Press, 2006), 26.

2. Ibid.

3. Paul Fussell, *The Great War and Modern Memory* (New York: Oxford University Press, 1975); Samuel Lynn Hynes, *A War Imagined: The First World War and English Culture* (London: Bodley Head, 1990). Important feminist critical studies have also approached wartime writing with a focus on masculinity but critically, for example, Elaine Showalter, *The Female Malady: Women, Madness, and English Culture, 1830–1980* (New York: Pantheon, 1985); Sandra M. Gilbert, "Soldier's Heart: Literary Men, Literary Women, and the Great War," in *No Man's Land: The Place of the Woman Writer in the Twentieth Century*, ed. Sandra Gilbert and Susan Gubar (New Haven, Conn.: Yale University Press, 1989); and Joanna Bourke, *Dismembering the Male: Men's Bodies, Britain, and the Great War* (Chicago: University of Chicago Press, 1996).

4. Margaret Higonnet, "Authenticity and Art in Trauma Narratives of World War I," *Modernism/Modernity* 9, no. 1 (2002): 92, 91–107.

5. The period that covers 1875 to 1914, according to E. J. Hobsbawm, *The Age of Empire, 1875–1914* (New York: Pantheon, 1987).

6. See, for example, Richard Badenhausen, "Mourning Through Memoir: Trauma, Testimony, and Community in Vera Brittain's Testament of Youth," *Twentieth-Century Literature* 49, no. 4 (2003): 421–448; Santanu Das, *Touch and Intimacy in First World War Literature* (Cambridge: Cambridge University Press, 2005); Ronald Smith, "Nick Adams and Post-Traumatic Stress Disorder," *War, Literature, and the Arts: An International Journal of the Humanities* 9, no. 1 (1997): 39–48; and Andrea Petersen, "Shell-Shocked in Somerville: Vera Brittain's Post-Traumatic Stress Disorder," in *Gender and Warfare in the Twentieth Century: Textual Representations*, ed. Angela K. Smith (Manchester: Manchester University Press, 2004).

7. As Jed Esty pointed out in 2004, there has been a surprising dearth of general studies on the relationship between Anglophone modernism and imperialism. Jed Esty, *A Shrinking Island: Modernism and National Culture in England* (Princeton, N.J.: Princeton University Press, 2004). This has changed with the growth of transnational approaches in the era identified as that of the new modernist studies.

8. The classic study is Fussell's. Fussell's argument that the war constitutes a rupture with everything that comes before it and has a decisive effect not only on literary history but history and culture generally reprises the modernist mantra "make it new" (*The Great War and Modern Memory*, 21–23). See also Allyson Booth, *Postcards from the Trenches: Negotiating the Space Between Modernism and the First World War* (New York: Oxford University Press, 1996);

Trudi Tate, *Modernism, History, and the First World War* (Manchester: Manchester University Press, 1998); and Vincent Sherry, *The Great War and the Language of Modernism* (Oxford: Oxford University Press, 2003).

9. Sigmund Freud, "Mourning and Melancholia" [1917], in *General Psychological Theory*, ed. Philip Rieff (New York: Collier, 1963), 164.

10. Ibid., 166.

11. Ibid.

12. Rebecca West, *The Return of the Soldier* (New York: Penguin, 1998), 38–39. Hereafter cited in the text.

13. See Victoria Glendinning, *Rebecca West: A Life* (New York: Knopf, 1987), for a description of the part it played in West's life.

14. All details of Monkey Island's history provided by Luke Over, "A Little History," in David Nash Ford's *Royal Berkshire History: Monkey Island Lodge, Bray, Berkshire*, 2002. http://www.berkshirehistory.com/castles/monkey_island.html.

15. Among others who take this position are Samuel Hynes, "Introduction," in West's *The Return of the Soldier*; Margaret Diane Stetz, "Drinking 'The Wine of Truth': Philosophical Change in West's *The Return of the Soldier*," *Arizona Quarterly* 43, no. 1 (1987): 63–78; Jane Gledhill, "Impersonality and Amnesia: A Response to World War I in the Writings of H.D. and Rebecca West," in *Women and World War I: The Written Response*, ed. Dorothy Goldman (New York: St. Martin's, 1993); and Laura Cowan, "The Fine Frenzy of Artistic Vision: Rebecca West's *The Return of the Soldier* as a Feminist Analysis of World War I," *Centennial Review* 42, no. 2 (1998): 285–308.

16. Hynes, "Introduction," x.

17. West, then still using her given name, Cicely Fairfield, declared in her opening of the review in the *Freewoman*, "There are two kind of imperialists: imperialists and bloody imperialists." Cicely Fairfield, "The Position of Women in Indian Life" [1911], in *The Young Rebecca: Writings of Rebecca West, 1911–17*, ed. Jane Marcus (New York: Virago, 1982), 12. This bold move became a signature of the precocious West and drew her to the attention of older, famous writers.

18. Rebecca West, *Henry James* (Port Washington, N.Y.: Kennikat, 1968), 27.

19. Dominick LaCapra, *Writing History, Writing Trauma* (Baltimore, Md.: Johns Hopkins University Press, 2001), 58.

20. While some readers note the fantasmatic qualities of the past represented on the island, they have not connected these to the framing device and considered how that device throws into relief the politics of witnessing and the conflicting interpretations of trauma the work elaborates. See Debra Rae Cohen, *Remapping the Home Front: Locating Citizenship in British Women's Great War Fiction* (Boston: Northeastern University Press, 2002); Marina MacKay, "The Lunacy of Men, the Idiocy of Women: Woolf, West, and War,"

NSWA Journal 15, no. 3 (2003): 124–144; and Patricia E. Chu, *Race, Nationalism, and the State in British and American Modernism* (Cambridge: Cambridge University Press, 2006).

21. Critics have focused on the novel's psychoanalytic dimensions but have overlooked the significance of the frame or its implications for reading alternative histories the novel invokes. Misha Kavka points out that the novel elaborates trauma as war neurosis but departs from this by offering a psychoanalytic theory that identifies the death of Chris's son as the traumatic event. However, the "actual trauma" is neither of these: "the war . . . marks the breakdown of the defenses of masculinity against the actual trauma, the knowledge of its own constructedness." Misha Kavka, "Men in (Shell-)Shock: Masculinity, Trauma, and Psychoanalysis in Rebecca West's *The Return of the Soldier*," *Studies in Twentieth-Century Literature* 22, no. 1 (1998): 151–171, 162. Wyatt Bonikowski, who does argue for the importance of Jenny as witness, claims that the cause is also war trauma, which diffuses into Jenny's narrative, but he maintains that the cause is internal to the characters, too: "war is not only something out there, happening in another place; rather war, like death, is present *within* the subject." Wyatt Bonikowski, "*The Return of the Soldier* Brings Death Home," *Modern Fiction Studies* 51, no, 3 (2005): 513–535, 514. Steve Pinkerton reads Margaret rather than Jenny as (psycho)analyst in the text and argues that among the causes of amnesia are Chris's son's death, but he also notes that other causes might precede this. He points to characterological, individual causes such as Chris's relationship to his father rather than wider historical causes the testimony invokes. Steve Pinkerton, "Trauma and Cure in Rebecca West's *The Return of the Soldier*," *Journal of Modern Literature* 32, no. 1 (2008): 1–12. For Susan Varney, both the trauma and recovery of the event are unrepresentable and linked to the impossibility of a foundation to social and sexual ties: "the concept of an intransigent social space within which social and sexual ties are possible (such as that represented in the ideal of Monkey Island) are repeatedly *not recovered*." Susan Varney, "Oedipus and the Modernist Aesthetic: Reconceiving the Social in Rebecca West's *The Return of the Soldier*," in *Naming the Father: Legacies, Genealogies, and Explorations of Fatherhood in Modern and Contemporary Literature*, ed. Eva Paulino Bueno, Terry Caesar, and William Hummel (Lanham, Md.: Lexington, 2000), 268. Varney refers to the "ideal" of Monkey Island, but her emphasis is on the novel's articulation of the impossibility of returning to a phantasmatic space rather than on the testimonial elaboration of the effacement of historical discord and struggle during the Victorian period.

22. Ruth Leys, arguing against the "literalist" interpretation of trauma offered by the influential readings of Cathy Caruth, compellingly makes this argument in her study of how trauma operates as a concept-metaphor through the entirety of Freud's corpus. Ruth Leys, *Trauma: A Genealogy* (Chicago: University of Chicago Press, 2000). Caruth reads Freud's text as articulat-

ing traumatic returns as literal, interruptive, and outside of all figuration. But Caruth's argument hinges on a reading of *Moses and Monotheism* and *Beyond the Pleasure Principle*'s discussions of accident neuroses (*Unfall Neurotiker*), which Freud distinguishes from *traumatisch Neurotiker*. Moreover, Leys has questioned Caruth's interpretation on the grounds that it is based on a limited number of Freud's writings. Situating the concept of trauma in a wider context, Leys maintains that figurations, displacements, and condensations are modes of traumatic returns. Although Caruth's pioneering contributions to the intersection of ethics, literary theory, and trauma cannot be denied, Leys's interpretation of traumatic returns seems more compelling because of its analytical breadth.

23. Jacques Derrida, *Demeure: Fiction and Testimony*, trans. Elizabeth Rottenberg (Stanford, Calif.: Stanford University Press, 2000), 29.

24. Though biographies and letters do not verify that West had read *Swann's Way* before composing the novel, with educated guesswork one can infer that she most likely had. An avid reader who circulated among writers who had read Proust's novel when it was first published, she was also a Francophile and had likely read the favorable review in the *Times Literary Supplement* in 1913. That review commended Proust for his literary and philosophical exploration of memory, a subject of central interest to West in her first novel. Glendinning notes that for West, "Of the acknowledged 'great men' among the moderns, only Proust was beyond criticism. 'The greatness of Proust! One cannot exaggerate it,' she wrote in the 1920s, and never changed her mind" (*Rebecca West*, 254).

25. Paul de Man, "The Rhetoric of Temporality," in *Blindness and Insight: Essays in the Rhetoric of Contemporary Criticism* (Minneapolis: University of Minnesota Press, 1983), 187–228.

26. Marcel Proust, *Swann's Way*, trans. C. K. Scott Moncrieff and Terrence Kilmartin (New York: Vintage), 151.

27. Ibid.

28. Ibid.

29. Ibid.

30. See Alison Smith, *The Victorian Nude: Sexuality, Morality, and Art* (Manchester: Manchester University Press, 1996), chaps. 5–6.

31. Luce Irigaray's reading of the "caress" in Levinas's study on ethics *Totality and Infinity* analyzes this doubled, asymmetrical articulation of woman. She must be relegated to animality, maternity, and materiality, "depths," in order to prepare man for the "heights" of ethical transcendence. But paradoxically, her materiality must also be annihilated, her history and "scars" removed to keep intact an ideal virginity. Luce Irigaray, *An Ethics of Sexual Difference* (Ithaca, N.Y.: Cornell University Press, 1993), 201–202. This scene confirms Debra Rae Cohen's claim that "Chris's nostalgic celebration of Margaret occludes the

reality of the life she has lived . . . she loses her socio-economic actuality to become a 'place out of time and history'" (*Remapping the Homefront*, 79). While Cohen also reads Chris's nostalgic shaping of Margaret on Monkey Island, she argues that this nostalgia is linked to a different tradition, that of the Georgian poets, and maintains that through a pastoral-classical pastiche "he evades his own complicity in the class and gender system he now rejects as oppressive" (78).

32. On the history of these movements see Lesley A. Hall, *Sex, Gender, and Social Change in Britain Since 1880* (New York: St. Martin's, 2000).

33. Smith, *The Victorian Nude*, 220.

34. "The idea that men could have sexual intercourse with whom they liked but women could have sexual intercourse only within marriage had the effect of encouraging men to be promiscuous; they were bound, the male mind being what it is, to engage in any activity involving pleasure with double satisfaction if it were forbidden to the women most nearly equal to them in status." Rebecca West, *1900* (New York: Crescent, 1982), 53.

35. West, *Henry James*, 27.

36. Contrapuntal reading "must take account of both processes, that of imperialism and that of resistance to it, which can be done by extending our reading of the texts to include what was once forcibly excluded." Edward W. Said, *Culture and Imperialism* (New York: Knopf, 1993), 66–67.

37. Fredric Jameson, "Modernism and Imperialism," in *Nationalism, Colonialism, and Literature*, ed. Fredric Jameson, Edward Said, and Terry Eagleton (Minneapolis: University of Minnesota Press, 1990), 51.

38. William Wordsworth, "Lines Composed a Few Miles Above Tintern Abbey," [1798], in *William Wordsworth: Selected Poems*, ed. John O. Hayden (New York: Penguin, 1994), 66. Hereafter cited in the text.

39. Whether "imperialism" defines Britain's relationship to Mexico remains debatable. In the period to which the novel directs readers, which I have called, following Hobsbawm, the age of empire, more significant than governmental involvement was private investment, facilitated by occasional interventions by the British state, and major collaborations with the Mexican government. "Between 1870 and 1914 . . . the key actors in the relationship between Latin America and Britain were businessmen, not the government." Rory Miller, *Britain and Latin America in the Nineteenth and Twentieth Centuries* (London: Longman, 1993), 68. Many historians argue, however, that Britain's relationship to Latin America can be defined as informal imperialism. Britain had a long history of commercial interests in Mexico; it was the latter's primary foreign investor in the nineteenth century and held most-favored-nation status in trade. A complicity between British and other foreign firms and a Mexican "collaborating elite" (Miller, *Britain and Latin America*, 22) in the final decades of the nineteenth century led to land seizures that bankrupted peasants. The

British state facilitated private British interests through diplomatic and other acts. British involvement in Mexico thus resembles a form of imperialism that chronologically postdates the novel, neocolonialism.

40. Peter Calvert, *The Mexican Revolution, 1910–1914: The Diplomacy of Anglo-American Conflict* (Cambridge: Cambridge University Press, 1968), 21.

41. Ibid.

42. I thank Benjamin Conisbee Baer for calling my attention to the overabundance of references to whiteness in the novel.

43. "Everything suggests, indeed, that the mainspring of narrative is precisely the confusion of consecution and consequence; what comes after being read in narrative as what is caused by." Roland Barthes, "Introduction to the Structural Analysis of Narrative," in *Image, Music, Text* (New York: Hill and Wang, 1977), 94.

44. See Marina MacKay, *Modernism and World War II* (Cambridge: Cambridge University Press, 2007); and Phyllis Lassner, "Rebecca West's Shadowy Other," *Rebecca West Today: Contemporary Critical Approaches*, ed. Bernard Schweizer (Newark: University of Delaware Press, 2006).

45. MacKay, *Modernism and World War II*, 55, 63.

46. Chu, *Race, Nationalism, and the State in British and American Modernism*, 103, 113.

47. West described the Nuremburg trials in terms that resemble the definition of trauma as an unexperienced experience: "Conducted by officials sick with the weariness left by a great war, . . . inadequately reported, constantly misinterpreted, it was an unshapely event, . . . stamping no clear image on the mind of the people it had been designed to impress. It was one of the events which do not become an experience." In *A Train of Powder: Six Reports on the Problem of Guilt and Punishment in Our Time* (Chicago: Ivan R. Dee, 2000), 246. See also Ravit Reichman, *The Affective Life of Law* (Stanford, Calif.: Stanford University Press, 2009), 103–133.

48. Rebecca West, *The New Meaning of Treason* (New York: Viking, 1964), vii.

49. Ibid.

50. Patrick Deer, *Culture in Camouflage: War, Empire, and Modern British Literature* (Oxford: Oxford University Press, 2009). Deer discusses the rise of popular imperialist rhetoric that sought to secure England and Britain's trust in the battle against fascism from fronts that were not contained within a single nation and that relied on the colonies. Despite propaganda's attempts to convince people they had an oversight of the war, a "the sense of vulnerability continued to haunt even the most patriotic of invocations of the heroic national landscape" (107). Pointing to Churchill's Dunkirk speech of June 4, 1940, as an example, Deer writes that "the organic integrity of the national landscape is penetrated and divided by the lines of battle, 'the fronts

are everywhere.' A disturbing vulnerability is revealed, and [Churchill] is forced to confront the frightening prospect of a literally de-centered empire" (107).

51. Rebecca West, *The Meaning of Treason* (New York: Viking, 1947), 186. Hereafter cited in the text.

52. In a letter to Lord Beaverbrook dated December 4, 1947, West writes, "This material about treason will go down the drain if I do not record it; and it is valuable not only to the historian but to everyone who wants humanity to survive. There isn't only the fact that treason in modern condition [*sic*] works out as cruelty to prisoners of war—that is the real fruit of my book, from an *immediate* point of view. There is the fact that treason is an attempt to live without love of country, which humanity can't do—any more than love of family." *The Selected Letters of Rebecca West*, ed. Bonnie Kime Scott (New Haven, Conn.: Yale University Press, 2000). West's words echo Churchill's description of the British empire as family, a description Alan Sinfield comments includes as secondary citizens those outside of England: "For the total mobilization of modern warfare, general acquiescence was not enough. So when Churchill spoke from the steps of Bradford town hall in December 1942, he celebrated the unity that he knew he had to produce: 'All are united like one great family; all are standing together, helping each other, taking all their share and doing their work, some at the front, some under the sea or on the sea in all weathers, some in the air, some in the coal mines, great numbers in the shops, some in the homes—all doing their bit' (Churchill, p 245). Notice how the speech's extended geographical itemizing effaces a possible hierarchical one." Alan Sinfield, *Literature, Politics, and Culture in Postwar Britain* (London: Athlone, 1997), 10. In contrast to Churchill, however, West does not extend kinship, even of a hierarchical nature, to British colonial subjects in this work.

53. Chu discusses the role of radio, national community, and collective fantasy. *Race, Nationalism, and the State in British and American Modernism*, 105–106.

54. Shoshana Felman, *The Juridical Unconscious: Trials and Traumas in the Twentieth Century* (Cambridge, Mass.: Harvard University Press, 2002), 5.

55. As Marina MacKay's writes of Esty's *A Shrinking Island*, "that the war and the loss of the empire were closely connected—politically and economically, as well as imaginatively—is nowhere registered . . . the endurance of the war in Britain is surely related to the island's shrinkage; it may even be the acceptable idiom for speaking of it" (*Modernism and World War II*, 17).

56. Esty, *A Shrinking Island*, 28.

57. Robert Cover, "Violence and the Word," in *Narrative, Violence, and the Law*, ed. Martha Minow, Michael Ryan, and Austin Sarat (Ann Arbor: University of Michigan Press, 1992), 203.

58. Ibid.

59. Christopher Menke, "Law and Violence," *Law and Literature* 22, no. 1 (Spring 2010): 2.

60. She titles her report on a lynching trial "Opera in Greenville," and she remarks that two of the Nuremberg trials "took off and left the earth, becoming phantasmagoric, chapters out of *The Mysteries of Udolpho*, not trials at all" (*A Train of Powder*, 239). She describes the main Nuremburg trial also as "a performance" (*A Train of Powder*, 247). In "Mr. Setty and Mr. Hume," she claims this murder trial in Britain operates as a kind of "morality play" (*A Train of Powder*, 202).

61. Mark Sanders, *Ambiguities of Witnessing: Law and Literature in the Time of a Truth Commission* (Stanford, Calif.: Stanford University Press, 2007), 23.

62. Jacques Derrida, "Force of Law: The 'Mystical Foundation of Authority,'" in *Deconstruction and the Possibility of Justice*, ed. Drucilla Cornell, Michael Rosenfeld, and David Gray Carlson (New York: Routledge), 6.

63. Ibid., 38.

64. Ibid., 35.

65. Ibid., 34–35; Jacques Derrida, *Force de loi* (Paris: Galilée, 1994), 87.

66. Derrida, "Force of Law," 23.

67. Ibid., 38.

68. Derrida cites Benjamin: "The admiring fascination exerted on the people by the 'figure of the great criminal' (281)" is elicited because "he is someone who, in defying the law, lays bare the violence of the legal system, the juridical order itself" (ibid.).

69. Ibid., 34.

70. Carl Rollyson notes that "To Henry's mother, Mary, Rebecca described Joyce as a 'little whippy jig-dancing sort of Irishman, quite ugly, but full of fight. He swaggered in and out of the dock, really very courageous indeed and made a very dignified appearance in court, on his appeal.' . . . This was the admiration of an adversary, but as a woman struggling against her own Irishness, and a sense of isolation. . . . No more than Joyce did she ever see herself as acceptable, an Establishment figure." Carl Rollyson, *Rebecca West* (New York: Scribner, 1996), 244.

71. The famous sentiment that "to write lyric poetry after Auschwitz is barbaric" (312) is elaborated upon in the essay "Commitment." Adorno addresses the issue of stylization of genocide, criticizing committed literature and art that "are willingly absorbed, as contributions to clearing up the past." In *The Essential Frankfurt School Reader*, ed. Andrew Arato and Eike Gebhart (New York: Continuum, 1982), 313. Adorno makes a distinction between "the so-called artistic representations" (312) of pain and suffering and art's non-representational or thematic practices of "imaging," instead, through form. He writes of the first, "by turning suffering into images, despite all their hard implacability, they wound our shame before the victims. For these are used

to create something, works of art, that are thrown to the consumption of the world that destroyed them" (312). The second, in contrast, makes no attempt to render it consumable, acknowledging that art is a betrayal of the event that demands art: "it is now virtually in art alone that suffering can still find its own voice, consolation, without immediately being betrayed by it. The most important artists of the age have realized this. The uncompromising radicalism of their works, the very features defamed as formalism, give them a terrifying power, absent from helpless poems to the victims of our time" (312).

72. For these theorists, this impossible and "incorrect" narrative act can facilitate clinical healing and at the same time reconfigure how we measure and understand historical truth. In clinical psychoanalysis, this is a basic premise. Dori Laub, for example, makes this point and offers as an example a Holocaust survivor who testifies to what is "false information" by disciplinary historical measures. Laub reads this woman's testimony as a way of reconfiguring the real in order to provide historical truth that exceeds empirical facts alone. The woman testifies that she'd seen four chimneys blow up at Auschwitz, but historians determined that only one chimney had blown up. Laub contends that "An essential part of the historical truth she was . . . bearing witness to" was the "bursting open of the very frame of Auschwitz." Dori Laub, "Bearing Witness or the Vicissitudes of Listening," in Shoshana Felman and Dori Laub, *Testimony: Crises of Witnessing in Literature, Psychoanalysis, and History* (New York: Routledge, 1992), 62.

73. Joseph Slaughter, *Human Rights, Inc.: The World Novel, Narrative Form, and International Law* (New York: Fordham University Press, 2007), 114–115.

74. Ibid., 115.

75. Ibid.

76. Roman Jacobson, "Two Aspects of Language and Two Types of Aphasic Disturbances," in *Fundamentals of Language*, by Roman Jakobson and Morris Halle (Berlin: Walter de Gruter, 1971).

77. "Fichte conceives of the state as an instrument of the nation and not vice versa. The territorial state and its institutions are an external mechanism of national culture that should be subsumed by the nation, infused with its vital spirit, and made to serve its work. Unless the state is rooted in the living nation, any plan to establish a perfect state will necessarily fail. It will be an abstraction imposed on an aggregate of people from the outside and realized as a mechanical construction of parts that do not cohere. The most glaring example of this is the French Revolution's culmination in the Terror: 'the state in accordance with reason [*vernunftgemasse Staat*] cannot be built up by artificial [*künstliche*] measures from whatever material may be at hand [*vorhandenen Stoffe*]; on the contrary, the nation must first be trained [*gebildted*] and educated [*herauferzogen*] up to it. Only the nation which has first solved in actual practice the problem of educating [*Erzeihung*] perfect men will then solve the problem

of the perfect state.' The Seventh Address explicitly reinscribes this topographical subordination of state to nation in terms of the oppositions between organism and machine, life and death." Pheng Cheah, *Spectral Nationality: Passages of Freedom from Kant to Postcolonial Literatures of Liberation* (New York: Columbia University Press, 2003), 131. Cheah demonstrates how this legacy survives and is reconfigured in various contemporary postcolonial nationalisms and literary stagings of *Bildung* as well.

78. As Slaughter writes, "Humboldtian *Bildung* describes a civic course of acculturation by which the individual's impulses for self-expression and fulfillment are rationalized, modernized, conventionalized, and normalized within the social parameters, cultural patterns, and public institutions of the modern nation-state. In this idealized model of socio-aesthetic modernization and enfranchisement, culture conducts a civilizing (or civicing) mission that has two complementary centripetal effects: centralizing the nation-state and centering its citizen-subjects" (*Human Rights, Inc.*, 113).

79. Cheah, *Spectral Nationality*, 128.

80. Homi K. Bhabha, "Of Mimicry and Man," in *The Location of Culture* (London: Routledge, 1994), 125.

81. As the trial reporter J. W. Hall recounts, "He was listened to by many in the beginning of the war, but then his listenership seriously dwindled. From being a sinister bogey-man, he had to many people, if not to most, become a figure of fun, about whom comedians sang songs on the wireless." *The Trial of William Joyce*, ed. J. W. Hall (London: William Hodge and Co., 1994), 9.

82. Bhabha, "Of Mimicry and Man," 127, 130–131.

83. Ibid., 131.

84. See Carey J. Snyder, *British Fiction and Cross-Cultural Encounters: Ethnographic Modernism from Wells to Woolf* (New York: Palgrave Macmillan, 2008); and Esty, *A Shrinking Island*.

85. Rebecca West, *The Strange Necessity: Essays and Reviews* (Garden City, NY: Doubleday, Doran & Co., 1928), 207.

86. Ibid.

87. Ibid., 207–208.

88. The details in this paragraph are taken from L. Perry Curtis Jr., *Apes and Angels: The Irishman in Victorian Caricature*, rev. ed. (Washington, D.C.: Smithsonian Institution Press, 1997), esp. 19–21.

89. West, "Opera in Greenville," 81.

90. She condemns Ben Bolt in particular: "When he was speaking of the FBI agents he said, 'Why, you would have thought someone had found a new atomic bomb, but all it was was a dead nigger boy.' This is not a specifically Southern attitude. All over the world there are people who may use the atomic bomb because they have forgotten that it is our duty to regard all lives, however alien and even repellent, as equally sacred" (ibid., 97).

91. Ibid., 105. Summarizing a letter from West to Emanie Sachs written during the trial, Rollyson comments that "She felt about the Irish as Southerners do about Negroes, Rebecca confided to Emanie: 'they just seem to me a different and repellent breed, whom one could like if they converted themselves into faithful servants.'" (*Rebecca West*, 244).

92. Ibid., 53.

93. Ibid.

94. Kieran Dolin, *Fiction and the Law: Legal Discourse in Victorian and Modern Literature* (Cambridge: Cambridge University Press, 1999), 30. West's remark in another trial report proposes something similar: "This murder trial . . . had the air of a morality play in its presentation of contrasting types of good and evil" ("Mr. Setty and Mr. Hume," in *A Train of Powder*, 202).

95. Peter Brooks, "The Law as Narrative and Rhetoric," in *Narrative and Rhetoric in the Law*, ed. Peter Brooks and Paul Gewirtz (New Haven, Conn.: Yale University Press, 1996), 19.

96. Gloria G. Fromm argues that the form of trials provided productive constraints on West's writing. She argues that the trial reports are more structured than writings such as *Black Lamb and Grey Falcon*, which "suffers from the extremist characteristics that mar her 'straight' fiction: looseness, a disproportionate emotional intensity, and portraits that seem almost like caricatures. These failings are less present (though by no means absent)" in the trial reports. "The courtroom proceedings provided a ready-made structure, and though her method was to weave psycho-social narratives about the men in the dock, there were limits or boundaries established by certain known facts" (51). I argue, conversely, that West fashions those pieces that were not facts into her own narrative to provide the trial more structure than actually existed. Gloria G. Fromm, "Rebecca West: The Fictions of Fact and the Facts of Fiction," *New Criterion* 9, no. 5 (January 1991): 44–53.

97. Alan Dershowitz, "Foreword," in *The Trial of William Joyce*, 58–59.

98. Menke, "Law and Violence," 2.

3. VINDICATING THE LAW: H. G. DE LISSER, V. S. REID, AND THE MORANT BAY REBELLION

1. While there are discussions of the rebellion in the Victorian literary and intellectual context, there is to my knowledge only one scholarly work that gathers together twentieth-century literary representations of the Morant Bay rebellion: Rhonda Cobham, "Fictions of Gender, Fictions of Race: Retelling Morant Bay in Jamaican Literature," *Small Axe* 8 (September 2000): 1–30. Petrina Dacres also discusses the importance of the rebellion, but in the context of visual culture, specifically sculpture: "'But Bogle Was a Bold Man': Vision, History, and Power for a New Jamaica," *Small Axe* 28 (March 2009): 112–134.

2. Paul Gilroy, *The Black Atlantic: Modernity and Double Consciousness* (Cambridge, Mass.: Harvard University Press, 1993), 19.

3. Alison Donnell, *Twentieth-Century Caribbean Literature: Critical Moments in Anglophone Literary History* (Abingdon: Routledge, 2006), 83.

4. Pascale Casanova, *The World Republic of Letters* (Cambridge, Mass.: Harvard University Press, 2007).

5. Donnell, *Twentieth-Century Caribbean Literature*, 82.

6. Ibid., 87.

7. For the most extensive treatment and corrective of the previous understanding of the rebellion as a spontaneous riot, see Gad Heuman, *The Killing Time: The Morant Bay Rebellion in Jamaica* (Knoxville: University of Tennessee Press, 1994).

8. Thomas C. Holt, *The Problem of Freedom: Race, Labor, and Politics in Jamaica and Britain, 1832–1938* (Baltimore, Md.: Johns Hopkins University Press, 1992), 299–300.

9. Rande W. Kostal provides an in-depth discussion of the process of inquiry under the JRC and writes that "under pressure of time, having to contend with uncomprehending, incomprehensible, obstinate, or, in one notable case, even menacing witnesses, the JRC questioned 730 people in the course of 60 hearings. Their testimony filled 1,100 large folio pages. The documents and appendices of the final report filled another 600 pages. It took another 41 pages for the JRC to summarize its findings. And although some of these findings later attracted critics, its methods and tenacity in fact-gathering did not. Even the lawyer-scrutineers retained by the Jamaica Committee, the men in the best position to know, did not dispute the fundamental integrity of the investigative process. . . . In the final result, moreover, the hearings generated evidence enough to support the criminal indictments of over a dozen military and civilian officers, including Edward Eyre." Rande W. Kostal, *A Jurisprudence of Power: Victorian Empire and the Rule of Law* (New York: Oxford University Press, 2008), 81–82.

10. *Statement of the Jamaica Committee, Bristol Selected Pamphlets* (1866), 3; contributed by University of Bristol Library, http://www.jstor.org/stable/60247170.

11. Ibid., 3–4.

12. For details, see Bernard Semmel, *The Governor Eyre Controversy* (London: MacGibbon & Kee, 1962).

13. V. S. Reid, "The Writer and His Work: V.S. Reid," *Journal of West Indian Literature* 1, no. 2 (December 1987): 5.

14. David Scott, *Conscripts of Modernity: The Tragedy of Colonial Enlightenment* (Durham, N.C.: Duke University Press, 2004).

15. In approaching these works this way, my exploration is influenced by Shalini Puri's study of Caribbean literature and hybridity theory, which asks,

"First, how does the national impede and/or assist transnational organizing? And second, how do transnational forces help constitute the national?" Shalini Puri, *The Caribbean Postcolonial: Racial Equality, Post-Nationalism, and Cultural Hybridity* (New York: Palgrave Macmillan, 2004), 10. Another important thinker of the difficulties and exigencies of negotiating movement in Caribbean as well as Pacific Islands discourses is Elizabeth M. DeLoughrey, who writes that "One of the central but unacknowledged ways in which European colonialism has constructed the trope of the isolated island is by mystifying the importance of the sea and the migrations across its expanse," and who explores "the complex and shifting entanglement between sea and land, diaspora and indigeneity, and routes and roots." Elizabeth M. DeLoughrey, *Routes and Roots: Navigating Caribbean and Pacific Island Literatures* (Honolulu: University of Hawai'i Press, 2007), 2.

16. Mervyn Morris, "H. G. de Lisser; the First Competent Caribbean Novelist in English," *Carib* (January 1979): 18–26.

17. Leah Reade Rosenberg, *Nationalism and the Formation of Caribbean Literature* (New York: Palgrave Macmillan, 2007), 67.

18. Ibid., 64.

19. Ibid., 66.

20. Donnell, *Twentieth-Century Caribbean Literature*, 9.

21. Brian L. Moore and Michele A. Johnson, *"They Do as They Please": The Jamaican Struggle for Cultural Freedom After Morant Bay* (Kingston, Jamaica: University of West Indies Press, 2011), 135.

22. Ibid., 5.

23. H. G. de Lisser, *Revenge: A Tale of Old Jamaica* (Kingston: Gleaner and Co., 1919), 76. Hereafter cited in the text.

24. Nasser Hussain, *The Jurisprudence of Emergency: Colonialism and the Rule of Law* (Ann Arbor: University of Michigan Press, 2003), 17, 21.

25. Ibid., 25.

26. Ibid., 109.

27. Ibid.

28. Ibid., 113.

29. Nathan K. Hensley offers an extensive critical analysis of the liberal disavowal of the violence of law during the Governor Eyre controversy and discovers a literary rebuttal to this disavowal in the poetics of Charles Swinburne. Nathan K. Hensley, "Form and Excess, Morant Bay and Swinburne," in *Forms of Empire: The Poetics of Victorian Sovereignty* (unpublished manuscript, 2012).

30. *Statement of the Jamaica Committee*, 11.

31. Ibid., 11–12.

32. Parliamentary Papers, *Royal Commission on Jamaica*, 1:1–3, cited in Catherine Hall, "The Economy of Intellectual Prestige: Thomas Carlyle, John Stuart Mill, and the Case of Governor Eyre," *Cultural Critique* 12 (1989): 189.

33. Hall, "The Economy of Intellectual Prestige," 192.

34. Ibid.

35. The most famous of the polemics it inspired was John Jacob Thomas, *Froudacity* (Philadelphia: Gebbie and Company, 1890).

36. J. A. Froude, *The English in the West Indies; or, The Bow of Ulysses* (New York: Scribner, 1888), 252.

37. Ibid., 235.

38. Ibid., 250–252.

39. Diana Paton, "Obeah Acts: Producing and Policing Boundaries of Religion in the Caribbean," *Small Axe* 28 (March 2009): 6.

40. Brian L. Moore and Michele A. Johnson, *Neither Led nor Driven: Contesting British Cultural Imperialism in Jamaica, 1865–1920* (University of the West Indies Press, 2004).

41. Patton, "Obeah Acts," 4.

42. For a discussion of these debates, see Nathaniel Samuel Murrell, *Afro-Caribbean Religions: An Introduction to Their Historical, Cultural, and Sacred Traditions* (Philadelphia: Temple University Press, 2010).

43. Ibid., 179.

44. Ibid., 253.

45. Dale Bisnauth, *History of Religions in the Caribbean* (Trenton, N.J.: Africa World Press, 1996), 178.

46. Murrell writes that "while Obeah is often described as a practice for individuals as well as groups, Myal is only described as a religious ceremony, an association based upon corporate duty, which featured charismatic leaders with identifiable groups of adherents" (*Afro-Caribbean Religions*, 251). See also Dianne M. Stewart, *Three Eyes for the Journey: African Dimensions of the Religious Experience* (Oxford: Oxford University Press, 2005).

47. Bisnauth, *History of Religions in the Caribbean*, 178.

48. Mimi Sheller argues that between 1858 and 1865 "well-developed networks of civil society allowed for the elucidation and articulation of a semi-peasant, semi-proletarian democratic ideology" and demonstrates how the Underhill Convention grew past the confines of Baptist missionaries into Native Baptist quarters with branches throughout the island, which gave rise to the colonial government's fear of a race consciousness and the mechanisms for distribution and communication to create black publics. Mimi Sheller, *Democracy After Slavery: Black Publics and Peasant Radicalism in Haiti and Jamaica* (Gainesville: University of Florida Press, 2000, 174). For a reading of how voudou operated during the Haitian revolution and was used by colonials to deny rational action to black rebellion, see Alan Richardson, "Romantic Voodoo: Obeah and British Culture, 1797–1807," *Studies in Romanticism* 32, no. 1 (Spring 1993): 3–28.

49. Murrell, *Afro-Caribbean Religions*, 257.

50. Ibid., 252.

51. Ibid., 253

52. Ibid., 256–257.

53. De Lisser revisits the theme of Obeah and reveals the power of Obeah and its effects on femininity in his 1929 novel, *The White Witch of Rosehall.* For an examination of this work in the context of Caribbean literature from the eighteenth through the twentieth centuries, see Erin Mackie, "Jamaican Ladies and Tropical Charms," *Ariel* 37, nos. 2/3 (April–July 2006): 189–219.

54. Froude, *The English in the West Indies,* 250.

55. F. M. Birbalsingh, "The Novels of H. G. de Lisser," *International Fiction Review* 9 (1982): 46.

56. As Cobham writes, de Lisser "needed the spectre of rape directed specifically at an English-born woman precisely because . . . his novel strives to conflate the interests of the plantocracy with those of the Crown and to portray all whites as solidly behind the version of events he presents . . . Eyre and his men become the protectors of Victorian women's honour" (*Fictions of Gender, Fictions of Race,* 9).

57. Birbalsingh, "The Novels of H. G. de Lisser," 46.

58. Vilashini Cooppan, "World Literature and Global Theory: Comparative Literature for the New Millennium," *symplokē* 9, nos. 1/2 (2001): 33.

59. Catherine Hall, *Civilising Subjects: Colony and Metropole in the English Imagination, 1930–1867* (Chicago: University of Chicago Press, 2002).

60. Simon Gikandi, "Comment," *Journal of British Studies* 42, no. 4 (October 2003): 510.

61. *The Routledge Reader in Caribbean Literature,* ed. Alison Donnell and Sarah Lawson Welsh (London: Routledge, 1996), 114.

62. V. S. Reid, *New Day* (New York: Knopf, 1949), 360. Hereafter cited in the text.

63. Holt, *The Problem of Freedom,* 381. Holt describes some of the problems that attended the 1938 riots: "International developments as well as developments within Jamaica had created an unprecedented unemployment problem. Nations that had absorbed Jamaica's excess labor force now closed their doors to her migrants. Industries at home that had provided export crops for whole-time and part-time peasants, such as bananas, were now prostrated by plant diseases. Production in the reorganized sugar industry, the focus of much of the recent discontent, was constrained by international trade agreements. Furthermore, the systems governing labor relations had not been modernized and rationalized at the same pace as the technical systems of production. Since there was no systematic representation of the workers' grievances to management, strikes could be used by extreme elements . . . and by those who were not concerned in the dispute to create disorder" (387).

64. Scott, *Conscripts of Modernity,* 70.

65. Ibid., 83.
66. Ibid., 91.
67. Ibid., 95.
68. Holt, *The Problem of Freedom.*
69. Scott, *Conscripts of Modernity*, 192.
70. In this sense, the liberal position resembles the French response to the Haitian Revolution, as Michel-Rolph Trouillot theorized in *Silencing the Past: Power and the Production of History* (Boston: Beacon, 1995). On the problem of recognizing the rebellion as an act by Jamaican rather than English—not even British—subjects, see Ian Baucom, *Out of Place: Englishness, Empire, and the Locations of Identity* (Princeton, N.J.: Princeton University Press, 1999), 43–54.
71. This notion of postcolonial, to be distinguished from post-colonial, is articulated by Elleke Boehmer, *Colonial and Postcolonial Literature: Migrant Metaphors* (Oxford: Oxford University Press, 2005).
72. Franco Moretti, *The Modern Epic: The World System from Goethe to García Márquez*, trans. Quintin Hoare (London: Verso, 1996), 51.
73. Ibid., 39.
74. Ibid., 59.
75. M. Keith Booker and Dubravka Juraga, *The Caribbean Novel in English: An Introduction* (Portsmouth, N.H.: Heinemann, 2001), 132. Other critics point to both its language and depiction of landscape as proving its "authenticity" as a truly national work. See for example Louis James, "Of Redcoats and Leopards: Two Novels by V.S. Reid," in *The Islands in Between: Essays in West Indian Literature*, ed. Louis James (London: Oxford University Press, 1968).
76. See Franco Moretti, *Graphs, Maps, Trees: Abstract Models for Literary History* (New York: Verso, 2007).
77. Moretti, *The Modern Epic*, 238.
78. Ibid.
79. M. Vargas Lhosa, *García Márquez: historia de un deicidio* (Barcelona: Barral Editores, 1971), 549; cited in Moretti, *The Modern Epic*, 242.
80. Benedict Anderson, *Imagined Communities: Reflections on the Origin and Spread of Nationalism*, rev. ed. (London: Verso, 2006), 26.
81. On the staging of the spiral as key figure of global modernity, see Nico Israel, *Spirals: The Whirled Image in Twentieth-Century Literature and Art* (New York: Columbia University Press, 2015).
82. On the history of the culture wars' debates of writing and speaking British English, see Moore and Johnson, *"They Do as They Please,"* 81–107.
83. Reid, "A Writer and His Work," 5.
84. Ibid.
85. Ibid.
86. George Lamming, *The Pleasures of Exile* (Ann Arbor: University of Michigan Press, 1991), 45.

87. Ibid.

88. "The experience of going away to the mother country to further one's education, the movement away, for however short or long a period, was an essential part of the experience of the old wave. The movement away was not only physical but psychic. Vic Reid, who has rarely left Jamaica, was none the less involved in that inner emigration, that Daedalus-Icarus leap out of the old patterns of the colonial emigration into a new consciousness, which all writers caught up in the catalyst of the 1938 populist-national upheaval experienced. Hence the title of his novel *New Day*. The movement away was bolstered up by the clear cut goal of a return to an independent Jamaica, with its own flag and anthem." Sylvia Wynter, "One Love—Rhetoric or Reality?—Aspects of Afro-Jamaicanism," *Caribbean Studies* 12, no. 3 (October 1972): 71.

89. F. Cudworth Flint, "Some First Novels: *New Day* by V. S. Reid; *We Fly Away* by Robert Francis; *Lonesome Valley* by Henry Hornsby; *Fire in the Morning* by Elizabeth Spencer; *The Hollow of the Wave* by Edward Newhouse; *The Melodramatists* by Howard Nemerov," *Sewanee Review* 58, no. 1 (January–March 1950): 146. Other readers found in the language a "naturalness" to which Reid's own comments on devising contest. "Here was a technical problem of the first importance. Davie, John, Tamah, and the others would seem stiff and unreal were they to speak standard English; yet if they spoke Jamaican how few would understand! . . . He has created a form of speech which is natural to the characters, which is easily understood, and which has extra-ordinary beauty." P.M.S., "*New Day*, A Novel of Jamaica by V. S. Reid," *Caribbean Quarterly* 1, no. 1 (April–June 1949): 32.

90. Hussain, *The Jurisprudence of Emergency*, 109.

91. Kostal, *A Jurisprudence of Power*, 71.

92. For an alternative reading to my own that sees the "epic sweep of the novel" registering the growing divisions between nation and world, urban and rural, see Michael Gilkes, *The West Indian Novel* (Boston: Twayne, 1981). Gilkes argues that "*New Day* is prophetic of the obdurate division between an urban political and social power and a rural economy, between elite and folk. With Garth, the bond between the Campbells and the land is finally broken. He returns from abroad as a legal engine (as Johnny sees him) on which a 'safety valve' has been welded, and his aim is political manipulation of the people for their own good. He is aware that he does not know his own people, and his dedication to their betterment is highly tinged with personal rhetoric" (122–123).

93. Reid, "A Writer and His Work," 5.

94. For a reading of how this functioned in the cultural politics of commemoration, see Dacres, "'But Bogle Was a Bold Man.'"

95. Scott, *Conscripts of Modernity*, 13.

96. On the theorization of this difference, see Mieke Bal, *Narratology: Introduction to the Theory of Narrative*, 2nd ed. (Toronto: University of Toronto Press, 1997).

97. V. S. Reid, *Sixty-Five* (Port-of-Spain: Longman Caribbean, 1968), 99. Hereafter cited in the text.

98. Scott, *Conscripts of Modernity*, 166.

99. Hussain, *The Jurisprudence of Emergency*, 108.

4. TESTIMONY AND THE CRISIS OF THE JURIDICAL ORDER IN NGŨGI WA THIONG'O'S *A GRAIN OF WHEAT*

1. See for example Seok-Ho Lee, "Ngũgi's Postcolonial Aesthetic Experiments: *A Grain of Wheat* and *Petals of Blood*," *British and American Fiction* 16, no. 2 (2009): 125–148; Olawale Awosika, "The Modernist Legacy in African Fiction: The Examples of Soyinka and Ngũgi," *Ekpoma Journal of Languages and Literary Studies* 2 (2004): 15–22; David Ker, *The African Novel and the Modernist Tradition* (Ibadan: Mosuru, 2003); Harry Sewlall, "Writing from the Periphery: The Case of Ngũgi and Conrad," *English in Africa* 30, no. 1 (May 2003): 55–69; Keith Carabine, "'No Action is Simple': Betrayal and Confession in Conrad's *Under Western Eyes* and Ngũgi's *A Grain of Wheat*," in *Conrad at the Millennium: Modernism, Postmodernism, Postcolonialism*, ed. Gail Fincham et al. (Boulder, Colo.: Social Science Monographs, 2001), 233–271; Byron Caminero-Santangelo, "Neocolonialism and the Betrayal Plot in 'A Grain of Wheat': Ngũgi wa Thiong'o's Revision of *Under Western Eyes*," *Research in African Literatures* 29, no. 1 (Spring 1998): 139–152; and Alissa Hamilton, "The Construction and Deconstruction of National Identities Through Language in the Narratives of Ngũgi wa Thiong'o's *A Grain of Wheat* and Joseph Conrad's *Under Western Eyes*," *African Languages and Cultures* 8, no. 2 (1995): 137–151.

2. Ngũgi wa Thiong'o, *A Grain of Wheat* (London: Heinemann, 1967), 23. All references are to the original edition, unless noted, and any discrepancies that do appear between passages cited are discussed.

3. Marshall Clough, "Mau Mau and the Contest for Memory," in *Mau Mau and Nationhood: Arms, Authority, and Narration*, ed. E. S. Atieno Odhiambo and John Lonsdale (Nairobi: East African Educational Publishers, 2003), 255.

4. Simon Gikandi argues that *A Grain of Wheat* displays an ambivalence between irony and allegory, which he defines as despairing and hopeful perspectives toward a postcolonial future in Kenya: "the romance of the land and the prophetic narrative have now given in to a self-conscious ironic discourse." Simon Gikandi, *Ngũgi wa Thiong'o* (Cambridge: Cambridge University Press, 2000), 100. Gikandi elaborates that "if his nationalist leanings make allegory a tempting linguistic figure for representing the past, taking an exact measure of decolonization seems to force him toward modes of narration that privilege

irony as the appropriate form representing complex, contested, and incomplete histories" (108).

5. Caminero-Santangelo, "Neocolonialism and the Betrayal Plot in *A Grain of Wheat*," 146. Peter Nazareth also proposes that Mugo's confession must be read in contrast to Razumov's confessions in *Under Western Eyes*: "Razumov's confession does not have a positive impact on anybody while Mugo's confession shows others the way. For if he was so courageous as to lay open his terrible secret before all, can others not bare their souls to one another?" Peter Nazareth, "Is *A Grain of Wheat* a Socialist Novel?" in *Critical Perspectives on Ngũgi wa Thiong'o*, ed. G. D. Killam (Washington, D.C.: Three Continents, 1984), 251.

6. "He was Polish, born in a country and a family that had known only the pleasures of domination and exile. He had learnt English late in life and yet he had chosen to write in it, a borrowed language, despite his fluency in his native tongue and in French. And what is more he had made it to the great tradition of English literature. Was he not already an image of what we, the new African writers, like the Irish writers before us, Yeats and others, could become?" Ngũgi wa Thiong'o, *Moving the Centre: The Struggle for Cultural Freedom* (Portsmouth, N.H.: Heinemann, 1993), 6.

7. Ngũgi wa Thiong'o, *Decolonizing the Mind: The Politics of Language in African Literature* (Portsmouth, N.H.: Heinemann, 2005), 76.

8. Ngũgi of course writes at length about the problems of writing in English, especially in his "farewell" text to English, *Decolonizing the Mind*. Evidence for the novel's formal staging as an attempt at overcoming its own limiting condition is that following the composition of this novel, Ngũgi undergoes a "crisis": "The English language opened the door to a wide range of fiction and it was this that eventually led me to the English department at Makerere in 1959 and hence to the kind of writing which climaxed in *Petals of Blood* which was published in 1977. But I was becoming increasingly uneasy about the English language. After I had written *A Grain of Wheat* I underwent a crisis. I knew whom I was writing about but whom was I writing for? The peasants whose struggles fed the novel would never read it. In an interview in 1967 with *Union News*, a student newspaper in Leeds University, I said: 'I have reached a point of crisis. I don't know whether it is worth any longer writing in English'" (*Decolonizing the Mind*, 72). Other of his writings that address the same subjects, the Mau Mau rebellion, counterinsurgency, and betrayal are written before this turning point and do not use the formal techniques that *A Grain of Wheat* uses. Both "The Return" and *Weep Not, Child* explore issues of detention through a much more linear narrative structure, foregrounding problems of witnessing and trauma in plot rather than through narrative strategies we find in Ngũgi's later novels.

9. Ngũgi, *Decolonizing the Mind*, 16.

10. Ibid., 76.

11. Ngũgi wa Thiong'o, "Writing Against Neo-colonialism," in *African Literature: An Anthology of Criticism and Theory*, ed. Tejumola Olaniyan and Ato Quayson (Malden, Mass.: Blackwell, 2007), 160.

12. Ibid., 161.

13. Ibid.

14. See David Maughan-Brown, *Land, Freedom, and Fiction: History and Ideology in Kenya* (London: Zed, 1985). This line of argument has been recently revived by Brendon Nicholls, *Ngũgi wa Thiong'o, Gender, and the Ethics of Postcolonial Reading* (Burlington, Vt.: Ashgate, 2010), and is reconfigured in Timothy Bewes's analysis of the novel, which argues that the failure to accomplish the revolutionary mission is met with shame, which takes over the text: "the expectations of its characters; the categories with which they orient themselves ethically ('betrayal,' 'fidelity,' 'madness,' 'collaboration,' 'sacrifice'; the unified narrative perspective, the linear chronological framing)." Timothy Bewes, *The Event of Postcolonial Shame* (Princeton, N.J.: Princeton University Press, 2010), 123.

15. Neil Lazarus, "Modernism and African Literature," in *The Oxford Handbook of Global Modernisms*, ed. Mark Wollaeger and Matt Etough (New York: Oxford University Press, 2012), 228–248.

16. Simon Gikandi, "The Short Century: On Modernism and Nationalism," *New Formations* 51 (2004): 25.

17. See in particular Sewlall, "Writing from the Periphery," and Kenneth Harrow, "Ngũgi wa Thiong'o's *A Grain of Wheat*: Season of Irony," *Research in African Literatures* 18, no. 2 (Summer 1985): 243–263.

18. Michael Rothberg, *Multidirectional Memory: Remembering the Holocaust in the Age of Decolonization* (Stanford, Calif.: Stanford University Press, 2009), 11.

19. Giorgio Agamben, *State of Exception*, trans. Kevin Attell (Chicago: University of Chicago Press, 2005), 4.

20. Ngũgi wa Thiong'o, *A Grain of Wheat*, rev. ed. (Oxford: Heinemann, 1986), 103.

21. Rothberg, *Multidirectional Memory*, 11. My emphasis.

22. As James Ogude notes, "in spite of the strong sense of loss, there is also a strong sense of retrieval paralleled by the desire for land restoration. And here land not only means the physical space, but more significantly it signifies the nation. As a physical space, Ngũgi embraces the rural topology as the signifier of genuine nationalism." James Ogude, *Ngũgi's Novels and African History: Narrating the Nation* (London: Pluto, 1999), 48.

23. For a feminist reading of the novel that points out the many ways in which the work conveys a "uterine textual organization" through its depictions of nationhood, see Nicholls, *Ngũgi wa Thiong'o, Gender, and the Ethics of Postcolonial Reading*.

24. Shoshana Felman writes, "The law always attempts to . . . throw a bridge over the abyss . . . by enclosing it within the rationality of its legal categorizations . . . in an attempt to cover up its bottomlessness . . . to assimilate the gap within known categories of the social or political or legal order"; in contrast, "the literary text casts open the abyss so as to let us look, once more, into its depth and see its bottomlessness." Shoshana Felman, *The Juridical Unconscious: Trials and Traumas in the Twentieth Century* (Cambridge, Mass.: Harvard University Press, 2002), 95.

25. Giorgio Agamben, *Homo Sacer: Sovereign Power and Bare Life*, trans. Daniel Heller-Roazen (Stanford, Calif.: Stanford University Press, 1998), 3.

26. Ibid., 7.

27. Ibid., 122.

28. Ibid., 6.

29. Ibid., 19.

30. Ibid., 123.

31. Benedict Anderson, *Imagined Communities: Reflections on the Origin and Spread of Nationalism*, new ed. (New York: Verso, 2006), 86.

32. See for example David Anderson, *Histories of the Hanged: The Dirty War in Kenya and the End of Empire* (New York: Norton, 2005); David French, *The British Way in Counter-Insurgency, 1945–1967* (Oxford: Oxford University Press, 2011); Andrew Mumford, *The Counter-Insurgency Myth: The British Experience of Irregular Warfare* (London: Routledge, 2012).

33. Caroline Elkins, "Detention, Rehabilitation, and the Destruction of Kikuyu Society," in *Mau Mau and Nationhood: Arms, Authority, and Narration* 194.

34. Achille Mbembe points out the link between the Nazi camps and colonialism: "Taking a historical perspective, a number of analysts have argued that the material premises of Nazi extermination are to be found in colonial imperialism on the one hand, and on the other, in the serialization of technical mechanisms for putting people to death—mechanisms developed between the Industrial Revolution and the First World War." Achille Mbembe, "Necropolitics," trans. Libby Meintjes, *Public Culture* 15, no. 1 (Winter 2003): 18. Mbembe cites Enzo Traverso, who connects the development of gas chambers and ovens to "a long process of dehumanizing and industrializing death, one of the original features of which was to integrate instrumental rationality with the productive and administrative rationality of the modern Western world (the factory, the bureaucracy, the prison, the army). Having become mechanized, serialized execution was transformed into a purely technical, impersonal, silent, and rapid procedure. This development was aided in part by racist stereotypes and the flourishing of a class-based racism that, in translating the social conflicts of the industrial world in racial terms, ended up comparing the working

classes and 'stateless people' of the industrial world to the 'savages' of the colonial world" (18). In addition, Mbembe reminds us that Hannah Arendt points to connections between national socialism and imperialism: "colonial conquest revealed a potential for violence previously unknown. What one witnesses in WWII is the extension to the 'civilized' peoples of Europe of the methods previously reserved for the 'savages'" (23).

35. Elkins, *Imperial Reckoning: The Untold Story of Britain's Gulag in Kenya* (New York: Henry Holt, 2005), 49. My emphasis.

36. Agamben, *Homo Sacer*, 122.

37. Elkins writes that the figuration of Kikuyu as animals to be eliminated "was everywhere. During a brief stop in Nairobi in the spring of 1954, journalist Anthony Sampson likewise observed what he later called the 'dehumanization of the enemy' by local settlers and colonial officials. 'I heard it everywhere I went,' he said. 'How many Kukes had to be gotten rid of, how many Kukes did you wink today. [It was] almost like they were talking about big game hunting'" (*Imperial Reckoning*, 49). Joanna Lewis demonstrates how the British press's coverage of the Emergency in the 1950s presented, through photographic "evidence," the characterization of the Mau Mau as inhuman savages while also rearticulating the Emergency from a state of exception to a situation in which colonial officers operated under the codes of civil law ("The British Popular Press and the Demoralization of Empire," in *Mau Mau and Nationhood: Arms, Authority, and Narration*).

38. Agamben, *Homo Sacer*, 170.

39. Bethwell A. Ogot explains that "Baring's plans for defeating the Mau Mau were contingent upon . . . Oliver Lyttelton, and his assurance that all Mau Mau irreconcilables would be detained indefinitely. The governor estimated that at least 12,000 detainees would never be redeemed, and instead exiled to remote camps. When Whitehall began drafting post-Emergency legislation, however, it realized that Article 5 of the Geneva Convention on human rights, with its provision of no detention without trial, would undermine Lyttelton's promise. Whereas Kenya could derogate from the conventions because a formal public Emergency existed during Mau Mau, it could not do so once the Emergency was lifted. As early as 1955 the Colonial Office realized it could not endorse large-scale detention after the Emergency. Ultimately, the Kenya government was assured of London's support in drafting indefinite exile legislation for a limited number of Mau Mau politicals, provided all other detainees were passed through the Pipeline. In effect, London was willing to derogate from the conventions, but only for those few detainees—specifically the alleged Mau Mau intelligentsia—who misled the Kikuyu masses and whose release would surely compromise the viability of continued colonial rule in Kenya" ("Mau Mau and Nationhood: The Untold Story," in *Mau Mau and Nationhood: Arms, Authority, and Narration*, 213).

40. Judith Butler, *Precarious Life: The Powers of Mourning and Violence* (London: Verso, 2004), 51.

41. Ibid., 52.

42. Ibid., 55.

43. Elkins has examined the structure of policing and law enforcement during the Emergency and shown how it was decentralized. This unaccountability of functionaries who operate like sovereigns by virtue of Emergency regulations was historically anticipated by and constituted through the British empire's policies in Africa before the Emergency. "The most defining characteristic of British colonial governance in Africa . . . was the looseness of its decentralized control. While there was a strong consensus for the British imperial mission, there were never any hard and fast rules about how this mission be carried out on the ground" (*Imperial Reckoning*, 7).

44. Initially critics, most famously the historian William Ochieng, criticized Ngũgi for failing to document accurately the era of the Emergency. Carol M. Sicherman's influential essay from 1989 was the first to question historians' criticism by reading the novel's interweaving of fiction and historical detail as a motivated effort to integrate personal histories into a national history: Carol M. Sicherman, "Ngũgi wa Thiong'o and the Writing of Kenyan History," *Research in African Literatures* 20, no. 3 (Autumn 1989): 347–370. Since then, others have provided varied, nuanced readings of the aesthetico-political uses of history in the text. See Kathy Kessler, who develops the implications of the novel's formal presentation of contesting histories: Kathy Kessler, "Rewriting History in Fiction: Elements of Postmodernism in Ngũgi wa Thiong'o's Later Novels," *ARIEL: A Review of International English Literature* 25, no. 2 (April 1994): 75–90; Robert Spencer, who claims that the novel's device of polyphony enables an excavation of subaltern agency inaccessible from the perspective of conventional historiography: Robert Spencer, "'This Zone of Occult Instability': The Utopian Promise of the African Novel in the Era of Decolonization," *New Formations* 47 (June 2002): 69–86; Tej N. Dhar, who investigates the "history-fiction interface" neglected by earlier critics: Tej N. Dhar, "Ngũgi's Retrospective Gaze: The Shape of History in *A Grain of Wheat*," *Kunapipi* 29, no. 1 (January 2007): 173–183; and Seok-Ho Lee, who challenges the scholarly overvaluation of the documentary at the expense of the aesthetic dimensions of the text ("Ngũgi's Postcolonial Aesthetic Experiments: *A Grain of Wheat* and *Petals of Blood*"). Ngũgi himself recently suggested that the protocols of documentary journalism were inadequate to the histories he wanted to tell, and he implies that these histories required the imaginative qualities of fiction writing: "As an undergraduate at Makerere, completely outside the classroom, I started contributing articles to the Kenyan press. . . . But despite the quantity and variety of issues tackled, I never felt that my literary journalism had made me come to grips with the whirlwind any more than I

had through the class essay. How could an article really capture the complexity of what I had experienced in colonial Kenya?" Ngũgi wa Thiong'o, *Globalectics: Theory and the Politics of Knowing* (New York: Columbia University Press, 2012), 17. He addresses here events represented in *A Grain of Wheat*, "horror stories of white officers collecting ears, noses, eyes, genitalia, or even heads of the vanquished as trophies" (17) and mentions also Hola camp, fictionalized in the novel.

45. "Screening is the one word in Kikuyuland today that is synonymous with British colonial rule during Mau Mau. In recounting their days in the detention camps and barbed wire villages, Kikuyu men and women never translate screening into their own language. Instead, they pause in their Kikuyu or Kiswahili and enunciate the English word *screening* in a slow, deliberate, colonial British accent. This is because there is no word in Kikuyu or Kiswahili that captures the same meaning" (Elkins, *Imperial Reckoning*, 62).

46. Ngũgi wa Thiong'o, *Detained: A Writer's Prison Diary* (London: Heinemann, 1981), 43.

47. Ibid., 61.

48. Ibid., 14.

49. Ibid., 13–14.

50. Ibid., 40.

51. Jean-François Lyotard, *The Differend: Phrases in Dispute*, trans. Georges Van Den Abbeele (Minneapolis: University of Minnesota Press, 1988), 9.

52. Ibid.

53. Elkins, *Imperial Reckoning*, 27.

54. Ibid, 27–28. This is true for both Elkins, who admits that even with all her extensive research she has only "scratched the surface" of oathing, and for the civilians and insurgents who pledged the oaths.

55. Ibid., 28.

56. Ibid., 26.

57. Ibid.

58. Nicholls, *Ngũgi wa Thiong'o, Gender, and the Ethics of Postcolonial Reading*, 94.

59. Harry Sewlall highlights the prevalence of silence, "a phenomenon so frequently portrayed in the novel as to lead one back to speculation on the universe in which the silence is set," and this, he maintains, is "the universe of the concentration camp" ("Writing from the Periphery: The Case of Ngũgi and Conrad," 257). In addition to Nazareth and Caminero-Santangelo, who read Mugo's confession as the mark of a hopeful future because it corrects silences and miscommunications, Kenneth Harrow also maintains that the silence and irony driving the work are repressive and, like Sewlall, contends that these reflect the concentration camp ("Ngũgi wa Thiong'o's *A Grain of Wheat*: Season of Irony").

60. Ngũgi, *Detained*, 61.

61. Ibid., 14.

62. Lyotard, *The Differend*, 13.

63. Ngũgi, *Decolonizing the Mind*, 76.

64. For example, see Spencer, "'This Zone of Occult Instability'"; Delia Krause, "*A Grain of Wheat*: Ngũgi's Tribute to the Armed Rebellion," *Wasafiri* 9 (December 1988): 6–10; Hamilton, "The Construction and Deconstruction of National Identities"; and Gikandi, who argues the structure implies that "postcolonial attempts to produce a stable and collective narrative about the past are bound to flounder in the face of competing interpretations, desires, and recollections"(*Ngũgi wa Thiong'o*, 116), and maintains the most pressing issue is not whether one can access some "true history" but instead "what character and value this history acquires in its remembering, figuration, and retelling" (*Ngũgi wa Thiong'o*, 118). Gikandi does not focus on precisely how this figuration and retelling take place, but I contend it is crucial to reading the ethics of responding to history to examine precisely how this happens.

65. Paul de Man, "Semiology and Rhetoric," in *Allegories of Reading: Figural Language in Rousseau, Nietzsche, Rilke, and Proust* (New Haven, Conn.: Yale University Press, 1979), 3–19.

66. Sigmund Freud, "The Uncanny," in *The Standard Edition of the Complete Psychological Works of Sigmund Freud*, trans. James Strachey (London: Hogarth, 1953), 17:241.

67. Authors who address this systematically include Sarah Kofman, Luce Irigaray, and Jacques Derrida. See Sarah Kofman, *The Enigma of Woman: Woman in Freud's Writings*, trans. Catherine Porter (Ithaca, N.Y.: Cornell University Press, 1985); Luce Irigaray, *An Ethics of Sexual Difference; This Sex Which Is Not One*, trans. Catherine Porter and Carolyn Burke (Ithaca, N.Y.: Cornell University Press, 1985), and *Speculum of the Other Woman*, trans. Gillian C. Gill (Ithaca, N.Y.: Cornell University Press, 1985); Jacques Derrida, *Spurs: Nietzsche's Styles/Eperons: Les Styles de Nietzsche*, trans. Barbara Harlow (Chicago: University of Chicago Press, 1981). For postcolonial responses to this critical tradition, see Gayatri Chakravorty Spivak, "Displacement and the Discourse of Woman," in *Displacement: Derrida and After*, ed. Mark Krupnik (Bloomington: Indiana University Press, 1983); "French Feminism in an International Frame," in *In Other Worlds: Essays in Cultural Politics* (New York: Routledge, 1987), 134–153; "Feminism and Deconstruction, Again" and "French Feminism Revisited: Ethics and Politics," in *Outside in the Teaching Machine* (New York: Routledge, 1993).

68. Spivak does this to show the usefulness of the uncanny for planet thinking rather than globe thinking. See Gayatri Chakravorty Spivak, *Death of a Discipline* (New York: Columbia University Press, 2003), chap. 3.

69. Nicholls, *Ngũgi wa Thiong'o, Gender, and the Ethics of Postcolonial Reading*, 86.

70. Freud, "The Uncanny," 224.

71. This argument is threaded in different ways throughout various readings of gendering in the novel. See in particular Charles Nama, "Daughters of Moombi: Ngũgi's Heroines and Traditional Gikuyu Aesthetics," in *Ngambika: Studies of Women in African Literature*, ed. Carole Boyce Davies and Anne Adams Graves (Trenton, N.J.: Africa World Press, 1986), 139–149; and S. W. Perera, "From Mumbi to Wanja: The Emergence of the Woman in Ngũgi's Fiction," *Commonwealth Essays and Studies* 14, no. 2 (1992): 69–78. The strongest riposte to such arguments is Nicholls's thorough reading of gender, nationalism, and subalternity in *Ngũgi wa Thiong'o, Gender, and the Ethics of Postcolonial Reading*.

72. Frantz Fanon, "The Trials and Tribulations of National Consciousness," in *The Wretched of the Earth*, trans. Richard Philcox (New York: Grove, 1963), a chapter Ngũgi has declared required reading in his interviews.

73. Ngũgi, *Globalectics*, 80–81.

74. Ngũgi is sympathetic to Fanon's critique of systemic violence inflicted by colonialism and understands anticolonialism as a structural violence of history that has the function of *Bildung* and therefore (national) independence. But Ngũgi rejects the notion that the historical, structural violence detailed by Fanon (and earlier by Hegel) can be read as Fanon's prescription for, rather than description of, specific acts of violence undertaken by individuals, which produce more physical and mental traumas (*Globalectics*, 24–25).

75. Fanon, *The Wretched of the Earth*, 5–6.

76. Montagu Slater writes that Kenyatta's trial "was a political trial of decisive importance to the immediate future of Africa: but this was something the prosecution was anxious to deny." Montagu Slater, *The Trial of Jomo Kenyatta* (Nairobi: Heinemann, 1990), 7. The prosecution wanted to claim *The Queen against Kenyatta and others* was a criminal, not a political case. "To describe it as a state trial would invest it with a halo it does not really possess," Crown Counsel maintained (7). In contrast, the defense maintained that rather than aiming toward truth, the trial was motivated by politics alone. "In his last speech in court Kenyatta argues that 'this case, from our point of view, has been so arranged as to make scapegoats of us in order to strangle the Kenya African Union, the only African political organization which fights for the African people.' In his eyes the trial was a Machiavellian political maneuver. Others went further and hinted that the whole policy behind the Proclamation of Emergency was of a similar character" (14).

77. Ngũgi, *A Grain of Wheat*, rev. ed. 212.

78. Ngũgi was criticized for his representations of violence, which led him to rewrite this scene in the revised version. While most seem to think he excised the rape, a closer look at the ambiguous orchestration of violence sug-

gests he was reluctant to jettison entirely this particular instance of depicted Mau Mau violence. The events are presented once through Koina's abbreviated narrative, which mentions only that "he felled the god with a panga," and once, earlier, through Dr. Lynd's perspective. This retelling suggests Lynd might have been raped but does not claim it directly: "They tied her hands and legs together and gagged her. She waited for them to kill her, for after the initial shock she had resigned herself to death. But what followed was no less cruel and barbaric than if they had killed her. Her dog had barked at the two men. But on seeing the houseboy it wagged its tail and held back its attack. But the houseboy hacked it to pieces" (45).

79. Gikandi, *Ngũgi wa Thiong'o*, 117.

80. Lyotard, *The Differend*, 13.

INDEX